RELIGIOUS INFORMATION SYSTEMS
VOL. 16

ANTI-CULT MOVEMENTS IN CROSS-CULTURAL PERSPECTIVE

GARLAND REFERENCE LIBRARY
OF SOCIAL SCIENCE
VOL. 913

RELIGIOUS INFORMATION SYSTEMS

J. GORDON MELTON
Series Editor

ANTI-CULT MOVEMENTS IN CROSS-CULTURAL PERSPECTIVE

edited by

Anson Shupe
David G. Bromley

GARLAND PUBLISHING, INC.
New York & London / 1994

Library of Congress Cataloging-in-Publication Data

Anti-cult movements in cross-cultural perspective /
edited by Anson Shupe and David G. Bromley.
    p.   cm. — (Religious information systems ;
vol. 16) (Garland reference library of social science ;
vol. 913)
    Includes bibliographical references.
    ISBN 0–8153–1428–0 (alk. paper)
    1. Anti-cult movements.   I. Shupe, Anson D.
II. Bromley, David G.   III. Series: Religious information systems series ; vol. 16.   IV. Series: Garland
reference library of social science ; v. 913.
BP604.A58   1994
291—dc20   94–29858
                                       CIP

Printed on acid-free, 250-year-life paper
Manufactured in the United States of America

TABLE OF CONTENTS

ANTI-CULT MOVEMENTS
IN CROSS-CULTURAL PERSPECTIVE

v

Part II. Modern Anti-Cultism in Europe

Part III. Modern Anti-Cultism in the Middle and Far East

INTRODUCTION
THE GLOBAL SCALE OF ANTI-CULTISM

Anson Shupe and David G. Bromley

That a volume of articles on the cross-national phenomenon of current anti-cultism is published in the mid-1990s would probably have shocked antagonists on both sides of the great cult/anti-cult struggle if, two decades earlier, they could have seen the future. Our personal fieldwork within both camps at that time tells us that neither side expected this protracted protest against various new religious movements (hereafter NRMs) to last: either because a damaging image of the anti-cult movement (hereafter ACM) as an intolerant, anti-constitutional, vigilante movement would have been successfully promoted by its opponents; or because, thanks to the ACM's mobilization of public officials and law enforcement agencies, health professionals, academics, and public opinion, the "innovative" NRMs would have been broken up, prosecuted, or deported.

Instead, both sides are undoubtedly disappointed with recent history. While none of the NRMs ever approached the ongoing core-member size of commonly touted ACM claims (e.g., that the Unification Church, as one oft-cited example, possesses 80,000 core members and 20,000 "associates"), they did nevertheless demonstrate a resilience and ability to adapt that has resulted in some of them becoming more or less permanent actors in the American religious economy. Rajneesh during the mid-1980s, and Guru Maharaj Ji a decade earlier, suffered major collapses (in part because of internal organizational problems). But others, such as the Unification Church, the Church of Scientology, and the Family (formerly the Family of Love, and before that the Children of God), seem to be here to stay, raising their first generation of non-converted members.

Likewise, few of the first "generation" of ACM activists during the early-to-late 1970s expected to be in a consuming counter-movement for more than twenty years. (And many were not; as soon as their young adult sons and daughters defected or were forcibly deprogrammed to disaffiliate, AMC activists generally disengaged). There was (in hindsight) a naive expectation that ACM spokespersons simply publicizing their complaints that authoritarian totalistic groups had recruited their family members would enlist the immediate attentions of police, prosecuting attorneys, courts, and legislators. When the realization came that this crusade to alter public apathy and public officials' inaction was no minor task, and that the counter-cult activists had to dig in for the long haul, the movement began (quite rationally) to shift its bases of leadership, its financial underpinnings, and its strategies. The result is that the ACM as well is now an established part of the American religious economy (see Shupe and Bromley, 1980 for a structural history of the ACM's first decade; see Shupe and Bromley, Chapter 1 of this volume, for events occurring since then).

The focus of this volume is on the ACM as an international social movement industry with far greater appeal than its North American founders originally envisioned. We contacted writers and scholars of, and from, various regions and cultures to analyze the fortunes of ACM efforts to thrive and influence officials/publics in those places. Before previewing their contributions toward this end, however, it is worth briefly reviewing what previous research on ACM activities abroad (i.e., outside the borders of the United States of America) has been conducted.

Previous Research

While, as religious studies scholar J. Gordon Melton has shown, evangelical Christian writers have been systematically elaborating a counter-cult literature since the beginning of the twentieth century (building on nineteenth-century anti-Mormon and anti-Catholic criticisms), the modern post-World War Two scholarly literature on anti-cultism did not start until the 1970s. As several sources (Shupe and Bromley, 1980, 1981, 1985; Shupe, Bromley, and Oliver, 1984; Bromley, 1989) clearly document, the ACM itself was generating pamphlets, newsletters, leaflets, and tracts, and various intramovement communications since its inception in 1971. Also, books more or less sympathetic to the ACM had emerged (e.g., Patrick and Dulack, 1976; Conway and Siegelman, 1977; Stoner and Parke, 1977; Verdier, 1977).

However, the first independent social science analysis of ACM existence was not published until several years after the countermovement had been active (Shupe, Spielmann, and Stigall, 1977). Thereafter, many scholarly monographs analyzing specific NRMs, or the social conflict they generated, paid more attention to the ACM "factor" in NRM's evolution (e.g., Bromley and Shupe, 1979; Beckford, 1985; Shinn, 1987; Biermans, 1988; Robbins, 1988; Bromley, 1989).

Research into the ACM's international activities began during the early 1980s. Such counter-movement groups appeared to have emerged in Western European countries as well as Japan for two reasons: (1) generic complaints of families that their offspring were being estranged and pointed away from conventional career/domestic trajectories by cultic (often communal) groups "greedy" for members' time and loyalty; and (2) active "missionizing" or spread of North American ACM ideology by counter-movement spokespersons (see, e.g., Roberts, 1978; Beckford, 1983, 1985; Shupe, Hardin, and Bromley, 1983).

Abruptly, however, such research ceased by mid-decade. European and other non-North American ACM groups seemed to mobilize nothing more than negative media reports, government concern (for a time, depending on country), and the general antipathy toward NRMs by the public. Scholars apparently lost interest, if publications are any indication.

The Current Status of Anti-cultism

Anti-cultism in the United States, as all authors seem to argue directly or indirectly in Part I, has matured. More specifically, we can say that it shows neither the "mom-and-pop" grassroots orientation of the 1970s nor the early rough-and-tumble deprogramming tactics (with a few episodic exceptions). Thus, the ACM has *institutionalized* in several ways.

First, its spokespersons are more likely to be professionals with degrees than impassioned family members of cult "victims." For example, over the years the ACM has been gradually constructing an ideological medicalization of religious deviance (e.g., Sirkin and Wynne, 1990; Singer and Ofshe, 1990) along the lines of a "coercive persuasion" or "mind control" model that has been promulgated by ACM activists but was poorly articulated during the early 1970s (e.g., Patrick and Dulack, 1976; Verdier, 1977).

Second, many of the ACM's current organizations have achieved the financial and membership stability that once eluded their predecessors (Shupe and Bromley, 1980; Shupe, 1985; see also Chapter

ix

1 in this volume). The major ACM outlets such as the American Family Foundation and the Cult Awareness Network in many ways do not resemble the financially precarious organizations of an earlier era. Third, the ACM has shown a continuing willingness to expand the definitional umbrella of what it will consider as a "cult." This tendency began in the early 1970s when the United States' original ACM group, FREECOG (Free the Children of God), expanded to unite with families of young adult offspring involved in other NRMs (Shupe and Bromley, 1980); continued during the 1980s as "religioeconomic corporations," including many quasi-therapeutic groups (from *est* to Amway), were drawn into the definitional arena (Bromley and Shupe, 1990); and has continued into the 1990s as the fear of a nationally organized Satanic cult underground abducting and/or ritualistically abusing children has spread (Victor, 1993; Richardson, Best, and Bromley, 1991). Since the United States of America's constitutionally unregulated religious economy serves as an unparalleled petri dish for religious innovation and development, and because of the realities of the cultural imperialism of commercial broadcasting by multinational corporations, it is not unreasonable to expect that new groups—many as yet unformed or unrecognized—will be added to the ACM's list of "destructive cults."

The Future of the ACM

Readers will undoubtedly draw their own conclusions, both from prior assumptions and the chapters in this book, about the global prospects for the ACM in the next century. However, in an era of fax machines, modems, and computer networks, it is inevitable that one nation's social movement industry can instantaneously become another nation's, or many nations'. Such seems to be the case, for example, in Australia where ACM imagery and spokespersons from the U.S.A. have been widening the list of "destructive cults" to groups most Americans have never encountered ("Own Your Own Life," 1991; Council Minutes, 1993; Mostyn, 1993; "The Case Against a Cult Watchdog," 1993). Meanwhile, various groups in both Europe and the United States on both sides of the "cult" issue maintain communications and advise each other of upcoming events.

The future of a global ACM industry is uncertain. Writing of the future of the North American ACM, we concluded several years ago that its ideological, scientific, and (ultimately) public resources were precariously held (Bromley and Shupe, 1987). Reasons we provided included the indefinitely inclusive definition of "cult" so often employed (which widens the potential list of opponents willing to make common defensive cause against it), the lack of credible evidence for a widespread social danger, and the failure of the ACM to align itself with, or identify itself as, a legitimate regulatory agency. America's pluralistic religious history, and its current high capacity for laissez-faire religious tolerance, mitigate awarding any such status to a private group.

On the other hand, American culture continually generates religious crises that seem to support some basic ACM tenets. In 1978 it was the Reverend Jim Jones and the Peoples Temple massacre in Jonestown, Guyana; in 1993 it was the 51-day siege and disastrous immolation of nearly all members of prophet David Koresh's Branch Davidians at Waco, Texas. And there are always charlatans, embarrassing kooks, and fanatics to reinforce stereotypes for all NRMs.

Further, there are continual individual crises which play no small role in perpetuating this particular counter-movement. For example, in 1992 an Amish farmer in LaGrange County, Indiana hired San Diego deprogrammer Ted Patrick, Jr. (at $25,000 cold cash in advance) to free his wife from the "mind control" of a cult. The cult, it turned out, was a progressive Amish Bible study group in which "cultic" topics like operating electric and automotive machinery, women's dress, and so forth were discussed. Patrick failed in the deprogramming when the woman escaped, and he departed immediately for the West Coast when she called the LaGrange sheriff (Shupe, 1992).

The husband and wife reconciled; Patrick kept the money and was never charged with a crime, but a fundamental pattern was present which may explain why the ACM can expect to be entrenched, at whatever level of success, well into the next century: the apparent willingness of some persons to medicalize, marginalize, or even criminalize religious unconventionality. This is not to claim religion cannot be harmful—physically, psychologically, or spiritually. Far from it. But the combination of bonafide abuses by religious leaders and groups with the fears and misunderstandings by many about unconventional religions fairly insure that some ACM, if not *this* ACM, will be with us for the foreseeable future.

THE CONTENTS: AN OVERVIEW

Part I offers a cross-section of ACM activity at the current time as well as in its historical dimensions and from several non-consensual perspectives. The Anson Shupe–David Bromley chapter addresses the first twenty years of the North American ACM, how it has evolved, and why; David Bromley attempts to identify the essential attributes of "subversiveness" by comparing the anti-religious and Satanic cult ideologies; while Soshanah Feher more narrowly examines the Jewish struggle with faith-maintenance and a persistent (Christian) missionary threat to Judaism in a Judeo-Christian culture more Christian than Judeo. Richard Bergeron, a Canadian scholar, examines a program for reconciliation or adjustment for families whose members do join NRMs. Alternately, Priscilla Coates and Steven A. Hassan, both visible non-academic activists at the national level of the American ACM, present their personal views of their goals and activities as persons "in the trenches" of this conflict.

Part II examines a variety of specific ACM efforts in European countries (England, France, Germany, the Netherlands, and Italy). James T. Richardson and Barend van Driel ambitiously plot the conflict between NRMs and ACM groups in four nations, drawing conclusions about the differences in each. Massimo Introvigne discusses details of the ACM in Italy. John A. Saliba, a scholar and Jesuit, analyzes the Vatican's response to NRM's within the framework of the Vatican II Council. And Reender Kranenborg shows why the Netherlands has proven to be unfertile ground for ACM efforts to expand.

Finally, Part III moves eastward. Benjamin Beit-Hallahmi illustrates the unique religious pluralistic situation of Israel and how ACMs as well as NRMs are defined there. Michael L. Mickler, himself a member of one of the NRMs often written about, examines ACM activities in Japan and their connections to regional politics. And John Malley, also a member of a "disputed" group, outlines how ACM ideology spread to Australia in 1993 and its continuities to other cases.

All authors, regardless of their personal feelings and opinions on the subject of this volume, have worked splendidly with us. We have attempted only the most stylistic revisions, allowing each to express herself or himself in words and phrasings as originally presented. We have not offered their works to each other for rebuttal or comment, for such feedback, while invaluable in a face-to-face conference, would be voluminous and impractical within our limitations of space. We extend our thanks to them for their help and maintain our respect for their sincerity.

REFERENCES

Beckford, James A., 1985. *Cult Controversies*. New York: Tavistock Publications.

------, 1983. "The 'Cult Problem' in Five Countries: The Social Construction of Religious Controversy," in Eileen Barker, ed., *Of Gods and Men: New Religious Movements in the West*. Macon, GA: Mercer University Press, pp. 195-214.

Biermans, John T., 1988. *The Odyssey of New Religions Today*. Revised Edition. Lewiston, NY: The Edwin Mellen Press.

Bromley, David G., 1989. "Hare Krishna and the Anti-Cult Movement," in David G. Bromley and Larry D. Shinn, eds., *Krishna Consciousness in the West*. Lewisburg, PA: Bucknell University Press, pp. 255-92.

------ and Anson Shupe, 1990. "Rebottling the Elixir: The Gospel of Prosperity in America's Religioeconomic Corporations," in Thomas Robbins and Dick Anthony, eds., *In God We Trust: New Patterns of Religious Pluralism in America,* Second Edition. New Brunswick, NJ: Transaction Publishers.

------, 1987. "The Future of the Anti-Cult Movement," in David G. Bromley and Phillip E. Hammond, eds., *The Future of New Religious Movements*. Macon, GA: Mercer University Press, pp. 221-34.

------, 1981. *Strange Gods: The Great American Cult Scare*. Boston, MA: Beacon Press.

------, 1979. *"Moonies" in America: Cult, Church, and Crusade*. Beverly Hills, CA: Sage Publications.

Conway, Flo and Jim Siegelman, 1978. *Snapping: America's Epidemic of Sudden Personality Change*. Philadelphia: J.B. Lippincott Company.

Melton, J. Gordon, ed., 1990. *The Evangelical Christian Anti-Cult Movement: Christian Counter-Cult Literature*. New York: Garland Publishing.

Mostyn, Suzanne, 1993. "MPs Told of Cult Leader's Sexual and Mental Abuse," *Sydney Morning Herald*. Sydney, Australia, August 12.

"Own Your Own Life," 1992, *Sydney Morning Herald,* Sydney, Australia, August 12.

Patrick, Ted and Tom Dulack, 1976. *Let Our Children Go!* New York: Ballantine Books.

Richardson, James T., Joel Best, and David G. Bromley, 1991. *The Satanist Scare*. New York, NY: Aldine De Gruyter.

Robbins, Thomas, 1988. *Cults, Converts, and Charisma: The Sociology of New Religious Movements*. Newbury Park, CA: Sage Publications.

Roberts, J., 1978. "Happiness Ginseng From Earth-Conquering Moonies," *Far Eastern Economic Review*, June 23:58-60.

Shinn, Larry D., 1987. *The Dark Lord*. Philadelphia, PA: The Westminster Press.

Shupe, Anson, 1990. "'Deprogramming' Flaunts Civil Liberties," *The Fort Wayne Journal-Gazette*, December 2.

------, 1985. "The Routinization of Conflict in the Modern Cult/Anti-Cult Controversy," *The Nebraska Humanist* 8, no. 2, pp. 26-39.

------, David G. Bromley, and Donna L. Oliver, 1984. *The Anti-Cult Movement in America: A Bibliography and Historical Survey*. New York, NY: Garland Publishing.

------, Bert L. Hardin, and David G. Bromley, 1983. "A Comparison of Anti-Cult Movements in the United States and Germany," in *Of Gods and Men: New Religious Movements in the West*. Macon, GA: Mercer University Press, pp. 177-93.

------, Roger Spielmann, and Sam Stigall, 1977. "Deprogramming: The New Exorcism," *American Behavioral Scientist* 20 (July/August), pp. 941-56.

------ and David G. Bromley, 1985. *A Documentary History of the Anti-Cult Movement*. Arlington, TX: Center for Social Research, University of Texas.

------, 1980. *The New Vigilantes: Deprogrammers, Anti-Cultists, and the New Religions*. Beverly Hills, CA: Sage Publications.

Singer, Margaret Thaler and Richard Ofshe, 1990. "Thought Reform Programs and the Production of Psychiatric Casualties," *Psychiatric Annals* 20 (April), pp. 188-93.

Sirkin, Mark I. and Lyman C. Wynne, 1990. "Cult Involvement as Relational Disorder," *Psychiatric Annals* 20, April, pp. 188-93.

Stoner, Carroll and Jo Anne Parke, 1977. *All God's Children: The Cult Experience–Salvation or Slavery?* Radnor, PA: Chilton Book Company.

"The Case Against a Cult Watchdog," 1993, *Sydney Morning Herald*. Sydney, Australia, April 26.

Verdier, Paul A., 1977. *Brainwashing and the Cults.* Hollywood, CA:
The Institute of Behavioral Conditioning.

Victor, Jeffrey S., 1993. *Satanic Panic: The Creation of a
Contemporary Legend.* Chicago, IL: Open Court.

THE MODERN ANTI-CULT
MOVEMENT IN NORTH AMERICA

CHAPTER I

THE MODERN NORTH AMERICAN
ANTI-CULT MOVEMENT 1971-91:
A TWENTY-YEAR RETROSPECTIVE

Anson Shupe and David G. Bromley

What social science now recognizes as the modern Northern American anti-cult movement (ACM), embodied in social movement organizations such as the American Family Foundation and the Cult Awareness Network, originated in the United States in 1971. It began as a decentralized grassroots effort to oppose the operations of unconventional religious groups, which scholars labeled new religious movements (NRMs). During the past two decades this countermovement has mobilized individual families/church groups/professional associations, conducted informational campaigns, lobbied public officials, engaged in vigilante-style abductions to "rescue" or "deprogram" persons who joined these religions, and sought regulatory legislation to restrict NRM activities (Shupe and Bromley, 1985a, 1985b, 1980; Shupe, Bromley, and Oliver, 1984; Shupe, Spielmann, and Stigall, 1977). The ACM as a social movement industry continues to be active in seeking to shape the public definitions of such groups as "destructive cults" and "pseudo-religions" in order to deter affiliations with them and to obstruct their organizational activities.

Elsewhere we have analyzed the structural strains within modern industrial American society, defined in terms of contradictions between contractual and covenantal forms of social relations, that undergird the cult/anti-cult struggle (Shupe, Busching, and Bromley, 1989; Bromley and Busching, 1988). There have been numerous other scholarly works chronicling either the larger new religious movements controversy (e.g., Saliba, 1990; Bromley, 1989; Robbins, 1989; Melton, 1986; Beckford, 1985; Bromley and Shupe, 1981; Shupe and Bromley, 1979; Bromley and Shupe, 1979a) or the trajectories of individual religious groups since the 1970s (Barker, 1984; Bromley and Shinn, 1989; Shinn, 1987; Bromley and Shupe, 1979b; Wallis, 1977). By comparison, there has been relatively little written directly on the ACM (Bromley and Shupe, 1987; Shupe and Bromley, 1980). However, the cult controversy cannot be put in proper theoretical or historical perspective absent a detailed analysis of the ACM, and the developmental histories of specific NRMs cannot be understood without reference to countermovement initiatives (e.g., Hall, 1988; Shupe and Bromley, 1979; Shinn, 1987). In this chapter we consider factors that have both facilitated and impeded the development of the ACM, and hence the role it has played in the cult controversy.

FACTORS IN ACM SUCCESS
AND DEVELOPMENT

Factors that have contributed to the ACM's successful development include (1) organizational consolidation, (2) professionalization and ideological evolution, and (3) target expansion. In each case the argument is not that the ACM has achieved some optimal state but rather that significant development on these dimensions has made the ACM a more cohesive and influential movement.

Organizational Consolidation

Any overview of the ACM's organizational evolution must relate how a far-flung set of similar family-based local groups repeatedly tried to merge and form increasingly larger coalitions. The driving inspiration behind such coalition-building was the awareness held by ACM leaders that their precarious countermovement lacked political clout and economic viability. The ACM began in the early 1970s as a series of grassroots groups arising spontaneously and independently across the continental United States. These groups were initially composed of parents who typically became alarmed about their offsprings' NRM affiliations upon learning some of the details of these religions' theologies, practices, and lifestyles. The religious groups in question initially included the Unification Church, Divine Light Mission, Children of God, and Hare Krishnas—all of which were organized communally. Parents levied charges of kidnapping or enslavement against these religious entities, but they encountered obstacles when the alleged "victims" countered that they were participating of their own free wills. Parents and families, in turn, charged that these predominantly young adults had been "brainwashed" or psychologically lured/coerced into joining and remaining in these groups. Formal agencies of social control proved to be of little use to the families. Many NRM converts were, after all, legal adults, and issues of religious freedom were involved. Thus, distraught parents who turned to the police, district attorneys, state and national legislators, psychiatrists, and even clergy often received a sympathetic hearing but little concrete assistance. The "cult" problem simply raised too many complex and thorny political issues for most public officials. The president of one ACM organization complained about the parents' resulting frustration in a 1976 ACM newsletter:

> Their offsprings' lives are surely being destroyed and their families torn apart because far too few are willing to investigate and then take positive action. Many Congressmen say it is a local problem while local officials are saying write your Congressman. (CFF, 1976)

Frustrating as such "put-offs" may have been, individual families became aware that they were not alone as they engaged in the process of expressing grievances to officials. Particularly through the media, they learned that other families were experiencing similar problems with what sounded like similar groups and situations.

It was at this point that families began to contact one another and meet to discuss their mutual concerns. Out of these contacts coalesced the first major ACM organization in 1972: The Parents' Committee to Free Our Sons and Daughters from the Children of God Organization, or FREECOG. The Children of God, interestingly enough, was not an exotic Eastern religion but rather was a home-grown offshoot of the late 1960s Jesus Movement. It did, however, totalistically separate converts from conventional lifestyles and commitments—the common denominator behind parental complaints. For two years FREECOG resisted pressures to expand its concerns beyond the Children of God. But gradually, as "atrocity stories" (Bromley and Shupe, 1979a) about other groups' alleged methods of indoctrination, fund-raising tactics, and totalistic lifestyles began to accumulate, FREECOG members became convinced that there was a more general "cult" problem.

Thus, in 1974 FREECOG expanded (after some organizational trial and error) into the Citizens Freedom Foundation (CFF), the largest

ACM group in the western United States and, for a time, in the entire country. CFF established a key "working precedent" that became the strategy of other ACM groups throughout the 1970s. CFF leaders reasoned that in order not to spread their limited resources too thinly they ought to focus on the NRM they perceived as the most powerful, visible, and dangerous of the "cults," the Rev. Sun Myung Moon's Unification Church. By 1976 Moon's multinational religion had become literally the "archetypal cult" that drew the most intense ACM opposition (Shupe and Bromley, 1980:97).

Meanwhile, the same word-of-mouth process by which FREECOG and then CFF attracted members was taking place simultaneously across North America as parents with similar problems banded together. By the mid-1970s there was a multitude of such groups, many surfacing for a time as autonomous entities, then dissolving or merging into larger coalitions. They possessed expressive names, such as Love our Children, Free Minds, Return to Personal Choice, Citizens Engaged in Reuniting Families, Citizens Organized for the Public Awareness of Cults, and the National Ad Hoc Committee Engaged in Freeing Minds.

By early 1976 sufficient national attention had been drawn to NRMs that local and regional ACM groups were aware of one another's actions and began to coordinate their attacks on the growing number of unconventional groups they termed "cults." The first national manifestation of this alliance came in February, 1976 when over 400 ACM members met with U.S. Senator Robert E. Dole of Kansas and other federal officials at a public hearing in Washington, D.C. to call for an investigation into the Unification Church (Shupe and Bromley, 1980:96-101, 186-90). Encouraged by this event, one year later the six largest regional ACM groups merged into a single national coalition (the International Foundation for Individual Freedom) because it alone had obtained tax-exempt status as an educational foundation. The merger, however, was never successful because regional groups were reluctant to relinquish their autonomy and identities, to disband their own leadership structures, or to pool their resources. Internal divisions persisted, and several months later the ACM returned to its earlier position as a loosely integrated movement consisting of decentralized regional organizations.

Only in the 1980s did the two preeminent, truly national ACM organizations emerge: the American Family Foundation (AFF), established in Lexington, Massachusetts, and the Cult Awareness Network (CAN), headquartered in Chicago. Unlike other ACM entities,

AFF solved a number of internal problems plaguing all such groups. For example, it operated on a "pay-as-you-go" basis. Instead of automatically counting as card-carrying members all persons who sent queries for information and maintaining artificially long mailing lists, it required subscriptions to its newsletter and publications. It sold reprints of transcripts of public hearings, legal documents, and its own reports on the "cult" problem as a means of raising funds. AFF leaders aggressively sought foundation grants and donations. In short, unlike many smaller ACM groups that eventually folded their tents, AFF established financial solvency and organizational stability. CAN, on the other hand, operated more as a network of confederated offices and outposts in cities across the United States. But it, too, adopted practices of information-dissemination that kept it financially stable.

Nevertheless, all ACM groups—both early and later—existed to serve the same four purposes: (1) to monitor and expose activities of a broad range of religious groups in the hopes of discrediting them; (2) to operate as clearinghouses of information and services (such as counseling or deprogramming) for parents who "lost" sons or daughters to such groups; (3) to provide expressive forums through which family members could express their anxieties; and (4) to lobby against NRMs as dangerous "pseudo-religions."

Alongside and loosely integrated with these grassroots groups was a smaller but highly visible component of the ACM: the deprogrammers. The deprogrammers were sometimes moral entrepreneurs, sometimes mercenary vigilantes who forcibly abducted and, if necessary, restrained members of various NRMs on the premise that these young adults had been beguiled, deceived, hypnotized, or *programmed* into joining the groups rather than being truly converted. Hence these devotees needed to be *deprogrammed.* The practice was conceived by a San Diego community action worker named Theodore "Ted" Patrick, Jr. (Bromley, 1988). Patrick possessed absolutely no formal academic or professional counseling credentials, but he claimed to have discovered a unique new mental health therapy capable of reversing the effects of cultic programming. Patrick and the generation of deprogrammers who learned their techniques from him relied on rough-and-tumble tactics, sometimes coordinating vigilante-style operations to capture NRM members and then engaging in marathon confrontations to convince the deprogrammee to defect. Most deprogrammers operated as individual entrepreneurs or in small groups on a fee-for-service basis, and they lumped together an amazingly diverse range of religions as dangerous. In fact, any group affiliation that families opposed became a potential case for deprogrammers of that period. This indiscriminate targeting by deprogrammers provided civil libertarians with powerful ammunition to attack the legitimacy of the ACM itself. Deprogrammers later discovered to their surprise that non-coercive tactics proved about as effective as physical abductions in achieving their objectives. The combination of increasing legal risks associated with coercive deprogramming and the discovery that non-coercive techniques were effective moved deprogramming toward the current practice that is termed voluntary "exit counseling."

There were other services as well. A motley assortment of individuals, ranging from licensed mental health practitioners to NRM apostates, offered counseling services to former NRM members. Periodically there also have been "clinics" or "recovery houses" (e.g., the Freedom of Thought Foundation in Arizona) operating with full-time counseling staff and legal representation (see Shupe and Bromley, 1980:136-142). These served as halfway houses, particularly for deprogrammed individuals who were in transition between NRM life and conventional society. And former members, sometimes in conjunction with counseling services, formed ex-member support groups that functioned as self-help therapy groups which allowed individuals readapting to conventional society to take stock of their experiences and plan for the future.

This integrated complement of services was critical to ACM organizational consolidation. Families were able to obtain information on NRMs about which they typically possessed only the most rudimentary information and then could pursue a variety of strategies, ranging from simply waiting to deprogramming, through ACM channels. While alternative sources of information about NRMs became available as time went on, there were few options to the ACM for families that decided on unilateral intervention in their offspring's NRM affiliations.

Despite the importance of the ACM organizations' provision of grassroots' services in the development of the movement, it has also been a persistent source of instability for the ACM. One problem has been that many families have utilized ACM services only so long as an offspring was affiliated with an NRM, then they deactivated as soon as their family conflict was resolved. The ACM thus faces continuing problems in generating a stable, long-term activist base. Another problem has been that deprogrammers have constantly flirted with the boundaries of the law; thus, allowing deprogrammers to recruit clients through the ACM network has risked eroding the ACM's public legitimacy as well as the support of therapists who insist on working only with clients who voluntarily solicit their services. Force and abductions simply are incompatible with the norms of the established therapeutic community, and, therefore, vigilante deprogrammers like Ted Patrick have increasingly been relegated to the sidelines, still symbolically honored by movement insiders as founding heroes but carefully screened from public view. These problems notwithstanding, the ACM projected a much more effective presence once organizational consolidation had been accomplished.

Professionalization and Ideological Evolution

Culturally, the cult/anti-cult struggle has been a war of definitions and labels. Each side has claimed the moral high ground, casting its opponents in the role of being dangerous to religious liberties and the social order. The ACM has portrayed new religions as *ersatz* religions operated by opportunistic charlatans who transform their followers into robotic slaves. Various new religions, for their part, have cried "witch hunt," appealing to American values of fair play and claiming that they are the victims of narrow-minded religious bigotry. In this symbolic struggle, a key element in ACM development, therefore, has been to develop legitimation for its coercive mind control ideology. Mental health professionals have played a central role in this legitimation process.

The lack of sophistication in the early ACM is attributable to the fact that the first ACM groups were basically grassroots, family enterprises. The founders of the ACM came from varied backgrounds, and they perceived their cause as a temporary or emergency stop-gap activity that would soon accomplish its objectives and/or be picked up by appropriate law enforcement officials. They never envisioned an organization combatting cults that would become a permanent feature on America's religious landscape. Though one could locate some professionals and university-credentialed persons among the ACM leadership during the 1970s, only a few in this first "generation" of leadership could in any way be considered mental health specialists. Most professionals involved were physicians, lawyers, businessmen, clergy, and educators (Shupe and Bromley, 1980:93-94). They became involved in the ACM when their offspring joined unconventional religious movements, and they rose to positions of leadership because their high levels of education made them articulate spokespersons for the movement. To be sure, there were mental health professionals and others sympathetic to the ACM in these "early days" (i.e., in the early-to-mid 1970s), but these were not its leaders even if they played an important role in attesting to the legitimacy of the counter-movement's subversion ideology.

ACM founders also did not bother to systematically work out the details of the alleged mind control techniques purportedly used by "cults." Early ACM activists defined the terms of the struggle with NRMs within the symbolic context of a mind control/subversion ideology. Ex-members of NRMs accounted for their conversions simply by claiming they were drugged or hypnotized, deprogrammer-entrepreneurs claimed that they possessed the knowledge and techniques to break cult-induced trance states, and a badly misinterpreted post-Korean War literature on the psychology of attitude change was co-opted to lend the color of scientific knowledge to their activities. This ideology was rapidly and easily absorbed into America's popular culture as a result of the deeply ingrained belief in Communist brainwashing techniques.

Occasionally, mental health professionals publicly affirmed this subversion mythology. For example, clinical psychologist Paul A. Verdier, writing in 1977 when the modern cult scare was shifting into high gear, claimed that awesome powers of persuasion were possessed by the Unification Church's founder, the Rev. Sun Myung Moon. Said Verdier (Verdier, 1977:8):

> [The Rev. Sun Myung Moon] knows enough about mass hypnosis, conditioning, and brainwashing so that he does not even have to conduct his sermons in English. Korean will serve his purposes equally well, although few of his converts understand a word of it. Mass hypnosis does not need reason and logic to be effective; gestures will serve equally as well.

Other ACM activists developed a more sophisticated approach, using popularized brainwashing stereotypes in public forums and more circumspect, less sensationalistic renditions in professional settings (Anthony, 1990). As a result, even though very few persons in the general public possessed even the most rudimentary knowledge of the tenets or practices of the Unification Church or Hare Krishna, most were confident that "Moonies" and Krishna devotees were brainwashed (Shupe, 1987; Bromley and Shupe, 1979a). A cult then became any group employing subversive mind control tactics.

By the mid-1980s the ACM had undergone a transformation. Not only had the larger groups, such as the Citizens Freedom Foundation (located in Southern California, America's "cult capital") and the American Family Foundation, achieved financial stability, but also the ACM's leadership had in many ways become professionalized. The ACM became infused with medical, psychiatric, and psychological activists who took it far beyond the non-institutionalized days of vigilante deprogrammers. They perceived what sociologist Thomas Robbins (1989:177) has called an *opportunity structure* "to develop new and prestigious roles as counselors and rehabilitators of 'cult victims'." These professionals, representing various mental health fields, co-opted ACM leadership positions and turned the movement into a "growth industry" for therapists by redefining "destructive cultism" to be an emotional illness or psychological pathology. Robbins and Anthony (1982) have termed this labeling process the "medicalization" of religious deviance.

This new level of involvement by mental health professionals is visible in the American Family Foundation, by the 1990s one of the ACM's two premier organizations. The AFF's monthly newsletter, *The Cult Observer* (formerly *The Advisor*) became a major clearinghouse of information about cult/anti-cult legal conflicts as well as the major forum for various professionals involved with the ACM to present their views. *The Cult Observer* even occasionally printed editorials and letters to the editor by researchers unsympathetic to ACM ideology. The AFF held annual conventions and promoted national conferences.

At the beginning of the 1980s the AFF appointed a psychiatric social worker, Jean Merritt, as its Director of Government Affairs in Washington, D.C. In Spring, 1981 the AFF announced the establishment of its Center on Destructive Cults, with Harvard affiliate faculty member and psychiatrist John G. Clark, Jr. (a long-time ACM sympathizer) as its Executive Director. Psychologist Michael D. Langone was named the Center's Director of Research. In addition to a number of well known ACM attorneys and religious figures on the Center's Advisory Board, other members from the behavioral science community included a sociology professor at Loyola University of

Chicago, a psychology professor at the University of Southern California, a physician who was also assistant professor of psychiatry at Harvard Medical School and Director of Postgraduate Education for the Department of Psychiatry at Massachusetts General Hospital, and the chief psychologist for Adult Outpatient Services at the Lafayette Clinic in Detroit (*Advisor,* 1981).

The Center on Destructive Cultism has published special monograph reports, such as *Destructive Cult Conversions: Theory, Research, and Treatment* (Clark *et al.,* 1981) and pamphlets such as *Destructive Cultism: Questions and Answers* (Langone, 1982). In addition, it has published semi-annually *The Cultic Studies Journal,* edited by Michael Langone, with articles conforming in organization and style to other professional behavioral science publications. According to a 1984 annual report, the subscription list of scholars and professionals had reached several hundred, and it has to grow in succeeding years (AFF, 1984).

This professionalization of the ACM has brought new, more scientifically "neutral" jargon to its subversion mythology. Devotees and converts are no longer "zombies" or "brainwashed automatons" but rather suffer from "post-traumatic stress syndrome," "dissociative states" or a "cult-imposed personality syndrome." Concepts and jargon from the lexicon of psychiatry have been created or redefined to reinterpret the crude "atrocity" accounts of the initial generation of "cult victims."

Such changes were inevitable once distraught families in the fledgling ACM reached out to the behavioral science community for allies. They had been largely rebuffed by many scholars studying NRMs whose research revealed that these groups did not correspond to ACM stereotypes and who began drawing parallels between the modern anti-cult movement and earlier anti-Mormon/anti-Masonic/anti-Catholic campaigns. The relatively few academics and health professionals who did take up the cause of the ACM made great inroads in recasting its tone and methods. To put it another way, higher education drove out lower education in setting the ACM agenda.

Ironically, it was these same mental health professionals, more than any lawsuits brought against deprogrammers or civil libertarian lobbyists, who finally delegitimated the deprogrammers. Unlike deprogrammers (who were drawn from the ranks of private detectives, attorneys, used car salesmen, and NRM apostates who lacked any training in mental health), these credentialed professionals were members of accredited therapeutic fields. They could not be associated professionally as peers of the vigilante deprogrammers. At the height of the deprogramming controversy we (Shupe and Bromley, 1981) posed the following rhetorical question: "If deprogrammers, otherwise untrained in any behavioral science or profession, can suddenly begin performing attitudinal lobotomies and do so more quickly and inexpensively than traditional healers, what does this bode for psychology and psychiatry?" The obvious answer was that it would not bode well at all. The mental health professionals appreciated this fact. Moreover, as entrepreneurs themselves they realized the potential for creating a vastly expanded clientele by redefining unconventional religiosity as psychological pathology.[1] Thus they moved to stake out their personal claims of expertise regarding "cult" membership and to reshape the ACM subversion mythology in order that it better approximated the analytic logic of science.

The strength of this ideological development was that it created allies for the ACM within the mental health establishment who possessed the power of defining mental health and illness and therefore offered significant "clout" in shaping public perceptions of new religious movements (Richardson, 1993). These new allies lent greater credibility to the ACM and redirected the ACM's concerns away from families' angst with errant offspring to issues of personal pathology, public health, and societal well-being. What had been primarily a private trouble could now become a public issue. Thus the infusion of psychiatric jargon and models of psychodynamics helped shift the terms of the cult controversy in a more sophisticated, scientistic direction. The impact of mental health professionals became particularly significant in the 1980s when ACM strategy evolved to ACM-sponsored civil suits brought in the names of former NRM members who alleged experiencing emotional trauma as a result of their NRM affiliations. Expert witness testimony from mental health professionals sympathetic to the ACM played a major role in these cases (Anthony, 1990; Bromley, 1989).

But there was also a weakness in medicalizing religious conflict. This strategy mobilized a counter-coalition of social science and religion scholars, clergy, and civil libertarians, among others. It thereby created allies for many deviant religious groups that might otherwise have found themselves without sympathizers. This coalition was most strongly united in opposition to coercive deprogrammings, which one civil libertarian likened to "spiritual gang rape" (Kelley, 1977:32). For their part, ACM activists insisted they were not opposed to religious liberty, which they defined in terms of *freedom of belief*. They continually reiterated that religious groups could hold any religious tenets, however exotic; it was "abusive" practices with which they were concerned. While this position may have disarmed some opposition, it did little to assuage those who recognized that the kind of identity transformation associated with conversion to "strict churches" (Kelley, 1972) would inevitably become vulnerable to challenge under such a definition. An uneasy standoff continues over this issue. These tensions notwithstanding, the greater ideological sophistication of ACM ideology and support from elements of the credentialed mental health community dramatically enhanced ACM credibility and influence.

Target Expansion: The Widening Cult Net

As the ACM achieved greater organizational stability and professional respectability in the late 1980s it found itself with a critical, if curious, problem. Primed with better organization and more resources than ever before to wage war on the communal NRMs, in many ways events had left the ACM behind. The groups that the countermovement began opposing in 1972 and shortly after had radically changed over two decades. Some, like the cult of Rajneesh, the Divine Light Mission, and the Children of God were in varying stages of organizational demise. The original archetypal cult, the Unification Church, was engaged in a major reorganization and retrenchment that saw its efforts and resources shifting from America to Asia and Eastern Europe (e.g., Shupe, 1990b). Meanwhile, the Hare Krishna movement had seriously fragmented, weakened by the death of its founder and a subsequent struggle for power that racked the movement during the 1980s (Shinn, 1987). Virtually all of these groups experienced a mix of low recruitment and high defection rates. None any longer seemed nearly so monolithic, invincible, or intimidating as they had when the ACM emerged.

What is more, the old ACM stereotypes of the surviving movements were seriously out of step with reality. Most significantly, the communal lifestyles to which families had initially been so opposed were evolving into forms less at odds with American culture, including more romantic love-based marriages, prenuptial engagements, and families living and raising children in their own nuclear residences (Shupe, 1990b, 1985; James, 1983). Further, street and airport solicitations by Unificationists and Krishnas had become mostly relics of the past. Both the Hare Krishna and Unification Church had vastly diversified their economic bases, which yielded more conventional career opportunities for members. Likewise, the non-economic ways by which the originally communal NRMs interacted with the public changed. There were academic conferences, festivals, outreach charitable programs for the urban poor, drug rehabilitation programs, and participation in local events and organizations such as parades and chambers of commerce (e.g., Rochford, 1987; Shupe, 1990b, 1985). Krishna temples, for example, began serving as cultural beacons in cities and communities where persons of Hindu ethnicity came to worship and contribute money. A number of temples started vegetarian restaurants that served the general public. Meanwhile, the Rev. Sun Myung Moon's declining American empire, while experiencing leadership and membership factionalism (Mickler, 1987), spent the latter 1980s attempting to forge an alliance with the conservative wing of the Republican Party. Its glossy magazine *The World and I* and its flagship newspaper the *Washington Times* became major outlets of respected conservative opinion. These sorts of changes in the most "spotlighted" communal religions, plus the fact that many groups simply did not survive the 1970s, meant that the ACM was faced with losing its original target group. Its most visible opponents were moving toward the mainstream, thereby creating fewer opponents and reducing the likelihood of negative media coverage. By the late 1980s such groups were of great concern only to the immediate families of NRM converts and the ACM.

The declining number of communal NRM members has been compensated for by an expansion in the number of groups that the ACM designated as "cults" or groups that manifest "cult-like characteristics." In fact, the total number of members of all the communal NRMs at any given time never exceeded 25,000 individuals. And consistent with the history of communes in the United States, most NRMs have been quite short-lived, at least as communes. From an organizational perspective, then, the extension of the anti-cult campaign to quasi-therapeutic groups (ranging from Scientology to Synanon), independent fundamentalist churches, and even militant political movements created a much larger pool of potential clients and greater visibility for the ACM.

Yet, it is not clear that the ACM deliberately pursued a strategy of target expansion. In part, expansion was due to the fact that the ACM gradually became aware of the broadly based search for community as reflected in the popularity and growth of secular communes, fundamentalist Christian churches, Orthodox Judaism and therapeutic communities, as well as communal NRMs. Any such high demand organization raised the specter of cultism. It is also true, however, that countersubversion campaigns thrive on an expanding enemies list and heightened danger.

The problem the ACM created in casting its net more widely is that some of the common attributes its initial targets shared by virtue of communal organization were muted or absent in later additions to the list of cultic groups. Various interest groups also began nominating groups as cults once the term "cult" achieved notoriety. For example, some Jewish interests designated the Jews for Jesus as a dangerous cult, quasi-economic organizations like Amway were compared to the Moonies, televangelists were referred to in the media as cult leaders, and some deprogrammers fancied a new market in intense romantic relationships which they described as composed of a cult leader and a cult of one (Bromley and Shupe, forthcoming) or what some psychologists popularly termed co-dependents. But while the expansion of target groups created problems in maintaining the credibility of terms like "cult" and "brainwashing," it also insured a steady supply of clients for the ACM.

INHIBITING FACTORS
IN ACM DEVELOPMENT

Factors that inhibited ACM development included (1) movement sequestration, (2) failure to mobilize state-authorized sanctions, and (3) inability to gain regulatory group status. None of these three factors has jeopardized the ACM's existence as a movement; however, each has limited its developmental potential.

Movement Sequestration

If the ACM is to broaden its narrow base as a movement combatting only "destructive cults," one strategy for doing so would be to build alliances with other groups around the structural tensions in American society to which the ACM and other related movements are responses. In fact, the ACM is not unique in the conditions to which it responds. It is potentially related either to groups opposing individual churches or sets of churches or to the numerous childsaving movements (Best, 1990). Either of these strategic avenues presents significant problems and liabilities, however, and, to date, the ACM has achieved only minimal success in either direction.

There is a significant number of anti-sectarian groups that oppose a specific established church, such as the Jehovah's Witnesses, Seventh Day Adventists, Christian Scientists, or Mormons. There also are umbrella anti-sectarian organizations that have targeted a whole range of sectarian churches as cults (Shupe, Bromley, and Oliver, 1984). When NRMs began to appear, both types of anti-sectarian groups simply extended their critiques to include NRMs as the "new cults" (see, e.g., Martin, 1980). The ideologies of some of these anti-sectarian groups do contain the same kind of undue influence and abuse of power themes central to ACM ideology, and some of these sectarian churches do bear resemblance to NRMs in terms of the level of membership commitment. However, the anti-sectarian groups primarily feature direct attacks on sectarian church theologies. In essence, the primary normative standard against which any religious group is measured is theological orthodoxy. This stance has posed a significant alliance impediment for the ACM. Becoming a coalitional partner with groups challenging the theological tenets of any church might seriously undermine the ACM's assertion that it is in opposition to organizational practices and not to theological beliefs. Further, confronting churches that have attained a considerable measure of public legitimacy would strengthen the coalition opposing the ACM.

An alternative coalitional partner with which the ACM has made contact is Fundamentalists Anonymous (FA), a group formed in New York City in 1985 as a support group for former fundamentalist Christians (Finn, n.d.). According to founder Richard Yao, characteristics of fundamentalism include authoritarian leadership, a belief that the group possesses a monopoly on the truth, an excessive and oppressive set of rules, a group persecution complex, strong control over members, and esoteric beliefs known only to insiders (Yao, 1985:4). Yao asserts that

> The strong urge to control, to impose itself on others, and to be intolerant of differing viewpoints are not accidental byproducts of fundamentalism; they are its essence. When a

person needs an authoritarian worldview that keeps him in a state of permanent psychological dependence, it is a disease of the mind that should be taken seriously. It is time to recognize that fundamentalism is hazardous to the psychological well-being of millions and that it is a social disease that threatens the ideals and basic assumptions of a pluralistic democracy (1985:1).

The themes of psychological dependence, disease, and authoritarian leadership all resonate with ACM ideology. The failure to form a coalition appears to be attributable in part to the fact that FA defines its objective as guiding *"dissatisfied* fundamentalists out of fundamentalism" (Yao, 1985:6, emphasis added). FA pointedly eschews "intervention" that involves "force . . . kidnapping . . . threats, innuendos, arguments, or promises" (Finn, n.d.:17). In addition, FA has modeled its "intervention" on the Alcoholics Anonymous model. On both counts, then, FA has elected for voluntaristic self-selection of clients that does not mesh easily with the more confrontive intervention techniques of the ACM. The price of the alliance, one that the ACM has been unwilling to pay, might well be moving away from an interventionist toward a support group orientation. Given the relatively widespread mistrust of religious fundamentalists in mainstream America, however, such an alliance might substantially enhance the visibility of the ACM cause.

The ACM also has alliance potential with one or more of the childsaving movements that have flourished over the last two decades. American families' capacity to control their children's lives has diminished in recent years while the influence of peer groups, school systems, social service agencies, and media and economic interests targeting youthful consumers has steadily increased. One result has been "a plethora of family-based, grassroots movements seeking to reassert control by nominating as social problems such family-related issues as drug use, missing and abducted children, heavy metal rock music, fantasy games, sexuality and violence in the media, child pornography, drunk driving, and teenage suicide and birth control/abortion (Bromley, 1991b:67). The objective of each of these movements has been to "save" children from some set of forces over which family control has declined. The ACM can usefully be viewed as one such childsaving group.

One set of childsaving groups with which the ACM has shown recent signs of coordinating is the Anti-Satanism Movement (ASM). Since 1980 there has been an outbreak of Satanic cult fears in the United States, Canada, and Europe that has reached roughly the same level of intensity as the 1970s religious cult scare (Richardson, Best, and Bromley, 1991; Hicks, 1991; Shupe, 1991, 1990a). In its most extreme form, ASM ideology sketches a massive conspiracy by an international, hierarchically organized cult which ritually abuses and sacrifices tens of thousands of children annually (Bromley, 1991a). Teenagers allegedly are induced to join the cult through dabbling in drugs, sex parties, subliminal messages in heavy metal music and participation in fantasy role-playing games. The ACM has divided on the credibility of ASM claims. On the one hand, an AFF report labels as "false" the international cult claims, as "highly suspect" testimonies from women claiming to be "ritual abuse survivors" who were used as "breeders" to provide a supply of infants for ritual sacrifice, and as "dubious" allegations that there are small, intergenerational Satanic cults that have perpetrated ritualistic child abuse over a long period of time (Langone and Blood, 1990:56-57). On the other hand, the Chairman of the CAN Ritual Abuse Advisory Committee stated:

> As involvement progresses, dabblers may participate in criminal acts such as desecration of graves, theft, selling drugs, and arson. When some members of the group become bored with animal sacrifices, the next step is human sacrifice or suicide. At this point many members become frightened and attempt to leave the belief system. To escape they may seek hospitalization, enter a substance abuse program, or commit suicide (Robert Simandl and Bette Naysmith, 1988:4).

Further, the Cult Awareness Network, in cooperation with police departments, entrepreneurial law enforcement "Satanism-experts," social service workers, and health care providers is now actively sponsoring and participating in workshops and seminars to "educate" a wide range of professionals about this Satanic cult threat. Given the high level of public anxiety over Satanic cult activity, these conferences and workshops have been valuable forums in which the ACM can regenerate concern with its traditional target groups.

Important points of ideological convergence between the ASM and ACM are the themes of brainwashing, abuse, and cults (Bromley,

1991a).[2] For example, in warning of the dangers of Satanic cults, the ACM is able to incorporate a number of "warning signs" it has traditionally associated with "religious cults," such as withdrawal from family and friends, personality changes, and erratic school performance ("A Parent's Primer," 1988:150). The ASM's high visibility on Satanism has dramatically increased the flow of request for information. CAN reports that it received 6 calls per month in 1987, 27 percent of the calls requesting information about specific groups, compared with 165 calls per month in 1989, 37 percent of the total calls the organization received during that year ("Satanism Concerns," 1990:2). Public concerns about Satanism obviously have facilitated ACM contact with the same segment of the population that it drew upon as clients during the 1970s religious cult scare.

Links with childsaving movements such as the ASM are not without risks. A primary obstacle to coalition formation with these groups is that each has propounded its own narrowly focused subversion ideology identifying "killer drunks," "drug pushers," or "child pornographers" as the specific source of subversion of children. The ACM replicates this subversion logic with its "maniacal guru," "cult," and "brainwashing" ideology. Each of the childsaving groups thus has developed a vested interest in its own subversion ideology and organizational base. Further no compelling evidence of Satanic cult activity has yet been found, and ASM ideology recently has come under the same kind of criticism that ACM ideology did in the previous decade (Richardson, Best and Bromley, 1991; Hicks, 1991; Carlson and Larue *et al.,* 1989). The ACM thus risks being discredited by association with the Satanic subversion claims. The ideological and organizational fragmentation of childsaving movements ultimately derives from their response to symptomatic conditions rather than root causes. The effect is that coalitions among them are difficult to forge. The ACM both contributes to and bears the consequences of this fragmentation.

Failure to Mobilize State-Authorized Sanctions

The ACM has persistently attempted to mobilize both governmental and private organizations that possess the capacity to influence public opinion or impose sanctions on NRMs. These initiatives have taken place at the local, state, and national levels, with consistently mixed results. In general, initiatives at the local level have been the most successful as civic leaders have sought to respond to community constituents. At the state and national levels countervailing principles and interests have yielded more ambiguous and unsatisfying outcomes for partisans on both sides of the cult controversy.

At the local community level throughout the 1970s and 1980s the ACM launched a series of community level educational campaigns, contacting church organizations, PTA's, chambers of commerce, newspapers, local businesses, and other civic groups in attempts to cut off any unwitting cooperation with "cults." In many cases local ACM groups organized protests to prevent NRM recruiting teams, campus groups, and local organizational affiliates from locating in their communities. Activists gave talks at Rotary, Kiwanis, and Lions' Club luncheons warning of the danger posed by cults. They paraded ex-Moonies, ex-Krishnas, and ex-premies before teenage audiences at Methodist/Baptist/Catholic youth fellowship groups and at church meetings. They stumped for their cause on call-in radio programs and television talk shows, and they offered interviews to any news reporters who would listen. These local activities often were relatively successful. For example, many local governments refused permits to NRM fundraising teams, local zoning boards encumbered property purchases, and local police officials even winked at abductions of NRM members by deprogrammers, viewing these as family conflicts.

The ACM also has been active at the state level, sometimes achieving symbolic victories through legislative resolutions mirroring its concerns or at a minimum raising the topic of new religions *on its own terms.* ACM workers helped inspire and promote hearings and investigations in states as diverse as California, Vermont, New York, Texas, Minnesota, Michigan, and Illinois. They almost succeeded spectacularly at legislating social control of new religions in the New York State Assembly in 1977. New York Assemblyman Robert Wertz, who became involved in ACM activities through having a close friend's son join a NRM, introduced a bill to amend the state's penal law. Titled "Promoting a Pseudo-Religious Cult," its goal was to make promoting such a "cult" a felony. The bill was narrowly defeated.

Soon thereafter a new bill was introduced—the objective of which was to establish a legal mechanism that would enable parents to gain legal custody of their NRM-affiliated adult offspring. The bill constituted an extension of the "temporary conservatorship" provisions, common to state civil codes. Conservatorships were created to allow emergency action by relatives in the event that a senile or unstable family member was in imminent danger of committing an irrevocably self-injurious act, such as an elderly relative about to squander savings. The ACM proposed to extend these provisions to cover adults who had been subjected to a "thought reform program." Parents would be able to petition a court for legal custody based on their own assertions and without the identified individual being present. Families would then be empowered by state authority to separate their offspring from an NRM and to conduct a deprogramming during the custody period. This bill passed both houses of the state assembly for two successive years. It was defeated only after intense lobbying by civil liberties groups, mobilized primarily by NRMs, prompted gubernatorial vetoes on both occasions.[3] Both the pseudo-religion and conservatorship bills contained a veritable summation of vintage stereotypes taken directly from the ACM's subversion mythology. In the end, no bills of this kind were successful despite continuing skirmishes across the country. Nonetheless, the hearings accompanying such legislation produced widespread media coverage that raised all of the ACM allegations against NRMs.

At the national level ACM members were encouraged to participate in repeated lobbying campaigns directed at congressional members and certain government agencies, such as the Internal Revenue Service and the Immigration and Naturalization Service. For example, they sought to have foreign members of NRMs deported or blocked from entry into this country and requested investigations into the financial dealings and tax-exempt status of groups such as the Unification Church and the Church of Scientology. In one such case the national ACM coalition mounted an extensive lobbying effort during 1977 to have a Unification Church official cited for contempt of Congress for refusing to testify before the "Fraser Committee" (the House Subcommittee on International Organizations, chaired by Representative Donald E. Fraser) during the "Koreagate" scandal. A professional lobbyist was even retained for visits to members of Congress while ACM members across the country participated in a letter-writing campaign to their representatives (Shupe and Bromley, 1980:187-189). After the 1978 massacre of over 900 members of the Peoples Temple at Jonestown, Guyana, the ACM felt emboldened by what it considered vindication for its worst fears and pressed harder for government intervention. Again there were hearings, but no tangible initiatives against cults. This effort is symbolic of the frustration the ACM experienced at the federal level, and ACM supporters were bitterly disappointed that even after a disaster of this magnitude they were unable to mobilize federal agencies (Shupe and Bromley, 1982; Shupe, Bromley and Breschel, 1989).

All of the ACM initiatives did not involve governmental agencies. In 1978, for example, a letter-writing campaign was conducted to generate support for an anti-cult resolution on "Pseudo-religious Cults" under consideration by the National Parent Teachers Association at its annual convention in Atlanta, Georgia. This resolution, drafted by the ACM's International Foundation for Individual Freedom, called on the PTA to establish seminar "workshops" and programs to educate youth about NRMs and to support federal investigation of such groups. The PTA's 900 chapter delegates ultimately approved the resolution (Shupe and Bromley, 1980:191).

The larger, better organized NRM's responded to this ACM campaign by using their sometimes-considerable financial assets to mount a legal defense. They went to court at both municipal and state levels to challenge restrictions on their right to fundraise and missionize in public places and to prevent rezoning of the land on which their centers and buildings rested. The Unification Church sent its own representatives to Senator Robert Dole's 1979 Washington hearings on "cults" to reassure America that they were not about to commit any Jonestown-style suicide. Representatives of other NRM's, frequently in the company of civil libertarians, made their way to various state houses to try to turn the tables on their detractors and allege religious discrimination. NRM's sponsored lawsuits in the names of unsuccessfully deprogrammed members against their deprogrammers in an effort to take the profit out of deprogramming.

What ensued then through the later 1970s and most of the 1980s was an escalating series of battles conducted in political and judicial forums. This escalation can, with some oversimplification, be exemplified in the following way: When young adults joined communal NRM's, they frequently distanced themselves from their families and former lifestyles. Parents often responded to this distancing with attempts to reassert their control. NRM members, with group encouragement, reacted by becoming more secretive about their activities and location. Parents began resorting to abduction/deprogrammings to reestablish previous family relations. NRM's then challenged local law enforcement officials' permissiveness toward abductions by deprogrammers. The ACM began helping parents obtain temporary conservatorship orders so that NRM members could be deprogrammed while in parental custody. NRM's and their civil libertarian allies contested the legality of these orders. The ACM then sought to extend conservatorship provisions to define NRM affiliation as psychologically incapacitating, as they did in New York. When conservatorship bills were defeated, the ACM began developing voluntary exit counseling procedures.[4]

And so it went. Each side savored its victories, or at least what were perceived as victories, in this religious trench warfare. The ACM won numerous symbolic resolutions of support from public and private agencies but little access to formal sanctions. Civil suits by embittered former NRM members not infrequently were successful in gaining convictions in local jury trials, but just as often decisions were mitigated or reversed in the appellate courts. Tax-exempt status for some NRM's was denied or revoked, but in some cases it was later reinstated. Deprogrammers did succeed in convincing a high proportion of their deprogrammees to leave NRM's, but deprogramming became an ever more precarious occupation. There were, of course, some visible highwater marks, such as Rev. Moon's 1982 conviction for federal income tax evasion, the deportation of the Bhagwan Shree Rajneesh, and the conviction of high ranking Scientology officials on burglary charges. In general, however, these legal actions were initiated by governmental agencies on the basis of their own interests rather than as support for the ACM. In the end, then, there have not been any decisive victories, as the earliest ACM activists had naively hoped. And so the chess game of legal maneuvering simply continues.

Inability to Achieve Regulatory Group Status

Another alternative open to the ACM was to assume the role of a private watchdog or regulatory group. In some cases, such as for charitable organizations that operate with little formal public accountability or governmental control, private regulatory groups in essence enunciate normative operational standards. These organizations collect and disseminate information on charitable groups and publicly identify groups that are deemed to be in non-compliance. The success of private regulatory groups obviously hinges on voluntary reporting and cooperation from the charitable groups.

In general, the ACM has sought to occupy independent regulatory status by collecting reports, often from former members of NRM's or media accounts, on cultic practices. These reports are then reproduced in movement publications and disseminated to interested parties requesting information from the ACM. Specific NRM's are added to a list of groups about which critical reports have been received. The major problem the ACM faces, of course, is that it lacks both an independent research capability and direct access to NRM's. Perhaps the most significant project seeking consensual participation the ACM launched involved an AFF "Proposal to Develop a Code of Ethics for Religious Influences Participating in a Pluralistic Society" (AFF, n.d.). AFF began by attempting to elicit support from Christian churches. If a broad spectrum of major Christian groups were to subscribe to a code of ethics negotiated under ACM auspices, the ACM might then be in a position to influence more marginal groups to alter specific practices. Even though this project has not succeeded to date, it exemplifies nicely the independent regulatory model. The major impediment to extending this type of project is that the ACM continues to co-mingle countermovement and regulatory agency attributes.

SUMMARY AND CONCLUSIONS

There has been a veritable avalanche of research on NRM's since 1970. By comparison, relatively little has been written on the ACM which formed in opposition to them, still less on its later stages of evolution. However, the full story of the late twentieth-century cult controversy is one of movements and countermovements in open conflict with one another and vying for coalitional partners who would support their respective causes. In this chapter we have examined some factors that have facilitated and impeded the development of the ACM as a countermovement. The ACM's organizational consolidation, professionalization and ideological evolution, and target expansion enabled it to become a significant influence in the cult controversy. But its failure to marshall allies from among the ranks of related movement organizations, its failure to mobilize state-authorized sanctions, and its inability to function as an independent regulatory group have frustrated attainment of its objective of vanquishing NRM's. It is often (correctly) asserted that the American religious economy is a relatively open one. However, understanding the interests which shape its actual openness at an historical moment requires observing not just new entries into the religious marketplace but also the control responses they evoke.

NOTES

1. It is not necessary to postulate either conscious planning or conspiratorial motives to explain this domain expansion by mental health professionals. On the one hand, they simply recognized an untapped pool of potential clients. On the other hand, the increasing cultural importance of voluntarism, autonomy, and rationality disposed them to regard movements in which the group was given priority over the individual as problematic. Once they began working with clients, it was a simple matter to fence off their new domain on the basis of acquired experience and insight.

2. The ASM also explains victimization in terms of drugs and terror tactics, ideological elements the ACM has largely discarded.

3. This political encounter was of some importance since New York serves as a model legislation state for many states lacking extensive legal staffing. Had the bill become law, its passage would have been used to build support for similar legislation that was already being introduced by ACM supporters in many other states at the time.

4. The maneuvering became even more intricate at each stage. For example, when NRMs learned that a conservatorship order was being issued against one of their members, they challenged the order immediately and had it rescinded before a deprogramming could take place. ACM attorneys then began attempting to obtain conservatorships late on a Friday afternoon just before court closing. By the time NRM attorneys challenged the orders in court on Monday morning, a deprogramming had already taken place.

REFERENCES

Advisor, The, 1981. Weston, MA: American Family Foundation. (April/May):3.

American Family Foundation, 1984. *American Family Foundation Report.* Weston, MA: December.

------, n.d. "Proposal to Develop a Code of Ethics for Religious Influencers Participating in a Pluralistic Society," Weston, MA: American Family Foundation.

Anthony, Dick, 1990. "Religious Movements and Brainwashing Litigation: Evaluating Key Testimony," in Thomas Robbins and Dick Anthony, eds., *In Gods We Trust: New Patterns of Religious Pluralism in America.* New Brunswick, NJ: Transaction, pp. 295-344.

Barker, Eileen, 1984. *The Making of A Moonie: Brainwashing or Choice?* New York: Basil Blackwell.

Beckford, James A., 1985. *Cult Controversies.* New York: Tavistock.

Best, Joel, 1990. *Threatened Children: Rhetoric and Concern About Child-Victims.* Chicago, IL: University of Chicago Press.

Bromley, David G., 1991a. "Constructing Social Subversion: A Comparison of the Anti-Satanism and Anti-religious Cult Campaigns." Paper presented at the annual meeting of the Society for the Scientific Study of Religion. Cincinnati, OH.

------, 1991b. "Satanism: The New Cult Scare," in James Richardson, Joel Best and David Bromley, eds., *The Satanism Scare.* Hawthorne, NY: Aldine de Gruyter, pp. 49-72.

------, 1989. "Hare Krishna and the Anti-cult Movement," in David G. Bromley and Larry Shinn, eds., *Krishna Consciousness in the West.* Lewisburg, PA: Bucknell University Press, pp. 255-292.

------, 1988. "Deprogramming as a Mode of Exit from New Religious Movements: The Case of the Unificationist Movement," in David G. Bromley, ed., *Falling from the Faith: Causes and Consequences of Religious Apostasy.* Newbury Park: Sage Publications, pp. 185-204.

------, and Bruce Busching, 1988. "Understanding the Structure of Contractual and Covenantal Social Relations: Implications for the Sociology of Religion," *Sociological Analysis* 49 (December), pp. 15-32.

------, and Larry Shinn, eds., *Krishna Consciousness in the West.* Lewisburg, PA: Bucknell University Press.

------, 1987. "The Future of the Anti-cult Movement," in David G. Bromley and Phillip E. Hammond, eds., *The Future of New Religious Movements.* Macon, GA: Mercer University Press, pp. 221-234.

------, 1981. *Strange Gods: The Great American Cult Scare.* Boston: Beacon Press.

------, 1979a. "Atrocity Tales, the Unification Church, and the Social Construction of Evil," *Journal of Communication* 29 (Summer), pp. 42-53.

------, 1979b. *"Moonies" in America: Cult, Church and Crusade.* Beverly Hills, CA: Sage.

Carlson, Shawn and Gerald Larue *et al.,* 1989. *Satanism in America. Final Report of the Committee for Scientific Examination of Religion.* Buffalo, NY: CSER.

Citizens Freedom Foundation, 1976. *Citizens Freedom Foundation News.* Chula Vista, CA. (April, May).

Clark, John G., Jr., Michael D. Langone, Robert E. Schecter, and Roger C. B. Daly, 1982. *Destructive Cult Conversion: Theory, Research, and Treatment.* Weston, MA: American Family Foundation Center on Destructive Cultism.

Finn, Deborah, n.d. "Fundamentalists Anonymous and Moral Discourse." Unpublished paper, Emory University, Institute of the Liberal Arts.

James, Gene J., ed., 1983. *The Family and the Unification Church.* New York: Rose of Sharon Press.

Hall, John R., 1988. "The Impact of Apostates on the Trajectory of Religious Movements: The Case of Peoples Temple," in David G. Bromley, ed., *Falling from the Faith: Causes and Consequences of Religious Apostasy.* Newbury Park, CA: Sage Publications, pp. 229-250.

Hicks, Robert D., 1991. *In Pursuit of Satan.* Buffalo, NY: Prometheus Books.

Kelley, Dean, 1977. "Deprogramming and Religious Liberty." *The Civil Liberties Review* 4 (July/August), pp. 23-33.

------, 1972. *Why Conservative Churches Are Growing: A Study in Sociology of Religion.* New York: Harper and Row.

Langone, Michael D., 1982. *Destructive Cultism: Questions and Answers.* Weston, MA: American Family Foundation Center on Destructive Cultism.

------, and Linda Blood, 1990. *Satanism and Occult-Related Violence: What You Should Know.* Weston, MA: American Family Foundation.

Martin, Walter, 1980. *The New Cults.* Santa Ana, CA: Vision House Publishers.

Mickler, Michael L., 1987. "Future Prospects of the Unification Church," in David G. Bromley and Phillip E. Hammond, eds., *The Future of New Religious Movements.* Macon, GA: Mercer University Press, pp. 176-186.

"A Parent's Primer on Satanism," 1988. *Woman's Day* (November 22), p. 150.

Richardson, James T., "Religiosity as Deviance: Negative Religious Bias in and Misuse of the DSM-III." *Deviant Behavior* 14, pp. 1-21.

Richardson, James T., Joel Best, and David G. Bromley, 1991. *The Satanism Scare.* New York: Aldine de Gruyter.

Robbins, Thomas, 1989, *Converts and Charisma.* Newbury Park, CA: Sage.

------, and Dick Anthony, 1982. "Deprogramming, Brainwashing, and the Medicalization of Deviant Religious Groups," *Social Problems* 29 (February), pp. 283-297.

Rochford, E. Burke, Jr., 1987. "Dialectical Processes in the Development of Hare Krishna: Tension, Public Definition, and Strategy," in David G. Bromley and Phillip E. Hammond, eds., *The Future of New Religious Movements.* Macon, GA: Mercer University Press, pp. 109-22.

Saliba, John A., 1990. *Social Science and the Cults: An Annotated Bibliography.* New York: Garland Press, pp. 618-652.

"Satanism Concerns on Decline?" 1990. *The Cult Observer* (November/ December), p. 2.

Shinn, Larry D., 1987. *The Dark Lord: Cult Images and the Hare Krishnas in America.* Philadelphia: Westminster Press.

Shupe, Anson, 1991. "The Modern Satanist Scare in Indiana and Across the U.S." Paper presented at the annual meeting of the Society for the Scientific Study of Religion. Pittsburgh, PA.

------, 1990a. "Pitchmen of the Satanist Scare," *Wall Street Journal,* March 9.

------, 1990b. "Sun Myung Moon's American Disappointment," *Christian Century,* August 22-29, pp. 764-766.

------, 1987. "Constructing Evil as a Social Process: The Unification Church and the Media," in Robert N. Bellah and Frederick E. Greenspahn, eds., *Uncivil Religion: Inter-religious Hostility in America.* New York: Crossroad, pp. 205-218.

------, 1985. "The Routinization of Charisma and Conflict in the Modern Cult/Anti-Cult Controversy," *Nebraska Humanist* (Fall), pp. 26-39.

------, and David G. Bromley, 1985a. "Social Responses to Cults," in Phillip E. Hammond, eds., *The Sacred in A Secular Age.* Berkeley: University of California Press, pp. 58-72.

------, 1985b. *A Documentary History of the Anticult Movement.* Arlington, TX: University of Texas at Arlington Center for Social Research.

------, 1982. "Shaping the Public Response to Jonestown: The People's Temple and the Anticult Movement," in Kenneth Levi, ed., *Violence and Religious Commitment.* College Park, PA: Penn State University Press, pp. 105-132.

------, 1981. "The Deprogrammer as Moral Entrepreneur." Paper presented at the annual meeting of the Academy of Religion. San Francisco.

------, 1980. *The New Vigilantes: Anti-Cultists, Deprogrammers, and the New Religions.* Beverly Hills, CA: Sage.

------, 1979. "The Moonies and the Anti-cultists: Movement and Countermovement in Conflict," *Sociological Analysis* 40 (Winter):325-366.

------, and Bruce C. Busching, 1989. "Modern American Religious Conflict," in Joseph B. Gittler, ed., *The Annual Review of Conflict Knowledge and Conflict Resolution.* New York: Garland Press, pp. 127-150.

------, and Edward Breschel, 1989. "The People's Temple, the Apocalypse at Jonestown, and the Anti-cult Movement," in Fielding M. McGhee II, ed., *Ten Years After Jonestown: Reconsidering Its Meaning.* Lewiston, NY: Edwin Mellen Press, pp. 149-174.

------, and Donna L. Oliver, *The Anti-Cult Movement in America: A Bibliography and Historical Survey.* New York: Garland, 1984.

------, Roger Spielmann, and Sam Stigall, 1977. "Deprogramming: The New Exorcism," *American Behavioral Scientist* 20 (July/August), pp. 941-956.

Simandl, Robert and Bette Naysmith, 1988. "Dabbling Their Way to Ritual Crime," *Cult Awareness Network News* (August).

Verdier, Paul A., 1977. *Brainwashing and the Cults.* No. Hollywood, CA: Wilshire Books.

Wallis, Roy, 1977. *The Road to Total Freedom: A Sociological Analysis of Scientology.* New York: Columbia University Press.

Yao, Richard, 1985. *Fundamentalists Anonymous: There Is a Way Out.* New York: Luce Publications.

CHAPTER II

MAINTAINING THE FAITH: THE JEWISH ANTI-CULT AND COUNTER-MISSIONARY MOVEMENT

Shoshanah Feher

In the early seventies, cars around the country were seen displaying bumper stickers with slogans such as "I've Found It" or "Jesus Saves." The Jewish community responded by sporting bumper stickers that read "I Never Lost It" or "Moses Invests." Why did the battle of the bumper stickers develop?[1]

The mobilization of the Jews took the form of the Jewish anti-cult and counter-missionary movement (JACCMM). In this chapter, I examine this movement and analyze how, historically, the JACCMM arose separately from the larger, secular anti-cult movement (ACM). I then analyze some of the problems that are unique to the Jewish community, taking into consideration the antagonism Jews have historically felt toward conversion. Finally, I consider the implications of conversion out of Judaism for the Jewish community in the United States, with a focus on the concerns articulated by spokespeople for the Jewish community.

HISTORICAL DEVELOPMENT OF THE ACM AND THE JEWISH ACM

The ACM in the U.S.A. formed in the early seventies out of the efforts of family members whose relatives had joined new religious movements. The individual anti-cult groups sprang up independently of one another, but they all had as their mission to provide solidarity for their members and to disseminate information (Shupe and Bromley, 1980). The rise of these groups, and the information they disseminated, enabled family members of recruits to realize that many others shared their situation. Initially, the members were relatives of Children of God recruits and were based in San Diego. Slowly, however, relatives of recruits from other cults began to join and, in time, spawned other groups concerned about other new religious movements such as the Unification Church, the Hare Krishnas, and the Church of Scientology (Bromley and Shupe, 1987).

The ACM grew to include concerned professionals—lawyers, clergy, mental health professionals, and social scientists—that were beyond the immediate families of the recruits. Ex-members of cults also began participating in the movement and played a role testifying that they had been "brainwashed." As the membership of the ACM expanded, so too did the movement's status and visibility to the public (Bromley and Shupe, 1987).

The anti-cult movement was initiated and shaped principally by secular groups (Zaidman-Dvir and Sharot, 1992; Bromley and Shupe, 1993). Starting as independent grassroots organizations that persistently strived to coalesce into a network, they later developed into much more professionalized confederations of voluntary associations. It seems likely that the JACM developed after the secular ACM had arisen, at least as a recognizably separate social movement. It is probable that initially Jewish families felt that they were in the same situation as others whose children joined particular new religions. Perhaps it wasn't until later that they became increasingly aware of the uniqueness of the Jewish situation and were led to form their own types of support. It is notable that the Jewish Federation Council's attempt to meet the needs of Jews and their families developed in the late seventies. Likewise, Rabbi BenTzion Kravitz began his battle with missionary groups in the late seventies, and it was not until 1985 that he established Jews for Judaism. This is not to say that Jews were not involved in the ACM earlier, only that they separated a few years later.

Very little has been written on the Jewish aspect of the ACM. Shupe and Bromley (1980) note that Jewish involvement is somewhat different from that of Protestants and Catholics. They state that the response of the Jewish community was "harsh" and explain that it was probably due to the Jewish community's interest in maintaining subcultural family values and its concern with anti-Semitism.

The most obvious difference between the Jewish and non-Jewish anti-cult movements is that the Jewish community is also concerned about Christian missionary groups. There are two large JACCMM's in the U.S.A. One is run by the Jewish Federation Council, which operates the Commission on Cults and Missionaries and a Cult Clinic. The commission is a branch of the Jewish Community Relations Council and focuses on educating the community on cults. The Cult Clinic, on the other hand, is run through Jewish Family Services and is both secular and non-sectarian, offering counseling and referral services to people who have been affected by a cult. This work, done in the Jewish Federation Council's New York and Los Angeles centers, is primarily anti-cult, or "cult awareness" in its orientation (Andres, 1992). The second active JACCMM in the U.S.A., Jews for Judaism, spends its energy on the counter-missionary aspect of its agenda. Founded in Los Angeles, this organization has six offices in North America, the majority of them on the East Coast. It is religious in nature and, for obvious reasons, works without the help of the non-Jewish ACM.[2] The focus of Jews for Judaism is on educating Jews and providing pastoral counseling.

Both of the JACCM groups I've discussed are concerned with educating the community and providing counseling, be it psychologically (Jewish Federation Council) or religiously (Jews for Judaism) based. Neither group does exit-counseling or deprogramming. Although they may refer interested individuals to people who use these tactics, these two organizations work only with those who voluntarily approach them. This is partially due to matters of philosophy, but mostly it is due to a question of resources; exit-counselors and deprogrammers require a great deal of time and unexpected hours.

CHRISTIAN EVANGELIZING AND THE JEWISH COUNTER-MISSIONARY MOVEMENT

For the Jewish community, losses through proselytization and losses through persecution are perceived similarly. Whether a Jew joins a new religious movement, becomes a Christian,[3] or dies, the loss is felt by the Jewish community the same way because in all of these situations the member cannot pass down the Jewish tradition to younger generations. Any membership loss therefore brings up memories of past losses to tradition, calling up shadows of the Holocaust. For this reason, the Key73 experience that was provided was unique for the Jewish community.

The birth of Key73 can be traced to June 1967, when an editor of *Christianity Today,* Dr. Carl Henry, called for an ecumenical pooling of resources in order to spread the Gospel. Its first meeting, made up of fundamentalists, was organized by Dr. Henry and the Reverend Billy Graham (*American Jewish Committee,* "Memorandum," 1972; *The Star,* 1973).

Four years later, in January of 1973, over 140 Christian groups began what was touted as the largest ecumenical evangelical campaign ever conducted. Their approach, dependent on mass-media and door-to-door canvassing, was to "call the continent to Christ" by confronting everybody in North America with the Gospel.[4] At this point, Key73 was no longer a fundamentalist group. It had also attracted mainline Protestant churches, Catholic dioceses, independent evangelical groups, church bodies, para-ecclesiastical groups (*Texas Methodist,* 1972; *American Jewish Committee,* "Memorandum," 1972; *New York Times,* 1973a) and groups that had never before worked together. The structure of Key73 was very loose: contribution was relative to the size of the group, local endeavors were financed by the local church, and participation was up to the parish or local church.

The Jewish community, led by Rabbi Marc Tanenbaum, National Director of the American Jewish Committee's Interreligious Affairs Department, responded to Key73 with alarm and concern. Tanenbaum's fear was that Jews would also be sought after and evangelized. Again, the Holocaust was invoked. Rabbi Tanenbaum explained that after the Nazis had destroyed one-third of the Jewish population, Soviet assimilation would wipe out the remaining third (*Texas Methodist,* 1972). The Reverend Theodore A. Raedeke, Executive Director of Key73,[5] assured Tanenbaum that the campaign had no anti-Semitic implications and would not "persecute, pressure, or force Jews to believe or do anything against their will" (*Texas Methodist,* 1973a; *New York Times,* 1973a). However, the Jewish community's fear persisted, knowing that groups specifically seeking to evangelize Jews would attach themselves to the national efforts (*Street'n Steeple,* 1972). That is in fact what happened. Messianic Jews capitalized on Key73, riding on its coattails as people with a special mission to the Jews.

Accordingly, the Rabbinical Council of America, which represents more than 1,000 Orthodox rabbis in the U.S.A. and Canada, said in a statement:

The enthusiasm which Key 73 will no doubt generate should alert the Jewish community, and we ask all segments of the Jewish community to be on the alert lest the over-zealousness of this effort begin to penetrate into the Jewish communities. Already we have had reports of such activities on the college campus and in a number of smaller Jewish communities (*New York Times,* 1973a).

Slowly, the churches involved began issuing formal statements that they were not targeting the conversion of Jews.[6] The Reverend Billy Graham also issued a statement, saying that proselytizing

seeks to commit men against their will . . . gimmicks, coercion, and intimidation have no place in my evangelistic efforts . . . I have never felt called to single out the Jews as Jews nor to single out any particular groups, cultural, ethnic, or religious. Lastly, it would be my hope that Key73 and any other spiritual outreach program could initiate nationwide conversations which would raise the spiritual level of our people and promote mutual understanding (*Texas Methodist,* 1973b; *Newsweek,* 1973).

While Billy Graham's statement carried a lot of weight among Evangelicals and was therefore a triumph as far as the Jewish community was concerned, the over-riding feeling among Jews was that Jewish-Christian dialogues in the past had all been for nought and future dialogue had been damaged by Key73 (*Methodist Reporter,* 1973; *Western Recorder,* 1973a, 1973b; *Maryland Baptist,* 1972; *New York Times,* 1973d). Thus, the Jewish community continued to be wary.

In a certain sense, the Jewish response backfired. Ironically, the Jewish community provided Key73 the momentum it required by getting more excited about it than many Christian groups themselves (*New York Baptist,* 1973). Prior to the Jewish response, Key73 had been virtually unable to get media attention (*United Methodist Reporter,* 1973a). Rabbi Siegman, Executive Vice-President of the Synagogue Council of America, noted that while many Christians had not heard of Key73, virtually all North American Jews knew about it. He was angered by ". . . the imputations of Jewish insecurity and internal weakness implicit in this defensiveness—as if Judaism stands on so frail a reed as to be blown away by the slightest wind that comes along" (*United Methodist Reporter,* 1973b; *New York Times,* 1973b). It is clear that the Jewish response was an important aspect of Key73's longevity. Dr. Raedeke remarked that "their [Jewish] reaction helped our cause" by keeping Key73 in the headlines (*New York Times,* 1973d; *New York Baptist,* 1973; *Texas Methodist,* 1973c).

The strong Jewish reaction to Key73 may have had a lot to do with timing. Rabbi Kravitz (1993) of Jews for Judaism notes that Key73 was "the launching pad" for Christian groups who proselytize specifically to Jews, such as Jews for Jesus. In the seventies, not only was the Jewish community fighting Christians, but they were simultaneously fighting cults and Messianic Jews. Thus, while the Christian community may also have felt the threat centered around cults, the Jewish community perceived itself as fighting the attack on three different fronts.

THE UNIQUE PROBLEMS
OF THE JEWISH COMMUNITY:
ANTI-SEMITISM AND THE HOLOCAUST

In order to understand why the Jewish community responded to Key73 as strongly as it did, we need to evaluate why proselytizing religions cause such a threat to the Jewish community and how this community differs from its non-Jewish counterpart. After all, it may be argued that a threat to the maintenance of family values is not specific to the Jewish community (Bromley and Shupe, 1980). But a threat that is sprinkled with doses of anti-Semitism, implicit or otherwise, carries different implications.

In the context of Jewish membership in NRMs, ascertaining the impact of anti-Semitism means asking two questions: What does conversion out of the Jewish community mean for Jews? And, what images does this conversion conjure? After all, anti-Semitism is not purely of historic importance, but rather it currently continues to affect and shape the texture of the community. National organizations exist and actively work to fight the problem (such as the Anti-Defamation League of the B'nai B'rith or the Simon Wiesenthal Center) and scholars often cite it as a way of gaining insight into the Jewish mind, both at the individual and societal levels (Glazer, 1972; Bershtel and Graubard, 1992).

When one member, even one Jewish child, converts, it is considered a loss to the community, a loss that further jeopardizes Judaism's future. Each child that converts means that one less person will pass the tradition on to the next generation. Given the relatively small size of the Jewish community, this loss is therefore perceived as a serious threat.[7] As Isser and Schwartz explain:

> the threat to the present and future generations of Judaism is great enough that united action in preventive and remedial measures is warranted. That effort must respond not only to the cults, however, but also to the total threat to the continuity of life (1980:72).

While this may be true of all communities—be they ethnic, religious, or political—it is particularly salient in the Jewish community given the persecution of the past. Particularly after the Holocaust, Jews are acutely aware of how numerically small their ethno-religious community is, making the "loss" of every and any Jew strongly felt (Brickner, 1978).

For many, conversion out of the Jewish community touches on old historic feelings. As a community that has been persecuted for centuries, it has maintained itself through its separation, either voluntarily or involuntarily, from the rest of society. This memory is deeply ingrained because the history of the Jews has alternated between persecution and forced conversion. Due to this oscillation, conversion for Jews oftentimes has the connotation of "joining the enemy" (Isser and Schwartz, 1980:63). Brickner (1978:10) notes that Christians have been trying to convert Jews for two thousand years and, for two thousand years, "Jews have been resisting with notable resiliency."

Oftentimes, those who assimilated did so by hiding their Jewishness, through name change, avoidance of Jewish family and friends, and conversion to Christianity. They severed their connection to their people and their past and traded in an ethnic and religious life (Bershtel and Graubard, 1992). For example, Jews who left their community during the Middle Ages were absorbed quickly, within a few generations, into the general population (Wirth, 1956).

For most of Jewish history, conversion is synonymous with Christianity. The other, the enemy, has been the Christian:

> They are Goyim,
> Foes of the faith,
> Beings of darkness,
> Drunkards and bullies,
> Swift with the fist or the bludgeon,
> Many in species, but all
> Engendered of God for our sins,
> and many and strange their idolatries,
> But the worst of the Goyim are the
> creatures called Christians.
>
> (Zangwill in Wirth, 1956:119)

Missionary activity continues to express an ancient hostility that seemingly threatened the existence of the Jewish people and, at the very minimum, still questions the legitimacy of Jewish survival in the modern world (Endelman, 1987). Those who did convert often had to contend with the notion of Jewishness as a hereditary trait. In strongly anti-Semitic societies, Jewish character was considered inflexible and thus impervious to baptism (Endelman, 1987). Indeed, Jewish character continues to be considered inflexible even within the Jewish community.[7]

Historically excluded from the larger society, Jews had little choice but to maintain their commitment to Judaism and the Jewish community. After all, leaving their religion would mean joining those who attacked friends, family, and community. Therefore, as long as societies were static and boundaries between them impermeable, as long as religious hatred and persecution of the Jews continued, the existence of the Jewish people was assured. When society opened to Jews, removing the barriers to assimilation, many began to leave Judaism (Danzger, 1989).

Today, Jewish youth in the U.S.A. have virtually no barriers at all. On the contrary, in this "land of the melting pot" they are oftentimes encouraged to assimilate. Rabbi Eckstein, president of the Holyland Fellowship of Christians and Jews, says survival is the Jewish mandate. It is not just current day survival that accounts for the objection of proselytization, but also historical survival. Jews have been proselytized for 2,000 years, and their reaction against proselytization incorporates those 2,000 years of historical baggage (*Christianity Today,* 1988).

While past persecution and proselytization could be fought, it may not be easy in the future, note Isser and Schwartz:

> What the Spanish failed to do in the Inquisition, what Pius IX failed to do through his edicts and actions, what the Nazis failed to do in the Holocaust, may yet occur through the apparent gentleness of the Krishnas and the "Moonies," the "Jews for Jesus," and others who speak the language of the disenchanted (1980:72).

Within the U.S.A., missionary activity did not represent much of a threat to Jews insofar as it was confined to a small fringe element of American Christianity and was low on the visible agenda of mainline Protestant or Roman Catholic bodies. Organizations such as the American Board of Mission to the Jews were also considered fringe bodies, and thus disregarded by both mainline Christian and Jewish organizations. While past missionary activity may not have been too problematic, this changed with the onset of missionaries from new religions.

The 1978 mass suicide of the members of the People's Temple intensified activities of the ACM (Melton, 1991). Within the Jewish community, it called to mind Holocaust concentration camps (Kollin, 1979; Hecht, 1985). The Divine Light Mission had the same effect on Zeitlin (1984:4), not because the adherents of this religious movement died, but because her son was "taken from" her by the cult and thus "turned the clock to Holocaust time."

The Holocaust is an image which arises in Jewish popular literature time after time. Some anti-cultists consider new religious movements to be so authoritarian and anti-democratic that they are dangerous to the society at large as well as to the devotees, at both the psychological and physical level. So much so, in fact, that cults have been likened to anti-Semitic movements and the fate of devotees to the fate of those who were interned in Auschwitz (Rudin and Rudin, 1980:29). Cult devotees also have reminded theologian Rich Rubenstein of Germans following Hitler (Dujardin, 1979). Elie Wiesel, a Holocaust survivor, writes, "I shall not soon forget one Holocaust survivor I met, a pious Jew who had come originally from Poland. He could not understand what had happened [when his adult child joined a marginal group], asking, "Did I survive in order to fail precisely where my ancestors triumphed? To give life to a renegade?" He sobbed, and I was barely able to console him" (Wiesel, 1988:161).

Many new religious movements are charged with anti-Semitism; the worst offense is the denial of the Holocaust by the cult leaders. The Way International, for example, has "promoted anti-Semitic propaganda claiming the Holocaust was a 'hoax'" (Schwartz, 1982:11). Neri (1984) corroborates this point when she notes that The Way describes the Holocaust as being "Zionist propaganda." The Unification Church is also considered anti-Semitic due to its explanation of the Holocaust: An ex-member notes Reverend Moon's explanation that the six million Jews who died in the Holocaust were paying indemnity for the crucifixion of Jesus (Silverberg, 1976; Warshaw, 1979).

THE JEWISH COMMUNITY IN THE FUTURE: MAINTAINING THE FAITH

In this chapter, I have addressed the history of the JACCMM and how its impetus for development was different from the larger ACM. One of the differences between the two movements is the Jewish community's great concern with maintaining the faith.

According to the Council of Jewish Federation's 1990 census, only 62 percent of the U.S.A. Jewish population who were born Jews are currently Jews. Sixteen percent were born Jews and claim no religious identification, 3 percent have converted out, 16 percent were born of Jewish parents but were, or are, being raised in another religion. In all, this makes for 19 percent who, despite Jewish parentage, claim another religious preference. On the other hand, only 3 percent of the Jewish population is made up of people who convert to Judaism (CJF 1990). In California, that notorious hotbed for new religious activity, Rachel Andres, Director of the Commission of Cults and Missionaries, points out that cults are the largest threat to the integrity of the Jewish community but not to its size (Andres, 1992).

John Hochman is a psychiatrist who has been actively involved with a variety of different branches of the anti-cult movement since the early 1980s. One of his current affiliations is with Jews for Judaism, primarily a counter-missionary group, where he fields the questions that come in regarding new religious movements. He is aware that Jewish defection is largely due to "all the noise that's out there, the competition and distractions which make it hard for Jews to keep their focus"

(Hochman, 1992). However, he believes that this inability to maintain focus on Judaism flows directly out of the failure of Jewish education. Jews, he says, need to ensure that they are teaching their children about being Jewish, teaching them certain religious observances, and teaching them to have a strong relationship to God. If all this is in place, Hochman believes, Jews won't look for other types of religious experience.

Founder and Director of Jews for Judaism, Rabbi Bentzion Kravitz, considers his "battle" to be against assimilation. It's a battle, he says, that many in the Jewish community are fighting on different fronts. Missionary activity is the one front in which he feels most qualified to engage. His answer to the assimilation problem is to more thoroughly experience Judaism, a lifestyle so fulfilling that the emptiness Jews are trying to fill with Christianity will be filled with their religion of birth (Kravitz, 1993).

A large number of spokespeople in the Jewish community believe that the future of their community is in danger due to the apathy and assimilation of its adherents (Geller, 1992; Cooper, 1992; Windmueller, 1992). The challenge for the community is to instill a positive identity. Now, after the Holocaust, they claim, the community must provide its youth with positive reasons to identify as Jews.

Jewish groups concerned with anti-Semitism, community relations, Jewish rights, and, of course, new religious movements and missionaries, all seem to point to the same problem: the assimilation and alienation of Jewish members of the community. Many groups are trying to deal with the root cause of these issues, focussing their efforts at trying to fully comprehend the root of the vague problem. Other groups, like the JACCMM, are aware that they are really trying to deal with, and put an end to, a symptom.

Thus, to Jews it is important to study the reasons certain new religious movements and evangelical Christian groups appeal to Jewish youth. Through a better understanding of their appeal, the Jewish community can develop positive ways of strengthening the Jewish faith and culture for its youth. In better understanding the "symptom" of Jews joining evangelical and new religious movements, the Jewish community will gain a fuller understanding of how to maintain its unique faith.

NOTES

1. For a more detailed account of the Christian bumper-sticker business and other religious products, see *The New York Times*, February 13, 1973.

2. Israel's most effective anti-cult organization is a religious group involved in the conversion of Jews to a religious perspective, trying to substitute Orthodox Judaism for the new religious movements (Jaidman-Dvir and Sharot, 1992).

3. Whether it be a Gentile or a Jewish/Hebrew Christian.

4. According to one of the Key73 leaders, in one or two years, the program could convert the world to Christianity. According to the leader, one-fourth of the world's population is Christian. If everyone converted one person within the year and all converted the rest, in two years everyone would be Christian (Bernards, 1973).

5. Key73 was administered by an executive director on loan from one of the major Lutheran bodies (*Texas Methodist,* 1973a) and by a 50-member central committee (*American Jewish Committee,* "Memorandum," 1972).

6. On February 10, the California-Arizona Conference of the United Methodist Church issued a formal statement that the purpose of this organization's participation in Key73 was not to convert Jews. One month later, Southern Baptist leader, M. Thomas Starkes of Atlanta stated that Jews were not being singled out as special targets of evangelism (*Western Recorder,* 1973c; *The Maryland Baptist,* 1973). Likewise, the U.S. Bishops' Ecumenical Committee issued a memorandum telling Catholics in the participating Key73 dioceses not to look for converts in the Jewish community (*Newsweek,* 1973).

7. Jews make up approximately 2.5% of the U.S. population (Roof and McKinney, 1987; Danzger, 1989; Eisenberg, 1988).

8. This sentiment is expressed in a traditional Jewish joke. There are many variations on this joke but the idea is always the same:

Four Jewish apostates met on a train in Russia and began to relate the reasons that prompted them to accept Christianity. The first apostate said that he had saved himself from a pogrom by changing his religion. "The Cossacks killed almost every Jew in the village," he explained, "so I converted." The second apostate stated that he had wanted desperately to attend the university, but since Jews were not admitted he had become a Christian so that he might continue his education. The third apostate explained that he had fallen madly in love with a beautiful Gentile girl and that she would not marry him unless he accepted her faith. When the fourth apostate related his story he said, "I became a Christian because I was convinced that Christianity is superior to . . ."

"Now wait a minute," interrupted one of the Christian converts, "tell that to your Gentile friends!" (adapted from Spalding, 1969).

REFERENCES

The American Jewish Committee Memorandum, 1972. "Some Issues Raised by Forthcoming Evangelism Campaigns: A Background Memorandum," by Rabbi Marc Tanenbaum. New York: American Jewish Committee, June.

Andres, Rachel, 1992. Director, Commission of Cults and Missionaries, Jewish Federation Council, Los Angeles. Personal communication, Fall.

Bernards, Solomon, 1973. "Key73—A Jewish View," *The Christian Century* 3:12-14, January.

Bernstein, Rachel, 1993. Director, Cult Clinic, Jewish Federation Council, Los Angeles. Personal communication, Winter.

Bershtel, Sara and Graubard Allen, 1992. *Saving Remnants: Feeling Jewish in America.* New York, NY: The Free Press.

Brickner, Balfour, 1978. "Christian Missionaries and a Jewish Response," *Jewish Digest,* 23:10-19, Summer.

Bromley, David and Anson Shupe, forthcoming. "Organized Opposition to New Religious Movements," in David Bromley and Jeffrey Hadden, eds., *Sects and Cults in America.* Greenwich, CT: ASR/SSR/JAI Press.

-------, 1987. "The Future of the Anti-Cult Movement," in David Bromley and Phillip Hammond, eds., *The Future of New Religious Movements.* Macon, GA: Mercer University Press.

Christianity Today, 1988. 'Fulfilled' Jews or 'Former Jews'? October 7:66-68.

Cooper, Abraham, 1992. Associate Dean, Simon Wiesenthal Center. Personal communication.

Council of Jewish Federations, 1990. *Highlights of the CJF 1990 National Population Survey.* New York, NY.

Danzger, Herbert, 1989. *Returning to Tradition: The Contemporary Revival of Orthodox Judaism.* New Haven, CT: Yale University Press.

Endelman, Todd, ed., 1987. *Jewish Apostasy in the Modern World.* New York, NY: Holmes and Meier Publishing.

Geller, Laura, 1992. Director, American Jewish Congress, Jewish Federation Council, Los Angeles. Personal communication.

Hecht, Shea, 1985. *Confessions of a Jewish Cultbuster.* Brooklyn, NY: Tosefos Media, Inc.

Hilewitz, Yehuda, 1984. "The Alamo Story," *ADL Bulletin* 41:10-12, December.

Hochman, John, 1992. Consultant, Jews for Judaism. Personal communication, Fall.

Isser, Natalie and Lita Linzer Schwartz, 1980. "Community Responses to the Proselytization of Jews," *Journal of Jewish Communal Service* 57:63-72, Fall.

Kravitz, BenTzion, 1993. Founder and Director, Jews for Judaism. Personal communication, Winter.

Kollin, Gilbert, 1979. "Perversity," *The Jewish Spectator* 44:61-62, Summer.

Glazer, Nathan, 1972. *American Judaism.* Chicago, IL: The University of Chicago Press.

The Maryland Baptist, 1972, "Jewish, Christian, Theologians Discuss 'Civil Religion,'" by Mike Creswell, November 23.

------, 1973. "Starke Answers Jewish Criticism of Key73," March 15.

Melton, Gordon, 1991. Director, Institute for the Study of American Religion. Personal communication.

Methodist Reporter, 1973. "Rabbi Charges that Key73 'Validates' Radical Groups," March 23.

Neri, Judy, 1984. "Combatting Cults," *B'nai B'rith International Jewish Monthly* 98:43-45, June/July.

Newsweek, 1973. "Jews for Jesus," March 19.

The New York Baptist, 1973. "It Looks as Though Our Jewish Friends are Giving Key73 the Lift-Off Thrust!," February 15(5):2.

The New York Times, 1973a. "104 Church Groups Join in Huge Evangelical Drive," by Eleanor Blau, January 7.

------, 1973b. "Rabbi Questions Critiques of Key73," by Edward Fiske, January 28.

------, 1973c. "Bible Bumper Stickers Big Business Over U.S.," February 13.

------, 1973d. "Major Evangelical Drive Appears a Failure Over All," by Eleanor Blau, September 2.

The Providence Journal, 1979. "Jewish Theologian Believes Cultists are Searching for Sense of Worth," April 23.

Roof, Wade Clark and William McKinney, 1987. *American Mainline Religion.* New Brunswick, NJ: Rutgers University Press.

Rudin, James and Marcia Rudin, 1980. *Prison or Paradise?.* Philadelphia, PA: Fortress Sage.

Schwartz, Alan M., 1982. "Watch Out for the Way," *ADL Bulletin* 39:11-13, October.

Shapiro, Jerry, 1992. Associate Director, B'nai B'rith Anti-Defamation League, Los Angeles. Personal communication, Fall.

Shupe, Anson and David Bromley, 1980. *The New Vigilantes.* Beverly Hills, CA: Sage Publications.

Spalding, Henry D., ed., 1969. *Encyclopedia of Jewish Humor.* New York, NY: Jonathan David Publishers.

The Star, 1973. "Rabbi Describes Conversion Drive Aimed at Some Jews," by Phyllis Feuerstein, February 1.

Street'n Steeple, 1972. "Evangelism Actions of General Conference ," 6(3):1-2.

Texas Methodist, 1972. "Christian Evangelism Blasted," December 22.

------, 1973a. "Key73 Head Responds to Jews," January 26.

------, 1973b. "Billy Graham Clarifies Key73 Jewish Stance," March 16.

------, 1973c. "Key73 Originator Denounces 'Wolf Cries' Against Evangelism," April 20.

The United Methodist Reporter, 1973a. "Key73 Inertia Cited by Pastor, Rabbi on Panel," May 18.

------, 1973b. "Rabbi Sees Key73 as '73 Challenge to Judaism," 1(36), August 24.

The Western Recorder, 1973a. "Key73 Negates Jew's Relationship to God, Rabbi Says," April 7.

------, 1973b. "Nature of Evangelism is Key73 Problem—Tanenbaum," April 7.

------, 1973c. "Jewish Criticism of Key73 Answered," March 3.

Windmueller, Steven, 1992. Director, Jewish Community Relations Committee, Jewish Federation Council, Los Angeles. Personal communication, Fall.

Wiesel, Elie, 1987. "The Missionary Menace," in Gary Eisenberg, ed., *Smashing the Idols.* Northvale, NJ: Jason Aronson, Inc.

Wirth, Louis, 1956. *The Ghetto.* Chicago, IL: The University of Chicago Press.

Zaidman-Dvir, Nurit Sharot, and Stephen Sharot, 1992. "The Response of Israeli Society to New Religious Movements: ISKCON and Teshuvah," *Journal for the Scientific Study of Religion* 31(3):279-295.

Zeitlin, Marianne Langer, 1984. "Regaining a Child from a Cult," *The Jewish Digest* 29:3-5, May.

CHAPTER III

THE SOCIAL CONSTRUCTION OF SUBVERSION: A COMPARISON OF ANTI-RELIGIOUS AND ANTI-SATANIC CULT NARRATIVES

David G. Bromley

The decades of the 1970s and 1980s each witnessed major subversion episodes characterized by widespread fears of cultic subversion and the subsequent mobilization of aggressive countersubversion campaigns. During the 1970s subversion fears centered on a cohort of new religious movements (NRM's) that emerged beginning in the late 1960s (Bromley and Shupe, 1981). Throughout much of the 1970s it was the communally organized groups with world-transforming ideologies, such as the Unification Church, the Hare Krishnas, and The Family (at the time named the Children of God), that were labeled religious cults and drew the most intense opposition. Toward the end of the decade, when the NRMs, who precipitated subversion fears in the 1970s, were experiencing a rapid decline in membership, a new countersubversion campaign was mobilized against Satanic cults. During the 1980s subversion fears centered on a putative underground cult of practicing Satanists believed to be responsible for coordinating a variety of Satanic activity (including, for example, worship of Satan in Satanic churches, luring youth into cults through dissemination of occult material in fantasy games and heavy metal rock music, precipitating criminal homicides, and carrying out widespread grave desecrations and animal mutilation operations).

The 1970s countersubversion campaign against NRM's was founded on the assertion that there existed a set of pseudo-religious groups, referred to as "religious cults," whose primary defining characteristic was the utilization of a potent psychotechnology, referred to as "brainwashing" or "coercive mind control," to secure and control members. Cult recruitment campaigns allegedly targeted naive young adults who were particularly susceptible to the idealistic appeals employed by cult recruiters. The gurus who led religious cults were portrayed as motivated by a quest for political/economic power. This impulsion was evidenced in their political and financial empire-building and their dictatorial leadership style, which together led to the exploitation of individual followers. Religious cults successfully evaded legal controls, it was claimed, by clothing their organizations and activities in the mantle of religion and by operating through a variety of apparently legitimate "front groups." As a result, the number, size, power, and wealth of these monolithic, ruthless, authoritarian groups increased dramatically, making them a grave threat to the social order. (This counter-subversion campaign did not end with the 1970s; it continues today, though with shifting targets and emphases of targets. Thus, groups such as the Unification Church and the Family are still foci of concern for anti-cultists.)

The 1980s countersubversion campaign against Satanism, which has now extended into the 1990s, is premised on the conviction that there exists a vast international, secret network of tightly organized, hierarchically structured "Satanic cults."[1] The central characteristic of Satanic cults is their knowledge and application of a sophisticated combination of drugging, terrorism, and brainwashing techniques as a means of enslaving the young children whom they target. Satanists seek primarily enhancement of their personal pleasure and power through exploitation of children. Victims are forced to perform as sexual partners for the pleasure of adult Satanists or as actors in pornographic films that finance cult activity, and Satanists ritualistically sacrifice children in the belief that the victims' life energy can thereby be appropriated. Satanic cults also seek political power and religious status as a means of shielding their organization and activity from legal prosecution. Satanists have already managed to infiltrate some vulnerable institutions, most notably preschools and daycare centers, that provide them with unrestricted access to children. The startling rise in the number of individuals claiming to be "ritual abuse survivors" is presented as dramatic evidence of the rapidly growing power and danger posed by Satanic cults.

Subversion episodes are significant even if relatively rare social phenomena.[2] Alleging that others are engaged in subversion constitutes an extreme level of claimsmaking activity. Subversives are constructed as evil tricksters, traitors, and destroyers.[3] They mask their true intentionality by either concealment or deception; they betray the groups to which they publicly pledge loyalty by forming an alliance with the enemy; and they actively conspire to undermine a central form of group adaptation, thereby converting that form into its alien opposite. This chapter analyzes the structure of countersubversion ideologies, which are a critical element in the social construction of subversives because they delineate in appropriate cultural symbolism the shape of subversion. In the two cases examined here, the countersubversion ideologies are similar in that each identifies the same subversive agents (cults), subversive powers (brainwashing), and subversion targets (children).[4]

RELIGIOUS AND SATANIC CULT COUNTERSUBVERSION IDEOLOGIES

Countersubversion ideologies are constructed as narratives that describe in detail the nature of subversion.[5] They involve the following elements: (1) the historical origin and present location of the subversive force, (2) the nature of subversive organization, (3) the source and nature of the subversives' power, and (4) the impact of subversive power and organization.

Origin and Location

Countersubversion narratives provide a context for interpreting the apparently sudden appearance of extreme evil in the contemporary social order through identifying the source of subversion in spatial and temporal terms. Subversives are depicted as originating in territory outside of the everyday social world, either in an entirely separate realm or in contested terrain at the margins of conventional society, and they possess the capacity to infiltrate the everyday world. Further, subversives are portrayed as being part of some kind of confederation with an extended, independent history. The contemporary outbreak of subversion is often portrayed as a new and particularly sinister eruption of these historical forces that have recently begun making incursions into conventional society.

Anticult accounts of NRMs often stress the remote, secretive sites cults occupy. A one-time member of the Unification Church offers the following retrospective account of arriving at a rural Unification Church recruitment center in California (Swatland and Swatland, 1982:22-23):

> I woke just after midnight as we began to bump along a rough
> country road. The headlights of the bus illuminated a sign
> reading 'BOONVILLE IDEAL CITY RANCH' and close by
> there was another sign, 'PLEASE DO NOT ENTER
> WITHOUT PRIOR PERMISSION OF OWNER UNDER
> PENALTY OF LAW'. An eight-foot high barbed-wire fence
> surrounded the farm. . . . We clambered over a rickety
> suspension bridge. . . . I lay awake for a while wondering
> why a farm would need warning notices and those high
> barbed-wire fences. I was still wondering when I fell asleep.

Ted Patrick, one of the founders of the anti-cult movement and the
originator of the practice of deprogramming (Shupe and Bromley,
1981b; Bromley, 1985a), provides a similar account of a rural Children
of God commune (Patrick with Dulack, 1976:62):

> The security precautions at Woodland Park were the toughest
> I'd seen. The colony was way up in the mountains, some
> twenty-four miles back on a dirt road five miles off the main
> highway. There was nothing else on the road except the
> colony, which consisted of three buildings—old farm buildings
> —surrounded by a seven-foot-high fence with a locked gate.
> There were 350 kids living there. The grounds were patrolled
> by three vicious German shepherds. And one of the buildings
> was topped by a watchtower so that no one could come up that
> road without being detected at least five minutes before he
> reached the gate.

In describing his visit to this commune, Patrick creates the specter of a
prison in which residents are held captive (Patrick with Dulack,
1976:48): "The problem was it wasn't going to be easy to escape. You
were under constant surveillance. And it was pretty clear by now that
these Children of God weren't above employing ungodly rough stuff to
keep you there." After later returning home from the commune, he
responds to his wife's inquiry about where he has been by constructing
his trip as a journey to another realm: "I've been in hell, darling. . . .
You're looking at Lazarus," . . . "I just came back from the Kingdom
of the Dead" (Patrick with Dulack, 1976:52).

   Renderings of Satanic cults emphasize their underground, secret,
hidden nature in contested terrain such as cemeteries, isolated wooded

sites, or the criminal underworld. In a recent California court case, for example, two daughters and the granddaughter of a 76-year-old woman testified that the woman had forced them to engage in a variety of perverted sexual acts, infanticide, and even cannibalism. One of the daughters asserted that the rituals in which she had been forced to take part were conducted *in secret caves* that probably were located in the surrounding San Bernardino mountains ("Forced to Kill Her Baby, Woman Says," *Los Angeles Times*, 21 March 1991). In *Cults That Kill* (1988:vii), investigative journalist Larry Kahaner describes how he discovered an entire underworld Satanic domain in the course of investigating surface-level manifestations of Satanism.

> I found a hidden society, much larger and more disquieting than the world of Satanism alone, a place few people know exists . . . It is the underworld of "occult crime." . . . The crimes are frightening: a homicide where the decapitated victim is surrounded by colored beads, seven coins and chicken feathers; ritual sacrifices at wooded sites where black-robed cultists mutilate animals on alters; other homicides where the corpses are found drained of blood with symbols such as a pentagram or inverted cross carved into their chests; drug and pornography rings with nationwide connections to occult groups; carefully executed grave robbing; Satanic rituals and human sacrifices involving children—fantastic stories told by hundreds of children in scores of preschools throughout the United States, all of them relating similar horrors.

Historical continuity for religious cults is created primarily through defining their conversion techniques as brainwashing; and knowledge of this esoteric practice is then traced to communist thought reform programs in China and the former Soviet Union that were used initially to control internal dissidents and, later, American soldiers captured during the Korean War (Richardson and Kilbourne, 1983).[6] As the parent of a young woman who joined the Unification Church put it (Shupe and Bromley, 1981a:179):

> We think the brainwashing is very similar to what happened to our prisoners of war in Korea. It's a system of mind control the Orientals know very well, but we know very little about.

Social scientists Richard Ofshe and Margaret Singer (1986:18) link NRM thought reform techniques with those employed by communist regimes through the concepts of "first and second generations of interest," distinguishing the latter as a potent attack on the core as opposed to the periphery of the self:

> Second generation programs of coercive influence and behavior control appear to directly attack the core sense of being—the central self-image, the very sense of realness and existence of the self. In contrast, the attack of first generation programs is on the peripheral property of self, one's political and social views. . . . The inner person was not the focus of attack. The newer programs can make the target feel that the 'core me' is defective.

Conway and Siegelman (1979:37) likewise maintain that contemporary cult mind control techniques are unique. They aver that "Our culture has never witnessed transformation of precisely this kind before, although there have been many similar examples throughout the history of religion." This historically unprecedented process can be distinguished from brainwashing, which was "designed simply to change political belief and induce full cooperation among Chinese citizens and captive Westerners."

Similarly, contemporary Satanism is represented as the most recent in a long series of incursions by Satanic forces that have extended over countless human generations and even societal histories. These eruptions of Satanism have appeared in diverse forms in different historical eras, and sometimes their true source has not been correctly identified by contemporaries of the period (see, for example, Hill and Goodwin, 1989).[7] One "cult crime specialist" places the current outbreak in historical context while distinguishing the unique and virulent current outbreak in daycare centers (*Geraldo*, "Satanic Cults and Children," November 19, 1987):

> Well, cults have always existed throughout history, but it's only been recently that they've really become very active in this country. 1982 is a period or cycle for them that's known—every 28 years is the "feast of the beast" and it last occurred in 1982. And it gives them a whole new game plan on what

they're doing. Well, part of their game plan was to infiltrate preschool centers and such and to bring others into their service.

Certain forms of Satanism activity, particularly self-styled Satanic activity, has been linked to such groups as "outlaw bikers," extremist groups with occult interests, and serial killers. It is argued, for example, that serial killers have a long history and that they have naturally been drawn to Satanism:

> . . . if a serial killer picks and chooses beliefs that fit his aberrant needs, mixes this with signs, symbols and machinations of Satanism, conceives personal rituals and adds to all of this a liberal use of drugs, a frightening picture emerges: an evil, drug-lubricated butchering machine who justifies his behavior by exalting Satanism. (B.A.A.D., n.d.)

In other accounts, contemporary Satanists' brainwashing and drugging of victims is traced to medical experiments conducted by Nazi physicians. The doctors who developed these techniques (and a mysterious, infamous Dr. Green, in particular) were also Satanists who brought their pernicious knowledge with them when they fled Germany and settled in the United States.[8]

Power

Subversives are represented as having access to a source of power that is capable of overwhelming their targets' defenses. This power is described as *irresistible* (all individuals are vulnerable and any contact or involvement is immuring), *inexorable* (vulnerability to subversive control is progressive and capacity for resistance continuously declines), and *irreversible* (once individuals become ensnared they are unable to extricate themselves from subversive control, even if involvement results in self-destruction). The danger posed by subversive power is increased by its captivating quality: individuals find themselves alternatively paralyzed, fascinated, or even attracted to it.

At the height of the religious cult subversion episode, brainwashing was regarded as so highly coercive that even a perfunctory encounter with cultists might result in loss of free will. Following a lecture by a deprogrammer on the danger of cults, for example, one curious young adult asked if it would be possible to attend a Moon meeting "to find out about it" and then leave at the end of the night. The deprogrammer replied it would be risky, especially since a few reporters and investigators attempted to do so and found themselves "slipping under." Some, he added ominously, never returned to finish their stories ("Do Cults Brainwash Members?" *Burlington, NJ County Times*, 29 August 1976).

Deprogrammer Ted Patrick has provided a vivid account of how this potent psychotechnology is implemented by cultists (Bromley, 1985a). According to Patrick, typically cult street recruiters approach an individual and initiate a conversation on some subject of mutual interest. Imposing mind control involves making eye contact with the individual and then gaining their attention and trust. The objective is to get the individual thinking in a "single frame of mind." This corresponds to an unconscious state which, Patrick asserts, most normal individuals are in naturally about one-third of the time. Then, with just eye contact, the cult member can place the individual in a complete hypnotic trance without, of course, the individual's knowledge or permission. This capacity, Patrick claims comes from brainwaves which are projected outward through the cult member's eyes and fingertips. The target individual's mind then switches from a conscious to an unconscious state and a post-hypnotic suggestion is placed. Individuals in this state might continue to do what they are doing or to say what they are saying, but the suggestion that has been placed in their minds leaves them open to brainwashing. They might even walk away from the recruiters, totally negative toward them and the groups they represent. However, they later find themselves returning to meetings and cannot understand why. NRM apostates have frequently testified to being subjected to such techniques. One such individual (Edwards, 1979:60) recounts that:

> She took my hand and looked me straight in the eyes. As her wide eyes gazed into mine, I felt myself rapidly losing control, being drawn to her by a strange and frightening force. I had never felt such mysterious power radiate from a human being before.

In a more sophisticated formulation, *Snapping: America's Epidemic of Sudden Personality Change*, Flo Conway and Jim Siegelman

(1979:134-135) argue that snapping is a novel phenomenon that goes beyond intense physical experiences and psychological stresses by incorporating a "different kind of information." This information:

> . . . consists of the potent rhetorical ploys, individual and group techniques, and mass-marketing strategies that make up America's technology of experience, everything from fervid lecturing and earnest personal confrontation to slickly packaged appeals, from casual conversation to active role playing and guided fantasy. It is this set of instruments which may be systematically orchestrated to engage the entire range of an individual's communication capacities, from the most rudimentary and automatic biological functions to the highest reaches of human awareness. This all-encompassing verbal and nonverbal assault, charged with challenging new beliefs, suggestions, and commands, may build up profound and often conflicting feelings . . . which may prompt the individual to seek release from a troubled past or from more immediate and pressing problems. Then, . . . the individual may yield to some call, either from within or without, to surrender, to let go, to stop questioning, to relinquish all hold upon the will. And more than anything else it is this act of capitulation that sets off the explosion we call snapping. . . . In that moment, something quite remarkable may happen. With that flick of a switch, that change of heart and mind, an individual's personality may come apart.

Once individuals have been initially compromised by cult members, they may be permanently enthralled through the inculcation of self-programming procedures. As a deprogrammer instructed one deprogrammee (Bromley, 1985a:11):

> In order to keep you in this frame of mind, they have to make it impossible for you to ever think, or make decisions, or act on your own, except what they tell you. . . . That's when it turns into auto-suggestion and self hypnosis. . . . Every time you go to think, every time you have doubts, every time you go to do things other than the rules, to have emotion or ego, you are self-hypnotized.

The result, anti-cult proponents contend, is that cult members remain in a dissociated state, which results in mental disorder and prevents individuals from being able to express their individual autonomy. According to Appel (1981:134):

> What the Moonies and the Krishnas and the Scientologists and all the other dangerous cults do is to maintain the dissociation. They keep the parts of the mind—the connections inside the central nervous system—divided in function, in action, and in their connection with the outer world. It's a way of controlling them, and the longer it goes on, the further apart all of this gets to be—like the chronic schizophrenic.

Ex-cultists testify that once compromised in this way they became deployable agents, participating in brainwashing others. One former NRM member recalls that "I learned to hypnotize people and went out to witness to bring in new people." He claims that he hypnotized recruitment targets on the street when he would "walk up to them, stare at their eyes, get their attention and hold their attention" (Shupe and Bromley, 1981a:202-203).

According to the Satanic cult countersubversion ideology, brainwashing is practiced upon very young children, who are extremely vulnerable and who may be under the control of Satanists for years at a time. This combination of high vulnerability and prolonged exposure creates an enormous capacity for control:

> The process of ritual abuse takes place over an extended period of time, often for years. The process includes a variety of exercises and ceremonies, each with an intended purpose, and which collectively attack all levels of the child's normal orientation. This form of brainwashing forces the children to tune out all other societal influences and instills fear which eventually opens the door to psychological dependency (Massachusetts State Police, *Roll Call Newsletter*, January, 1989, pp. 3-4).

Therapists who treat individuals designated as "ritual abuse survivors" have attempted to discover the nature of the brainwashing techniques employed by Satanists, based on the material elicited from clients during the therapy process. One therapist (Snowden, n.d.), who has compiled a list of these techniques, asserts that Satanists induce dissociation to fragment the personality, shatter emotional spontaneity, disrupt the developmental process, and destroy all memory of the brainwashing process. She describes the brainwashing process, which is often combined with drugging, as ". . . sophisticated hypnosis which involves the associative pairing of induced pain/terror & the cult message & the trigger cue(s) . . . planted in the unconscious. . . . They are later utilized by the cult to control the survivor without his or her conscious awareness."[9]

Once children have been brainwashed or terrorized into submission, they may then be used as recruiters to ensnare others. One woman, who claims that as a child she was sexually terrorized and abused by being forced to engage in cannibalism and sexual intercourse with corpses and by being repeatedly impregnated by cult members who seized newborn infants for ritual sacrifice, reports that she later became a cult recruiter. She asserts that "women like her are raised by Satanists to infiltrate day-care centers and kidnap children" ("Stories Could Lead to Witch Hunt." *El Paso Herald Post* 21 September 1988). Some victims remain affiliated with Satanic cults as a result of being terrorized. One woman who reports that she finally escaped the Satanic cult with which she had been associated recounts that she witnessed and participated in several ritual sacrifices. In some of these cases the sacrifices were conducted specifically as a warning to her to maintain her silence: "As part of her grooming, Sam was required to watch other children being sacrificed; then she was forced to witness and participate in cannibalism. If she told anyone, she was warned, she would be killed. Sam had seen enough to believe the admonition." ("Satan's Victim: One Woman's Ordeal," *Style Weekly*, 19 January 1988).

Organization

Countersubversion narratives sharply differentiate subversive and conventional forms of organization. Establishing categorical distinctions is critical since subversive organizations often deliberately imitate their conventional counterparts as part of a concealment strategy. The ideologies depict subversive organizations as uniquely evil in their structure and operation. Subversives create complex organizations that deliberately and dispassionately engage in and then ritualistically celebrate destructive activity. These attributes typically are symbolized through descriptions of subversive organization as the *inversion* of conventional organization.

In the case of NRMs, anti-cult ideology explicitly distinguishes cults from legitimate religious groups that appear to share attributes in common. For example, Schwartz and Kaslow (1982:7) maintain that while "Spokespersons for those groups generally designated as cults perceive themselves as little different from the early Christians who broke with Judaism almost 2000 years ago," in actuality the differences are profound. They acknowledge some superficial similarities but, based on a comparison of eight groups (Lubavitcher Chassidim, Amish, Roman Catholics and Mormons compared with the Unification Church, Church of Scientology, Alamo Foundation, and Children of God), they assert that (1982:7):

> Although all eight groups compared . . . require substantial or complete "submission to authority" and some financial contribution to the group, only four practice restriction of communications, physiological (diet, sleep) deprivation, and generate feelings of fear and hatred toward non-members that border on paranoid delusions. . . . These same four also have charismatic leadership undemocratically selected.

The attributes of NRMs are defined so as to be opposed to the characteristics of mainstream churches. Thus NRMs are depicted as nothing more than economic scams or schemes for amassing personal of political power. One former NRM member asserts that it is just one big money-making scheme and they brainwash you into thinking you're doing God's work: "It's the greatest rip-off of them all" ("He Was Walking Zombie," *New York, NY Knickerbocker News*, 16 May 1976). Deprogrammer Ted Patrick expressed the same sentiment about NRM leaders in more colorful language (Patrick with Dulack, 1976:11): "Moon's got nothing to do with religion! . . . Moon's a crook, plain and simple. They're all crooks. You name 'em. Not a brown penny's worth of difference between any of 'em." A former member of the Unificationist Movement adopts a similar position, contending that Rev. Moon is engaged simply in a quest for power. He "wants to control the government and rule the world. . . . If he gets enough people in his cult, according to Doug, Moon can elect his own senators, congressmen and even the President. . . ." ("Woman, Man Tell of Religious Cult

Experience," *Waseca, MN Journal*, 16 April 1976). Much is made in this regard of the complex, international corporate organization of some NRMs.[10] There are even hints that religious cults are not independent groups but rather act in concert.

Satanic cult activity is represented as being highly structured through a set of interrelated activities and organizations. Four distinct levels of organization typically are identified in the ideology (Hicks, 1990:283). At the lowest level are *Dabblers*, young people who experiment with Satanic materials such as heavy metal rock music and fantasy games like Dungeons & Dragons. The second level consists of *Self-styled Satanists*, criminals who create or borrow Satanic themes as a rationale for their anti-social acts. A third level involves *Organized Satanists*, members of public, Satanic churches such as the Church of Satan and Temple of Set. At the highest level are the *Traditional Satanists*, individuals organized into a secret cult network engaged in child abuse and sacrifice. Involvement is thought often to begin at lower levels and subsequently lead to involvement at the higher levels. These descriptions of Satanic cult networks highlight the carefully organized, complex organizations created specifically to undertake anti-social activities and escape surveillance and intervention.

The polar opposition of conventional and subversive organization is represented nicely in descriptions of daycare centers that have been infiltrated and taken over by Satanists. In congressional testimony on ritual child abuse, Kee McFarlane, who interviewed children at the McMartin Preschool, drew a graphic picture of a large, powerful, well-financed, underground organization: "I believe we're dealing with an organized operation of child predators designed to prevent detection. The preschool, in such a case, serves as a ruse for a larger, unthinkable network of crimes against children" (*New York Times*, 18 September 1984). Satanists allegedly have used children in daycare centers and preschools as subjects in pornographic films, which are marketed to finance cult activity. Numerous ritual abuse survivors have begun reporting memories of participation in Satanic rituals involving filming of sexual activity. According to one such account:

> My experience was initially I was involved in the rituals. I was used by the Satanists in the rituals. And probably within a year of that initiation, there were a large number of children taken to a warehouse. We were photographed in sexual acts with

other adults, with other children, and in sexual acts with animals. There were generally large numbers of us. It was not home equipment. There were big cameras, big lights. There was a large number of children.

If Satanic cult organizations are consciously destructive, the rituals in which Satanists participate glorify destructiveness. Indeed, the central Satanic ritual involves the ceremonial sacrifice of victims through which participants seek to expand their personal power by literally absorbing the life energy of their victims at the moment of death. As one law enforcement official pieced together the elements of rituals based upon the accounts of survivors:

> The ritual is performed within a circle on the surface of the sacrificial area. The circle serves as a containment field for the energy released from the victim. It is believed that there is a great amount of energy unleashed when the victim is killed and those who conduct the sacrifice must guard against being overwhelmed by the force. The slaughter is preceded by silent concentration, incantations, and burning of incense. A gradual build-up of excitement (sic) culminates in a frenzy at the time of death and the discharge of blood from the victim. An even greater frenzy is reached if there is a simultaneous release of sexual energy through orgasm (Massachusetts State Police, *Roll Call Newsletter*, January, 1989:3).

Thus these rituals celebrate destruction of the very essence of innocent children for the purpose of self-enhancement.

Impact
Subversives possess extraordinary power which they are capable of projecting from the terrain they occupy into the very heart of normal society. The enormity of their power is evidenced by their infiltration of societal institutions, an explosion in the number of individuals who exhibit signs of being compromised by it, and the inability of individuals so afflicted or agents working on victims' behalf to reverse its effects. The infiltration of institutions typically is expressed in terms of the previously discussed inversions. In addition, personal attributes are designated as signs that individuals have been compromised.

Religious cults are depicted as constituting an unprecedented menace that is international in scope. They exist in virtually every locale, which means that there is no safe haven:

> Never before have religious cults been so geographically widespread. They are in every area of the United States, in every major city and on college campuses throughout the nation. They have spread to Canada and to Western Europe, Great Britain, France, Holland, Denmark, Italy, and West Germany—where governments are alarmed about their rapid growth. There are cult centers also in Asia, Africa, South America, Israel, Australia, and New Zealand. (Rudin and Rudin, 1980:16)

Likewise the number of cultists has reached disturbing proportions. For example, estimates of the membership of both the Unification Church and Hare Krishna have been as high as 250,000 members each in 1978 and 400,000 and 375,000, respectively, in 1981 (Appel, 1981:12-13). Given the large number of groups labeled cults, total cult membership is formidable indeed. For example, therapist Margaret Singer, "a cult expert, who counsels former cult members," estimates that "there are 2 to 3 million people in these groups" (Rudin and Rudin, 1980:15-16).

Estimates of the size of Satanic cult membership are extremely elusive since no direct, physical evidence of the cult's existence can be produced. The size of the cult network is therefore inferred from signs of its activity and from reports of ritual abuse from survivors who have managed to escape from the clutches of the cult. For example, local incident reports suggest a massive problem if generalized to the nation as a whole. Dale McCulley, a California law enforcement officer who produced a training film on Satanism, "estimates there have also been dozens of Satanic murders in Mendocino and Sonoma counties" based on the reports of children who have survived Satanic rituals ("Satanic Rituals Emerge in Empire," *The Santa Rosa, CA Press Democrat Empire News*, 29 January 1989). He goes on to report that one investigator is pursuing a Satanic cult case that spans nine separate states. There are many other similar reports to the effect that:

> In virtually every state in the nation, authorities are investigating some form of Satanic activity. In 22

municipalities in Los Angeles County alone, detectives and
social workers are enmeshed in investigations of child-porn
rings with ritualistic overtones. Cult murders are being reported
at a fantastic rate, graves are being robbed in New England,
skulls are sold to N. Y. practitioners of devil worship (Joel
Norris and Jerry Allen Potter "The Devil Made Me Do It,"
Penthouse January, 1986, p. 48).

Another source of estimates is the number of missing children. It is
sometimes claimed that most of these children are Satanic ritual victims,
which has yielded the widely publicized figure of as many as 50,000-
60,000 ritual sacrifice victims annually. These estimates of large
numbers of Satanic incidents and ritual victims, of course, suggests a
vast network of practicing Satanists.

One of the most common means of revealing signs of subversive
power is to identify the special "stigmata" exhibited by its victims.
Enumerating such signs moves subversion claims beyond abstract
numbers and global projections to specific individual characteristics that
demonstrate subversives are at work. Such stigmata also are extremely
useful during countersubversion campaigns when specific individuals
who have been compromised must be identified, quarantined, and
treated. Anti-cult ideology enumerates a series of personal characteristics
associated with religious cult involvement. These include linguistic
changes (e.g., truncated vocabulary); monotonic, inflection-free voice
level; fixed, permanent smile ("with mouth only"); glassy eyes and
dilated pupils; facial skin rash (due to vitamin A deficiency in diet); ill-
fitting, cheap, out-of-style clothing; overall physical debilitation (gaunt
facial appearance, hollow eyes); and hyperactivity, extreme nervousness,
and hunched frame (Shupe and Bromley, 1981c:255). Cultic
brainwashing often is suspected when family members begin observing
such characteristics. In one such account, for example, "His parents
noticed with alarm that he was becoming pale, withdrawn, nervous and
acting almost as if he were in a trance. . . . He was becoming a
walking zombie and nothing at all like the son we had known" (Shupe
and Bromley, 1981c:256). Similar lists of bizarre behaviors by young
children have been constructed as indicators of ritual abuse
victimization. These behaviors include, for example, preoccupation with
urine and feces; aggressive play that has a marked sadistic quality;
mutilation themes predominating in play behavior; fear of ghosts and

monsters; fear of "bad people" taking the child away, breaking into the house, killing the child or the parents, burning the house down; and preoccupation with the devil, magic potions, supernatural power, and crucifixions (Hicks, 1991:245-246).

Those involved in the countersubversion campaign against religious cults confess their defenselessness against brainwashing. According to Conway and Siegelman (1979:59), "The cult experience and its accompanying state of mind defies all legal precedents. It has also taken the mental-health profession by surprise: The conceptual models and diagnostic tools of psychiatry and psychology have proved inadequate to explain or treat the condition." Ted Patrick makes a similar claim: "Please try to understand this: I haven't found a psychiatrist, or any attorney, or a doctor or anyone else who knows anything about brainwashing and mind control" (Patrick with Dulack, 1976:82). The anti-cult movement did develop "deprogramming" as a technique for cultic programming. However, even in cases where individuals are deprogrammed, for an extended period they are left in a condition referred to as "floating" that renders them highly susceptible to losing control again, particularly if they come in contact with cult members or materials. Former members also report that they have been terrorized by cult leaders if they manifest sufficient strength of will to defect. One former NRM member asserts that "I fear for my life. I was told repeatedly that if I left the Church I would be killed" (Shupe and Bromley, 1981a:201). Other apostates have offered accounts of former members dying under strange circumstances shortly after defecting.

Satanic countersubversion ideology suggests that because Satanic cults operate underground and have long-term control over children, the effects of their mind control and terror tactics may be even more damaging. As one law enforcement officer commented about the capacity of police agencies to combat Satanists, "When confronted with those criminals who are led or controlled by supernatural evil beings, philosophies, or motivations, traditional police tools are not effective" (Hicks, 1991:55). One ritual abuse survivor recounts an instance of two undercover police officers attempting to infiltrate the cult with which she was involved, with the result that "one ended up joining and the other was murdered" (Hicks, 1991:173). Ritual abuse survivors contend that they have been subjected to such a thoroughgoing brainwashing program that control over them can be reestablished through "trigger cues" that were implanted in their minds during the brainwashing process. In some ritual abuse survivor networks members avoid phone calls and even greeting cards in the fear that Satanists have planted trigger cues in those materials. One therapist recounts the story of a patient, whose family he suspected of being part of an intergenerational Satanic network, who received a card from her family and then tried to commit suicide. When the family later sent a second identical card to her, she once again attempted suicide. At this point, the therapist became suspicious of the card. Upon examination of the card he discovered a variety of Satanic numbers and symbols embedded in the card's message and artwork (Hicks, 1991:164).

SUMMARY AND CONCLUSIONS

Between the 1960s and 1990s, the United States, and a number of other Western nations as well, witnessed two major subversion episodes. Countersubversion campaigns were launched first against religious cults and subsequently against Satanic cults. Subversion allegations serve as the basis for extreme claimsmaking. Both of the countersubversion campaigns discussed in this chapter have sought legitimation through child endangerment claims, the first concerning adolescents making the transition to adulthood and the second concerning infants moving outside the protection of the family for the first time. This chapter has addressed one important issue in the social construction of subversion— the development of a countersubversion ideology through which the shape of subversion is symbolically depicted.

At the core of creating subversives is the construction of negative transcendence. Transcendence denotes "structural principles or relations of a level lying above or outside the level of structure taken as the point of reference" (Turner 1977:69), in this case the contemporary conventional social order. When human groups are confronted by high levels of structural tension, one common response through history has been to conceive that source of tension as an external, transcendent force with which the group is in conflict. Countersubversion ideologies construct negative transcendence in four ways.

First, subversives are located outside the conventional social order temporally and spatially. Both religious and Satanic cults are described as being simply contemporary outcroppings of evil with a much longer tradition. Subversives thus transcend the present and possess an independent existence, but subversive history has periodically intersected societal history. In both ideologies this extended history is symbolized through linkages to social forms regarded as anti-social, such as Nazism, communism, and organized crime. Similarly, subversives are located beyond the boundary of conventional society, creating for them an independent physical existence. Both types of cults are located in contested sites at the margins of society where the exercise of social control is weakest. It is to these locations that victims are transported and from them that subversives incursions are launched. This separate terrain is crucial to the creation of subversives because it identifies not only their origination point but also a location in which forms of power and organization alien to conventional society may exist.

Second, subversives are endowed with a form of power that is incompatible with and destructive to the functioning of normal human society. This power is described as inherently corrupting and dis-integrating to members of normal society. For religious and Satanic cults alike, this power involves in some combination brainwashing, terrorizing, and drugging of targets. Even seemingly inconsequential contact with this form of power may be sufficient to undermine an individual's capacity for resistance. Dabbling with occult materials or attending a cult-sponsored lecture, for example, renders individuals vulnerable to a form and level of power they are unlikely to be able to withstand. Armed with this potent force, subversives attack the fundamental basis of adaptation within the society. In the two cult countersubversion ideologies the target is individual identity that is necessary for adult development and autonomy. The resulting individual disintegration is symbolized as a cult-imposed personality which leaves victims fragmented, with split or multiple personalities. Even more devastating is that this power is self-replicating as cultists both re-program themselves and join the ranks of perpetrators in search of new victims. The esoteric, corrosive power wielded by subversives is critical to the construction process because it exemplifies the essential social "otherness" of subversives.

Third, subversives are endowed with a transcendent quality through organizational forms that are qualitatively different from their conventional counterparts by being uniquely dedicated to destructive principles and practices. They employ their transcendent power specifically to undermine normal, natural individual and group functioning. Because subversives seek to avoid detection and lure innocents by mimicking conventional organizations, the unique attributes of subversive organizations must be identified. Religious cults are carefully distinguished from conventional churches as are cult front groups from legitimate business and civil libertarian groups. Likewise, activities and enterprises infiltrated by Satanists, such as churches and childcare facilities, are contrasted with their legitimate counterparts. The essence of their subversive form is conveyed in the fundamental contradiction they embody. Subversive organizations expropriate conventional social forms to undermine and destroy those very forms. Thus religious cultists pervert the intrinsically valuable quest for the sacred by transforming religious organizations into utilitarian political and economic enterprises advancing the power and profit of cult leaders. And religious cults exploit youthful idealism to transform journeys of spiritual liberation into journeys of spiritual captivity. Rather than functioning as surrogate families with a sacred trust to nurture and protect children in their care, Satanic cults operate with ultimately calculative callousness, treating children as mere human commodities to be exploited in order to maximize organizational profit. This inversion of legitimate social principles and practices is epitomized for both types of cults in rituals that destroy individual identity.

Fourth, the transcendence of subversives is symbolized by the rate at which normal individuals succumb to subversive power, the way in which it transforms individuals, and the persistence of its effects in the race of treatment and control processes that are effective against other pathological conditions. The rapidly swelling ranks of religious cultists and Satanic ritual abuse victims indicates the awesome potential of subversive power. Additional evidence of subversive power is found in its capacity to transform specific individuals, leaving them bearing the marks of their exploitation. Subversive power is all the more awesome because it is extremely resistant to reversal by conventional treatment and control agents who only dimly understand its nature and operation and have few effective means for combatting it. Finally, subversives are capable of projecting their power so as to reclaim individuals who apparently had escaped their control.

The essence of constructing subversives symbolically, then, lies in depicting in culturally appropriate terms a group having an independent existence and history that transcends the society into which it has now penetrated. Subversives possess forms of power and organization that originate outside the social order, but once operating within the boundaries of the impacted social order are capable of transforming institutions and individuals alike into their alien opposites. Treatment and control agencies find themselves virtually defenseless against subversive forces. It is precisely this cultural depiction, when combined with the equally important construction of social agency for subversives, that is capable of producing the kinds of social scares observed in both the religious and Satanic cult subversion episodes. We can turn to historians to learn just how long this form of cultural collective behavior has been occurring in Western civilization.

NOTES

1. There are, in fact, several Satanic countersubversion narratives. The narrative considered in this chapter concerns the presence of Satanists in daycare centers. The countersubversion activities associated with this narrative involve parents allying with therapists against daycare center workers based on the testimony of young children. In another narrative, adult children ally with therapists against family members, who are accused of being members of an intergenerational Satanic cult. For a general treatment of the countersubversion campaign, see Richardson, Best and Bromley, 1991.

2. As social forms, subversion episodes involve a number of additional elements beyond the countersubversion ideologies considered here. Such episodes are rooted in profound structural tensions, which create countervailing behavioral imperatives for specific groupings of individuals. Both subversion episodes analyzed in this chapter can be traced to tensions between the *contractually* organized public sphere, in which individuals pledge to specific performances rather than to the other's well being and in which social relations are structured and authorized by the state and economy, and the *covenantally* organized private sphere in which individuals pledge to the other's well being and in which social relations are structured by family, church, and community. (For an elaboration of contractualism and covenantalism, see Bromley and Busching, 1988; for an analysis of the impact of contractual-covenantal tensions on the two countersubversion campaigns, see Bromley, 1991 and Bromley and Shupe, 1993). Second, in addition to the construction of a countersubversion ideology, countersubversion campaigns involve the creation of a subversive agency. That is, subversives must not only be described culturally but also empowered such that demonstrable effects can be attributed to subversives. Finally, countersubversion campaigns involve establishing a power base through which the subversive label can be imposed on certain targeted individuals or groups.

3. The matter of precisely who subversives are is quite complex. Subversion as a form of power and organization originates outside of the impacted social order. Subversives here refer to individuals within the social order who act as agents of that external power and organization. All individuals associated with subversive groups are not themselves labeled subversive, however. Some individuals may confess to subversive activity but be designated victims rather than perpetrators.

4. It has sometimes been argued that one distinction between anti-religious and Satanic cult ideologies is that the former groups actually exist while the latter do not. However, a cult, as described in anti-cult ideology, is in fact an amalgamation of characteristics of a variety of groups which the anti-cult movement opposes, and there are some individuals who belong to Satanic churches as well as individuals and groups which employ Satanism to account for their actions. This distinction therefore is difficult to defend.

5. Swidler (1986:279) defines ideology as "a highly articulated, self-conscious belief and ritual system, aspiring to offer a unified answer to problems of social action."

6. It is also worth noting that separate domain is created for such practices as they occur "behind the iron curtain."

7. For example, critics of Satanic countersubversion ideology have challenged ritual abuse survivor accounts by pointing out strikingly similar stories by individuals claiming to be UFO abductees. Ideology proponents speculate that the UFO stories may have been planted in the memories of ritual abuse survivors to shield the true source of their psychic trauma.

8. Personal communication with Robert Hicks.

9. Satanists also allegedly employ other forms of mind control. Teenage "dabblers" may be lured into deeper involvement in Satanism through subliminal messages, referred to as "backward masking," placed on Satanic rock music. Masking is evident to the conscious mind when the records are played backward. Instead of the garble usually heard on a normal version, words are plainly

discernible. These messages cannot be heard with the conscious mind when the record is played normally, but the subconscious mind retains them (Koenig, 1985:65).

10. For a description of the international organization of the Unificationist movement, see Bromley, 1985b.

REFERENCES

Appel, Willa, 1981. *Cults in America: Programmed for Paradise*. New York: Holt, Rinehart and Winston.

B.A.D.D. (Bothered About Dungeons and Dragons), Inc., n.d. "Advanced Ritualistic Crime Seminar." Richmond, VA.

Bromley, David G., 1991. "The Satanic Cult Scare." *Society* (May/June), 1-11.

------, 1985a. "Deprogramming as a Mode of Exit from New Religious Movements: The Case of the Unificationist Movement," in David G. Bromley, ed., *Falling from the Faith: Causes and Consequences of Religious Apostasy*. Newbury Park: Sage Publications, pp. 185-204.

------, 1985b. "The Economic Structure of the Unificationist Movement." *Journal for the Scientific Study of Religion* 24, pp. 253-274.

------, and Bruce Busching, 1988. "Understanding the Structure of Contractual and Covenantal Social Relations: Implications for the Sociology of Religion." *Sociological Analysis* 49, pp. 15-32.

------, and Anson Shupe, 1993. "Organized Opposition to New Religious Movements," in David Bromley and Jeffrey Hadden, eds., *The Handbook of Cults and Sects in America*. Greenwich: Association for the Sociology of Religion and JAI Press, pp. 177-198.

------, and Anson Shupe, 1981. *Strange Gods: The Great American Cult Scare*. Boston: Beacon Press.

Conway, Flo and Jim Siegelman, 1979. *Snapping: America's Epidemic of Sudden Personality Change*. Philadelphia: Lippincott.

Edwards, Christopher, 1979. *Crazy for God*. Englewood Cliffs, NJ: Prentice-Hall.

Hicks, Robert, 1991. *In Pursuit of Satan: The Police and the Occult*. Buffalo, NY: Prometheus Books.

Hill, Sally and Jean Goodwin, 1989. "Satanism: Similarities between Patient Accounts and Pre-Inquisition Historical Sources." *Dissociation* 2, pp. 29-44.

Kahaner, Larry, 1988. *Cults That Kill: Probing the Underworld of Occult Crime*. York: Warner Books.

Koenig, Frederick, 1985. *Rumor in the Marketplace: The Social Psychology of Commercial Hearsay*. Dover: Auburn House.

Ofshe, Richard and Margaret Singer, 1986. "Attacks on Peripheral versus Central Elements of Self and the Impact of Thought Reforming Techniques." *The Cultic Studies Journal* 3, pp. 3-24.

Patrick, Ted with Tom Dulack, 1976. *Let Our Children Go!* New York: Ballantine Books.

Richardson, James and Brock Kilbourne, 1983. "Classical and Contemporary Applications of Brainwashing Models: A Comparison and Critique," in David G. Bromley and James T. Richardson, eds., *The Brainwashing/ Deprogramming Controversy: Sociological, Psychological, Legal and Historical Perspectives.* New York: Edwin Mellen Press, pp. 29-46.

------, Joel Best and David Bromley, eds., 1991. *The Satanism Scare.* Hawthorne, NY: Aldine de Gruyter.

Rudin James and Marcia Rudin, 1980. *Prison or Paradise? The New Religious Cults.* Philadelphia: Fortress Press.

Schwartz, Lita and Florence Kaslow, 1982. "The Cult Phenomenon: Historical, Sociological, and Familial Factors Contributing to Their Development and Appeal," in Florence Kaslow and Marvin Sussman, eds., *Cults and the Family.* New York: Haworth Press, pp. 3-30.

Shupe, Anson and David G. Bromley, 1981a. "Apostates and Atrocity Stories: Some Parameters in the Dynamics of Deprogramming," in Bryan Wilson, ed., *The Social Impact of New Religious Movements.* New York: Rose of Sharon Press, pp. 179-215.

------, 1981b. *The New Vigilantes: Deprogrammers, Anti-Cultists and the New Religions.* Beverly Hills: Sage Publications.

------, 1981c. "Witches, Moonies, and Accusations of Evil," in Thomas Robbins and Dick Anthony, eds, *In Gods We Trust: New Patterns of Religious Pluralism in America.* New Brunswick: Transaction Books, pp. 247-262.

Snowden, Kathy K., n.d. "Satanic Cult Ritual Abuse." Unpublished manuscript.

Swatland, Susan and Anne Swatland, 1982. *Escape from the Moonies* London: New English Library.

Swidler, Ann, 1986. "Culture in Action: Symbols and Strategies." *American Sociological Review* 51:273-286.

Turner, Terence, 1977. "Transformation, Hierarchy and Transcendence: A Reformulation of Van Gennep's Model of the Structure of Rites

De Passage," in Sally Moore and Barbara Myerhoff, eds., *Secular Ritual*. Van Gorcum: Assen, Netherlands, 1977, pp. 53-70.

CHAPTER IV

AN ALTERNATIVE TO THE ANTI-CULT MOVEMENT GROUPE ALLIANCE IN CANADA

Richard Bergeron

The anti-cult movement is the most visible and serious response to the phenomenon of the new religions and spiritualities. The movement has appeared as a coalition of groups and centers which share the same negative vision of the new religious movements and which are more or less loosely united.[1] The movement unites three categories of members: (1) those who have a loved one in a new religion: parent, spouse, friend; (2) former adherents who had a negative experience in a new religious group; and (3) specialists who offer analysis and the underlying ideology of the anti-cult movement. In a real, if ironic sense, much of the research focusing on the new religions has been mandated by the anti-cult movement.[2]

The anti-cult movement, at both popular as well as scientific levels, is almost exclusively centered on the deviance, the abnormality, and the dangers of the religions. This has consequently created an intense fear. Since that fear seems disproportionate in relation to the immediate danger, Kilbourne and Richardson speak of *cultphobia:* and, according to them, one is able to "demonstrate conceptually how the *psychopathology argument*—applied to the adherents by the anti-cult movements—can also be applied to members and sympathizers of the ACM."[3]

The anti-cult movement postulates that the majority of new religious movements are destructive for the individual, for the family, and for society. The individual is allegedly seduced, alienated, and pressured to the point where it is no longer possible for him or her to voluntarily leave the group. Following the joining of a member, the nuclear family is divided and society's structures and dominant values are threatened. Hence, the anti-cult movement has appropriated for itself the mission of protector of individuals, families, and society against this new scourge. It lobbies government for severe anti-cult legislation; it forewarns the public by using large numbers of negative testimonies by disappointed former adherents, and it uses more or less doubtful means to de-convert the adherents (deprogramming, exit counselling). It considers the new religions *a priori* either as socially dangerous groups or along the lines of dangerous heretics. This initial prejudice leads to a reaction centered around condemnation, denunciation, and fear.

What is, then, the alternative to the anti-cult movement? In Montréal a team from the Centre d'information sur les nouvelles religions, composed of psychologists, theologians and specialists in religious science, and social workers, has worked steadily for several years to conceive an approach which is not essentially centered on others (i.e., the groups and their adherents, but on oneself). This approach stems from the conviction that the new religions constitute an important socio-religious phenomenon in our secular society, and a challenge to the large established churches, for society in general and for the individual, especially for those with a loved one in a new religion or spirituality. Can we conceive of a psycho-spiritual approach offering an open and critical interpretation of this new religious phenomenon? An approach seeking to face the challenge and the summons to respond of the new religions, and to transform the fear and the "danger" into a springboard for psycho-spiritual growth and personal development? Can we turn the suffering of seeing a loved one converting to a new religion into a creative movement of psycho-spiritual growth and personal development, so that the relational impasse would become a road to life? Can we conceive of an approach where, instead of starting a war, the individual is mobilized by the new religions to undertake a new quest of self-discovery?

It is in order to respond to such concerns that the approach of Groupe Alliance was born. Groupe Alliance addresses all who have a loved one (parent, spouse, child, friend) in a new religion and who are profoundly affected and troubled by this situation which threatens marriage relationships, the family, and friendships. Groupe Alliance gathers together those men and women who have in common the disappointment and "loss" caused by the allegiance of a loved one to a new religion. The group is founded on the conviction that only a change in their attitude will help them to resolve the crisis, and its counselors seek to integrate this new reality into a deeply valued relationship, to live through the situation with confidence and peace, and to allow for personal growth. The goal, in other words, is to reinterpret loved ones' experiences as growth opportunities, both for their loved ones and relatives and for themselves. In doing so, the fact (and stigma) of having a close relation in an unconventional religious group loses its power to dominate and disturb non-members' lives. They realize that all their efforts to change the other only produces biased judgements, traumatizes them, and worsens the situation.

Of course, it is well understood that the Groupe Alliance adheres to no particular church or religious denomination. It does not engage in any controversy and doesn't presuppose, at the beginning, any particular religious conviction.

Objectives

Groupe Alliance was conceived to help those with a loved one in a new religion to integrate that new fact into their married life, their family life and in their friendships, and to grow personally in the new situation. The approach proposes, then, to promote the psycho-spiritual relief of these people, to lead them into a state of interior serenity and peace and to help them better understand and love their dear ones engaged in a new religious option, in order to establish a new dialogue with them. Unlike other North American "anti-cult" groups, it does not immediately establish an antagonistic, fearful relationship between a family and the conventional group in which one of its members is now a member.

Approach

To attain its objectives, Groupe Alliance proposes an approach inspired and already largely proven in those self-help groups called "anonymous." The approach, which is composed of ten steps, forms the roadbed upon which we are able to build only slowly and will bear fruit only if we supply effort and good will. The ten steps are articulated around the four themes which constitute the great moments of the program.

First Moment

In the first great moment, the person is brought to look squarely at the situation, to recognize that she or he has no power over the freedom of another and consequently, that she or he is *not able to change* the religious choice of their loved one. The first steps are contained in this first great moment. The first then can be formulated as follows:

> 1. I have decided to look at the situation squarely in the face and to seek to identify with that which makes me suffer.

The difficulty for someone who is troubled is to take the "authentic" measure of a personal situation and to identify the source of his or her suffering. The next step is then dedicated to situating the problem in a larger context, to provide an explanation of the global phenomenon of new religions and to give an adequate knowledge of the group to which the new adherent has converted.

With that done, we are able to identify the precise nature of the malaise. The person is led to identify: (1) what type of emotions they feel: aggressiveness, grief, fear, insecurity, guilt, hate, resentment? (2) precisely in which circumstances these feelings appear? what behavior, attitudes, or ways of being and speaking of the new adherent? in religious, familial, or conjugal areas? and (3) why does he or she feel like that? What is it that causes the shock, the trouble, triggers aggressiveness? Where, precisely, is he or she touched: in religious conviction, in pride, in prejudices, in what is experienced as rejection, in the dreams one had for one's own children? The precise identification of that which makes them suffer is foundational in the proposed approach. With that done one moves to the second step.

> 2. I admit that I am powerless in front of the religious choice of my loved one and that relations have become difficult, if not practically impossible.

This step is difficult to clear because of the prejudiced atmosphere which denies the possibility of a free choice and which affirms easily that the adherents of the new religions are all seduced, conditioned, brainwashed, or programmed. And that seems confirmed by the change in behavior and ways of being and reactions of the new adherent. The approach of Groupe Alliance is often the last recourse, when everything else has been tried to deconvert the new adherent: anger, emotional blackmail, discussion, recourse to specialists, and subtle persecution. Nothing works. All the efforts have done nothing but reinforce the new adherent in his attachment and has produced nothing except frustration, disenchantment, and hurting.

Having exhausted all resources, the time comes to let go. It is often as a result of despair that people take the approach of Groupe Alliance. And how difficult it is! It will not happen until one recognizes one's impotence in front of the religious choice of one's loved one and until one finally renounces the desire to deconvert him or her. Recognizing one's powerlessness is fundamentally a positive attitude of non-resistance, of letting go: on one hand, it prevents one from exhausting oneself in frustrating approaches which cannot issue in anything but a hardening of positions, and on the other hand, it permits one to channel one's energies positively and to experience the emotional detachment so necessary in the situation.

3. I have recognized the right of the other to her own religious affiliation.

In the midst of the current pluralism, it is readily accepted that each person has the right to adhere to the religion of his or her choice. This usually doesn't cause problems as long as we are dealing with religions considered "respectable" and "worthy of faith." But when we are dealing with the new religions, this tolerance often breaks down. Worries and genuine concerns (as well as feelings of loss) reveal that many participants are afraid to see the other "lost forever." "If the new religion made a little bit of sense . . ." "If the new adherent was truly free . . ." Then, one could recognize the right for him or her to get involved. This is what is thought by most.

Even if a new religion offered little respectability and involved practices dishonest and prejudicial to the psychic health of the adherent, that would not injure the right of an individual to opt for the religion of his or her choice. It would show only that the choice is "dangerous." Respecting the right of the other is not real unless one accepts the other's decision, even though this decision could have been conditioned in many ways, as are the better part of our human decisions. This acceptance implies that one is able to express his dissention, where there is dissention. Of course, the zone of dissention is possibly large. But that doesn't remove the acceptance of the other and their right to the religion of their choice.

Upon clearing this very difficult step, one is able to proceed to the second moment.

Second Moment.

In the second moment, one is invited to examine oneself and to become aware of one's own involvement in this situation.   This constitutes the fourth and fifth steps of the journey.

   4.   I have decided to examine myself in reference to this situation.

Once one admits that one has no power over the decisions of the new adherent and over the behavior following from their choice, one's only recourse to change the situation is found within oneself. Groupe Alliance teaches that everyone has the power to change him or herself and to change his or her attitudes and behavior. The new adherent is not the only one responsible for the conflict. If relations have deteriorated, it is not exclusively the fault of the adherent to a new religion. The spouse, friend, relative, also has something to do with the situation as it is.

At this point in the approach it is necessary to cease looking at the adherent and to look at oneself, to examine one's personal attitudes and behavior. These attitudes may be of a nature such as rejection or argumentation that provokes a hardening on the part of the adherent, i.e., "driving" them further into the group. For example, all words or actions which work towards deconversion, or which are critical of adherents' groups or which let it be understood that they have been programmed—all that is of such a nature as to provoke the "hardening" of the adherent, who feels assaulted. And that's how the situation becomes more irksome and painful to loved ones on the outside.

This self-examination leads to the question that loved ones must ask themselves:who have I become, as an historical subject and a concrete person? Each of us is fashioned by a myriad of little events, happy or unhappy, which one has experienced and carries in oneself: one's own injuries, one's shames, one's sorrows, one's fears. It is all of this which expresses itself in the interaction with the adherent.

Responsibility, however, doesn't mean culpability. The temptation to feel guilty is strong in these circumstances. For example, what is it that I have done wrong which has pushed my partner, or my child to join a new religion? Most who follow the approach are guilt-ridden. Hence, there is the need to distinguish between culpability and responsibility. Looking for who is guilty is not the issue. The issue is responsibility. This is not the place to look for culpability. It stirs one to responsibility. Not the responsibility we have in the choice the other makes in a new religious option, not the responsibility which we have in the choice the other makes in a new religious option, but the responsibility which we have *now* in the situation which causes suffering. Altogether, we struggle to make a good examination of conscience: this will make it possible to move on to the next step.

5.   I have decided to begin a journey of reconciliation towards my loved one whom I have harmed by my attitudes, judgements, or accusations.

In this step, one continues to examine oneself, looking especially at one's injuries and suffering, of which the new adherent is the cause or the occasion. I have been harmed by their attitudes, their judgements, their accusations, and hurt by the leader or members of the new religion. I am pained by the suffering of "losing" a loved one. Hence, the feelings of bitterness, of hate, vengeance.

At this step in the journey, one is invited to go from an attitude of hate and denunciation to one of forgiveness. It is not necessary to obtain the forgiveness of the new adherent, but it is important to enter into a global attitude of forgiveness. For only forgiveness is able to "unlock" the situation and to allow life to continue to flow. To forgive is, indeed, to remember that the other is greater than the injury they have inflicted on me. To forgive is to refuse to make final judgements on the new adherent, to classifying him or her once and for all in negative categories. That is to lock him or her up in his or her present way of being and doing.

Having entered into this attitude of forgiveness and having become aware, through the previous step, that the adherent has been hurt by one's judgements, accusations, unpleasant or even hostile comments, what must one do? One must reconcile. This reconciliation must take place at two levels. First it is an *interior journey* which consists essentially in an attitude of availability arising from the regret of having injured the other, of compassion toward him/her, and of the desire to correct one's own faults in making honorable amends. This approach of reconciliation which takes place within the person fosters interior peace and cleans the heart.

Essentially interior as it is, however, reconciliation ought also to be expressed in words and actions as soon as possible. This exterior approach to reconciliation, in which one humbly recognizes one's errors and tactlessness, aims at renewing contact with the new adherent. It also prevents unavoidable misunderstandings and roadblocks from degenerating the situation. This contact reestablishes or, perhaps, improves an important element in the further development of the adherent and shows itself often, as the only critical stance in their journey.

Thus ends the second great moment of the approach. Having looked honestly at the situation and at oneself, one is ready to move to another decisive step. Up till now the approach has focused on clarifying the psychological and social field. People arrive at Groupe Alliance full of aggression, of fear, of worry, of rage, of guilt, of bitterness, hatred, and shame. The two first moments have permitted them to clean the psychological field and to differentiate between emotional outbursts and feelings. The approach has been hard, painful, the cost has been high in tears and violent outbursts, and it has demanded on the part of all the participants much understanding and comforting.

Third Moment.

Once the psychological field is loosened up, the participant discovers that the problem with which he or she is confronted is not at first psychological but, rather, spiritual. The question which is raised by the new adherent falls in the whole domain of values, of spirituality and of religion—in one word, the question of God. Thus the participant is confronted with the question of God. At the beginning of the approach, he or she is unable to hear the words God, Bible, or religion—since all of that has been the cause of "the loss" of his or her loved one. Now, he or she is ready to speak about it and to turn towards God.

In the third great moment of the approach, the person is invited to look at God. It will not do here to speak of God in an abstract or objective manner. But, rather, to place oneself personally in front of God and to integrate God into one's present life and journey.

6.   I have come to believe in a power superior to myself who is able to enlighten my personal journey and to help me to have the necessary discernment.

Until now the approach has allowed people to come out of their isolation in order to share with others who, living an experience similar to theirs, were capable of empathy and understanding. This opening towards others has allowed a first clarification in people's thoughts and feelings and a clean up of their interior world. Faced with one's powerlessness to change the decision of the adherent, the opening up to others has already produced beneficial fruits. What will happen then if one opens to The Other (with a capital O) that is, to the Superior Power? The words "I have come to believe" mean that in my powerlessness to change the adherent, I have awakened to the reality of this Superior Power which could bring understanding in my interior journey. People may have thought initially that this Power was able to "deconvert" the adherent; but, now they have come to believe that it is able to do something *for themselves.* It is them who need to change. And a Superior Power is able to help them do it.

7.   I have decided to confide in God, as I understand God, seeking to know God's will and allowing God to intervene in my life.

Having accepted the idea that one is able to receive help from a Superior Power, the participant is invited to trust his understanding to God. The approach of Groupe Alliance imposes no religious creed, neither Catholic, nor Protestant, nor Hindu, nor Buddhist, nor Islamic. The God in whom the person has resolved to confide is not the God of one religion, but his or her own God.

Having gone through this difficult step, the participant is on the same ground as the adherent. The latter, too, has decided to believe in a Superior Power and has accepted that God intervenes in one's life. And this has upset his or her life, modified their personality, and changed both their values and views on life. This is where the misunderstanding between the participant and the adherent was located. And it is precisely at this level that the participant is ultimately challenged by the adherent. So, at this stage, the participant is not only better able to identify his or her own situation but also to understand the new adherent from the inside.

And that allows one to enter into the last step of the approach which consists, on the one hand, of discovering the positive aspects of the adherent's experience and on the other hand, the source of one's own spiritual roots. Indeed, the spiritual experience of the new adherent, in challenging the participant's own spiritual vision, helps him or her to discern more clearly the content of his or her spiritual life.

8.   I sought to discover the positive aspects of the experience of the other and to welcome their spirituality.

Transformed by the previous steps, the participant is able to see the adherent in a new way. The latter may well continue to pretend to be pure and saved, in a world lost and unconscious, or to quote the Bible and the words of a Guru. However, the participant has gotten rid of feelings of aggression and hatred and of stereotypical judgements, and so is able to cast a fresh look at the adherent. He/she is thus able to see beyond the negative aspects and to seek to discover the experience which the adherent is trying to express through Bible quotes or new behaviors. The participant is able to see beyond the rigidity and the claim to possess all the truth made by the adherent. The participant then understands that the adherent is experiencing something which involves him or her completely and motivates all of his or her existence. This new religious option has perhaps allowed the adherent to discover the sense of his or her life, to come out of solitude, and to overcome the insignificance of a material existence or certain enslavements (alcohol, drugs, sex). Perhaps the adherent has discovered the beginnings of a new interior life in a one dimensional world; or he or she is given new values and morals.

Having discovered the positive sides, it is possible to move from accusation to openness, from negation to challenge. One discovers, then, that the new option of the adherent challenges one at the spiritual level and puts in question religious convictions, existential positions, and even a bourgeois existence. One feels directly challenged by the adherent; at the same time one's view has been enlarged and one discovers that the phenomenon of the new religions poses a great challenge to society and to the established religions.

9. I have decided to deepen my own spiritual allegiance or religious conviction through appropriate means.

The preceding step sends one directly to oneself as a spiritual subject. By their religious option, the adherent implicitly asks the following question: "And you, what is your spiritual allegiance?" Some participants think that by returning to religious practice, or to church, they are facing the challenge. But, at this step, the issue is not to return to religious practice or to become a more fervent Catholic or Protestant. The issue, rather, is to honestly find out where one stands with respect to one's life.

Whether one is a believer or an unbeliever, everyone has a spiritual allegiance, even if it is an allegiance to no religion. It is this spiritual allegiance which is important here. The spiritual allegiance consists of all the values to which a person adheres and by which one lives; it defines one's way of life and one's behavior towards oneself, towards money, goods, others, and society.

Obviously this quest for one's own values leads to the question of what is the foundation of these values and, that in turn, leads ultimately to the question of God.

This step raised and raises a passionate interest on the part of the participants. So much so that in order to respond to their needs and desires, we had to set in motion another process—that of the Groupe Appurtenance—which follows the process of Groupe Alliance and allows them to begin a journey centered around a common experience—that of having had or still having a loved one in a new religion.

There is a tenth step—which isn't quite a step: it brings the participants on the one hand to look back on the journey they have gone through and on the other hand, to start a new beginning which takes two directions: sharing this step with others and applying the main principles to all areas of life.

Functioning of the Group

1. *The Participants:* They are those who are deeply disturbed by the participation in a new religion of someone they hold dear; however, they are also psychologically sound. A person suffering from psychosis, from a nervous disorder, or from some other serious pathological condition would simply be unable to enter such a process. He or she

would be a major handicap for the functioning of the group. Such people ought to be supported on an individual basis through specialized psycho-spiritual counselling. The approach of Groupe Alliance unearths psychic and spiritual monsters buried within oneself, lifts up the veil on hidden aspects of one's life, and explores unsuspected recesses of one's being. That can sometimes be upsetting for the participants. An individual with serious traumas would run the risk of aggravating his or her situation. As a matter of fact, the group would not be able to provide support and guidance for such a person.

   2. *The Group Meetings:* The group consists of 10 to 15 people. It has been functioning for nine years. It meets each week for three hours with a specialist in new religions. The process lasts between six and eight months. Some choose to go through the process in whole or in part the following year in order either to go deeper in the process or to go through a step which has not yet been cleared. Each meeting begins by the reading of the ten steps. The meeting is composed of the following elements: explanation of the step, exchange on the step, and sharing on our experiences of the previous week. These three elements don't always occur in the same order, nor do they necessarily occur at every meeting. This sharing of one's experiences, emotions, thoughts, failures, and successes constitute the fundamental dynamic of the approach. The participants have so many things to share and so many emotions to express. They relate to one another at a deep level. And they quickly become a network of friends, so much so that after the meetings the telephone continues ringing. Each member of the group is furnished with an accompanying notebook of 70 pages, in which each step is explained, so that one is able to study and deepen the experience on one's own.

   3. *Type of Approach:* The approach, as has now become clear, is not mainly an intellectual one but, rather, a psycho-spiritual one. It is not an approach of critical understanding. Since, however, the understanding of the phenomenon of the new religions isn't a minor element, information and explanations designed to help in understanding the phenomenon are provided when appropriate during the course of the process.

   The approach hopes to be essentially one of integration, of becoming whole. It aims at integrating the new reality in the parental, conjugal, or friend relationship. If the integration is successful it makes parents become parents in a *different way,* spouses become spouses in a *different way,* and friends become friends in a *different way.* Numerous participants witness to this reality: "It is from the group that I acquired my new way of seeing my children." (Jacques); I was brought to better love my spouse." (Serge); "The steps helped me to be more honest with my friend" (Sylvie). If integration is successful, then all of life is integrated through this experience. The main principles of the approach are integrating elements of the psycho-social, spiritual, and even religious aspects of life.

The following testimonies witness to that. "The steps lead us to refuse mediocrity and to allow new life to surge in us." (Serge); "I was led to face myself. I broke down a wall." (Michel); "I became aware that I wore masks" (Sylvie). This integrating quality of the approach finds its best expression in the following witness: "I truly sensed a personal transformation operating in me which brought me peace and interior serenity. The approach moves us to find, first of all in ourselves, and then in the other, the forces which allow us to say that all is not finished. Thus the approach brings us beyond, to which at first sight seems closed, to unexpected possibilities. In other words, the approach opens us gradually to the religious and spiritual dimension of existence, beyond simply existing and beyond material comfort."

The approach of Group Alliance isn't a miracle recipe. The results are not guaranteed. Instead, they depend on the degree of personal involvement of each participant. The participants find the approach difficult and trying but, for the most part, appropriate to their needs. The trying difficulties are not the same for all—except for the initial difficulty which is to renounce one's anti-cultist crusade, to allow oneself to be called into question and to undertake to work upon oneself. Once that difficulty is overcome, one is then able to undertake the process during the course of which other roadblocks may develop. For some this happens at step 2 (letting go); for another, it will be at step 5 (taking responsibility and forgiveness); for another yet, step 6 (an opening to a Superior Power) and so on. But it is not necessary to have cleared completely one step in order to move onto another. Quite often a later step sheds light on a previous step and allows the hoped for passage. There is nothing mechanical about all of this; the steps are to be understood less like the degrees of a ladder where persons advance one rung after the other than as a movement which explores and liberates the various parts of their being and of life as they found themselves in the situation created by the new religious choice of a loved one.

NOTES

1. Shupe, Anson D., Jr. and David G. Bromley, 1982. "Shaping the Public Response to Jonestown: People's Temple and the Anticult Movement," in Ken Levi, ed., *Violence and Religious Commitment.* London: Pennsylvania Press, pp. 102-131.

2. Brock Kilbourne and James T. Richardson, 1986. "Cultphobia," *Thought* 61, p. 258.

3. Ibid., p. 259.

CHAPTER V

THE CULT AWARENESS NETWORK

Priscilla D. Coates

The Cult Awareness Network (CAN) is a non-profit, educational association comprised primarily of volunteers. CAN was established as a consumer protection coalition to document and record reports of organizations which are abusive to their members. CAN provides preventive education about destructive groups and serves as a resource and referral network for further data on the nature of destructive cults. CAN also provides support for all those victimized by destructive groups. CAN provides information about destructive cults whether they are destructive religious cults, therapy cults, political cults, or commercial cults.

> Congress shall make no law respecting an establishment of religion, or **prohibiting the free exercise thereof;** . . .[1] The subsequent cases interpreting these four words make it clear that while the free exercise clause provides absolute protection for a person's religious **beliefs,** it provides only limited protection for the **expression** of those beliefs and especially **actions** based on those beliefs. Freedom of belief is absolutely guaranteed, freedom of action is not.[2]

The Cult Awareness Network traces its beginnings to 1971 when a group of families in and around San Diego began collecting and exchanging data about a group called the Children of God. Those families called their organization Free the Children of God or FREECOG.[3] When the national television program *Chronolog* referred to FREECOG in its 1972 investigative report on the Children of God, FREECOG was surprised by inquiries from parents and siblings, teachers, clergy and friends from all over the country about a variety of religious groups. The network began when people around the country began to correspond and form groups similar to FREECOG.

By 1974, many small organizations of families, sometimes joined by former members of abusive groups, were meeting across the country to exchange information. They compiled first-hand experiences from former members and families of what appeared to be abuses such as slavery, privation, harassment and intimidation, deception, financial exploitation, and monetary fraud. The attorney general of the state of New York, Louis J. Lefkowitz, began an investigation into the Children of God.[4] Senator Mervyn Dymally, then a California State Senator, organized hearings on abusive groups in California.[5]

One community leader who spoke against abusive groups was Theodore (Ted) Patrick. In 1965, President Ronald Reagan, then Governor of California, appointed Patrick, a Democrat, Head of Community Relations for San Diego and Imperial Counties. Patrick's son, Michael, had been recruited briefly by the Children of God in 1971. As a result of that experience, Patrick began speaking with cult members to encourage them to allow themselves time to question and reflect. He called that process "deprogramming."[6] No coercion was suggested or required because in the early 1970s these groups were open organizations. Publications were freely distributed. Families and friends could have access to their loved ones.

On August 30, 1974 representatives from many of the small cult awareness groups met in Denver to unite to form a national consumer protection organization to educate the public about what they called spiritual frauds or destructive cults. They proposed a program of prevention through consumer education exposing the deception, fraud, and corruption. If recruiting became difficult, they reasoned, destructive cults would be forced to reform. The group meeting in Denver selected the name CITIZENS FREEDOM FOUNDATION (CFF). They established a nine-member board with staggered three-year terms to create bylaws, incorporate as an educational organization, seek tax exempt status, and establish a national office to compile and distribute information. They agreed to confine their concerns to illegal and unethical activities, manipulation, and deception. Those individuals represented many political perspectives, skeptics, and believers from a multiplicity of religions, occupations, and levels of education. The individuals involved today are just as diverse. Agreement on one issue remains constant: human beings are being hurt by destructive groups.

Similar cult awareness groups were also forming in England, France, and Germany by 1974.

Ted Patrick attended the meeting in Denver. He was not an organizer or a member, as some incorrectly allege. The minutes reflect he interrupted a speaker to endorse the formation of a national group and urged the selection of a national chairman. Patrick stated he would not be part of any parents' group and left the meeting before its conclusion.[7]

Those early CAN networks struggled to understand the social dynamics of the groups which spawned so many complaints. In trying to understand these self-proclaimed new religions, their members read extensively about religion and religious movements throughout history. They discovered new religions with bizarre beliefs which were benign. They compared their information with articles on a similar phenomenon of the 1800s when thousands of groups flourished and deteriorated within three years. Yet the new religions which were generating so many complaints seemed to have more staying power.

The founders of the CAN network turned to the early thought reform and brainwashing literature for explanations for the transformations they had witnessed in those who joined abusive groups. One book they recommended was Dr. Robert J. Lifton's book, *Thought Reform and the Psychology of Totalism: A Study of Brainwashing in China,* about the reeducation camps established in China by Mao Zedong. The Attorney General of New York had issued a preliminary report on the Children of God in January 1974.[8] That report included a chapter on the techniques of mind manipulation as employed by the Children of God to explain the reported submission by followers to solitary confinement, physical coercion, censorship of communications, and sexual abuse.

From 1974 to 1976, the network was encouraged because sociology researchers expressed interest in the network and its concerns. Many families and former members were interviewed. They trusted and exposed themselves as they relayed their stories. When articles began appearing which referred to the network as ACM, now known as the Anti-Cult Movement, and deprogramming was called the new exorcism, they felt deceived.[9]

The Cult Awareness Network is not an "anti-cult" group. CAN supports religious choice. CAN defends diversity of belief systems and celebrates the right of individual determination. The Cult Awareness

Network does not and will not judge doctrine or belief. CAN is concerned with actions which are totalitarian and segregated, abusive, and sadistic; actions which are illegal and unethical; actions which are used to recruit and retain members through undue influence and deception; actions which make a group institutionally dishonest.

In 1976 the first "coalition" of front groups for destructive groups was formed and called FOR, Freedom of Religion Committee. FOR's purpose was to appear to be composed of representatives of mainline religions who supported all "new religions." As FOR grew, its name was changed to APRL, Alliance for the Preservation of Religious Liberty. FOR and APRL established a networking relationship with the ACLU, American Civil Liberties Union, and many of its state chapters.[10] [11]

By 1977, many of the new religions had become secretive and closed. Families and friends had increasingly limited access to loved ones. Although court decisions had allowed limited conservatorship to families of cult members, most were eventually overturned. Some desperate families who sincerely believed their loved one's mental or physical health was in jeopardy resorted to kidnapping their progeny to obtain counseling, information, and assistance. CAN has never supported or condoned abduction. CAN has always supported voluntary exit counseling or voluntary deprogramming.

In 1974, the participants in the Denver meeting agreed to issue a newsletter to summarize the anti-social, unethical, and illegal activities of destructive cults and expose their deception and fraud. The Southern California volunteers' newsletter evolved as the national newsletter. The *CFF News* relied then, as *CAN News* does now, on volunteers who clip and send news articles from local newspapers. In 1982, responsibility for production of the newsletter was shifted to the national office. The national director now works with a committee to produce the *CAN News* each month. The early goal of establishing and funding a national office did not happen right away. Modest donations and volunteers enabled small local groups to survive but it could not staff or fund a national office. Even with little national coordination, the newsletters continued and small groups of dedicated volunteers fastidiously collected data and answered inquiries. The network continued.

Throughout the seventies and eighties, newspapers, radio and television programs, and books publicized the network. The number of inquiries kept increasing and the base and the scope of the network expanded. Inquiries continued from families, friends, and clergy and still more and more requests came from the media and former members. Press conferences and press releases were rare but, through documented newsletters and reasoned factual statements, the network earned the reputation as a resource for reliable information.

By the late seventies, the network began to receive increasing inquiries and complaints about organizations which did not call themselves religions or have anything to do with religion or spirituality. They were political, therapeutic, and commercial groups. The systems of social control were similar to the destructive cults; the abuses were the same. The network began to seek data and documentation on the operations of unconventional political, therapeutic, and commercial groups: what the network now frequently refers to as destructive "therapy cults," "political cults," and "commercial cults."

In 1980, the first annual Leo J. Ryan[12] award was presented to honor the individual who had done the most that year to alert the public to the dangers of destructive groups. And in 1980, the first national director was appointed. By 1984, the national office was receiving more than 5,600 queries per year. In 1985, the national board of directors voted to establish the national office in Chicago and change the association's name to the Cult Awareness Network. In preparation for that name change, the organization was called the Cult Awareness Network of Citizens Freedom Foundation. Cynthia Kisser has been the national director of the Cult Awareness Network since 1987. In 1991, the national office received more than 16,000 requests for information. Since then requests have remained steady.

In the early eighties, the network was inundated by complaints and inquiries about what appeared to be fundamentalist Christian churches. Many of these complaints focused on severe physical and sexual abuse and neglect of children. In one year, three children were beaten to death in three different groups in three different states as three different leaders, respectively, directed and watched.[13] As information accumulated, it became apparent that some groups which called themselves "Christian" had become remarkably authoritarian and abusive. Many of these new, self-proclaimed "Christian" organizations were run by self-ordained dictators. Others were part of what some refer to now as the shepherding/discipleship movement.[14]

As the network grew, former cult members began to play a significant role on the national level. Former members are greatly respected by the network. They are intelligent, sincere, and articulate.

Most have left their abusive groups on their own and have solicited information from the Cult Awareness Network. Many former members and their children have been required to degrade themselves and betray their families through repeated humiliation, deprivation, and abuse by their destructive cults. Their experience and insight is very useful and accurate. Now, many hold influential leadership roles in the network.

Today, the Cult Awareness Network and its many affiliates provide preventive education through national and regional conferences, distribution of books and articles, and supplying factual and dependable information about destructive cults. The Cult Awareness Network extends support for former members, families and friends, and others who have been affected or exploited by destructive groups. As noted earlier, the national office of Cult Awareness Network in Chicago now receives and responds to more than 16,000 inquiries each year concerning destructive cults and the problems they pose to society. CAN's 2,000 supporters include health professionals, educators, clergy, law enforcement, ex-cult members, and their families.

The Cult Awareness Network will continue to oppose those actions by destructive cults which harm human beings, especially those which are contrary to our society and its laws. CAN will continue to demand an end to intimidation by destructive cults so former members and their families can live without fear and members will not be enslaved. CAN will continue to insist that mistreatment of children in destructive cults ceases. CAN will continue to expose fraudulent and illegal activities in destructive cults.

The Cult Awareness Network will continue and it will continue to urge that destructive cults be held accountable for their actions and be held legally responsible for making restitution for the damage they have caused.[15]

NOTES

1. United States Constitution, Amendment I, as cited in Wollersheim, Endnote 2.

2. *Wollersheim v. Church of Scientology,* B023193, California Court of Appeal, Second Appellate District, Division Seven, July 19, 1989.

3. Conway, Flo and Jim Siegelman, 1978. *Snapping: America's Epidemic of Sudden Personality Change.* J. B. Lippincott: Philadelphia and New York.

4. New York State Office of the Attorney General, Charity Frauds Bureau, 1975. *Final Report on the Activities of the Children of God* to the Honorable Louis J. Lefkowitz, Attorney General of the State of New York. Albany, NY.

5. *Volunteer Parents of America.* Newsletter. August 1974.

6. Conway, Flo and Jim Siegelman, 1978. *Snapping: America's Epidemic of Sudden Personality Change.* J. B. Lippincott: Philadelphia and New York. Patrick, Ted and Tom Dulack, 1976. *Let Our Children Go!,* E. P. Dutton & Co., Inc., New York.

7. Citizens Freedom Foundation. Minutes of meeting, Denver, Colorado, August 30, 1974.

8. New York State Office of the Attorney General, Charity Frauds Bureau. *Preliminary Report on the Activities of the Children of God* to the Honorable Louis J. Lefkowitz, Attorney General of the State of New York. Albany, NY.

9. Some publications include: Shupe, Anson D., Jr., Roger Spielman, and Sam Stigall. "Deprogramming: The New Exorcism," *American Behavioral Scientist,* Sage Publications, vol. 20, no. 6, pp. 941-956, July/August 1977. Shupe, Anson D., Jr. and David Bromley. "The Moonies and the Anti-Cultists: Movement and Countermovement in Conflict," *Sociological Analysis* 1979, 40, 4:325-334. Shupe,

Anson D., Jr., Roger Spielmann, and Sam Stigall. "Cults of Anti-Cultism," *Society,* March/April 1980, pp. 43-46. Bromley, David and Anson D. Shupe, Jr., 1981. *Strange Gods: The Great American Cult Scare.* Beacon Press: Boston.

10. Interview with former chairperson of Freedom of Religion Committee.

11. In 1977, a bizarre and incredible little pamphlet began circulating. It was entitled "Deprogramming: The Constructive Destruction of Belief: A Manual of Technique" and was dedicated to Ted Patrick. Headings in the pamphlet include: Food Termination, Sleep Withdrawal, Shame-inducement Through Nudity, Physical Correction, Verbal Stress, Destruction of Holy Works, Sex, and the Deprog Tech. The pamphlet referenced the British cult awareness group, Family Action Information and Rescue, FAIR. It appeared to imply FAIR sanctioned the booklet. FAIR had nothing to do with the manual. FAIR's charter, practices, and public statements totally contradict the manual's absurd contents. It was discovered that the "group" POWER, which was also cited, was one man who vanished. In his book, *Carnival of Souls,* (Seabury Press, NY, 1979) Joel MacCollam notes, "(M)any observers feel that the manual is not a legitimate production but rather the combined effort of several cults. . . ." The manual has no author and no one has ever claimed credit for it. Yet many destructive cults appear to still use versions of this manual to dissuade followers from meeting with their families and friends.

12. The Leo J. Ryan award is named for Congressman Leo J. Ryan, who was assassinated on November 18, 1978, on an airstrip in Guyana. Congressman Ryan courageously traveled to Guyana to investigate the People's Temple on behalf of his constituents and former members. Along with Congressman Ryan, *San Francisco Examiner* photographer Greg Robinson, NBC newsmen Don Harris and Bob Brown, 913 followers of cult leader Jim Jones were murdered or committed suicide. Each year on the anniversary of the Jonestown massacre, the Cult Awareness Network honors an American citizen who exhibits "extraordinary courage, tenacity, and perseverance in the battle against tyranny over the mind of man."

13. "Not Guilty in Boy's Death, Cultist Pleads," *Chicago Tribune,* Section 1, p. 5, August 26, 1982. A three-year-old boy in the Covenant Community, DeMotte, Indiana died after a severe beating. American Human Society publication *Protecting Children,* "Children Abuse and Neglect in Cults and Religious Sects," vol. 1, no. 1, Winter 1984, p. 17. In July 1983, a twelve-year-old boy was beaten to death in the House of Judah religious community in Michigan. In August 1983, a husband and wife were convicted of involuntary manslaughter in the fatal spanking of their two-year-old son at Stonegate, a religious community in West Virginia.

14. Vinzant, Don, 1988. "Historical Roots of the Discipling Movement Among Churches of Christ," in Flavial Yeakley, Jr., ed. *The Discipling Dilemma.* Gospel Advocate Company: Nashville TN.

15. The address of the Cult Awareness Network is West Pratt Boulevard, Suite 1173, Chicago, Illinois 60645. Telephone (312) 267-7777.

CHAPTER VI

STRATEGIC INTERVENTION THERAPY: A NEW FORM OF EXIT-COUNSELING FOR CULT MEMBERS

Steven Hassan

Since Ted Patrick first introduced deprogramming in the early seventies, it continues to be a controversial method for rescuing people from destructive cult groups. Patrick wrote about his methods of deprogramming in his book *Let Our Children Go!* (Patrick and Dulack, 1976). Hundreds of distraught families turned to Patrick, and he was able to help many break out of the mental straight jackets of destructive cult membership. Patrick's success, however, was far from universal. Numbers of unsuccessful "rescue" attempts occurred, and angry cult members returned to their group and sued him as well as their own family members. No doubt in some of these situations the failed attempts caused further alienation, hardship, and pain—as well as legal convictions. His methods were sensationalistic: abduction in broad daylight, car switches, hidden locations for the deprogramming, and 24-hour security guards to prevent any escapes. The average price per case was reportedly around $10,000, but much higher figures have been quoted by some of his former clients.

Despite these issues, involuntary intervention was the only effective method in the 1970s to help those trapped by mind control. Successful deprogramming was like a miracle for family members. Tremendous anguish, fear, and hopelessness would dissipate as family members experienced the transformation of a destructive cult member from an often "trancy," programmed "stranger" back into an emotionally expressive, critically thinking individual. Naturally, the success of involuntary intervention would generate strong endorsements by family members and very often the ex-member (myself included initially).

They, in turn, would encourage other desperate families to try it. It was the only choice besides sitting back, waiting and praying, often for many, many years. In some cases families watched a loved one marry and have children within the mind control cult and would give up hope, not knowing what else they could do to make a positive difference.

Since that time, a new approach, exit-counseling, is emerging as the method of choice because of growing concern about the stress, risk, illegality, and often high cost involved with deprogramming. There are only a handful of people, mostly former cult members themselves, who are practicing full-time exit-counselors. Most of them do not have any formal counseling training, but through years of research and experience they have become competent, effective practitioners. Their primary orientation is through the sharing of information: documents, video and audio tapes, and first- and second-hand experience. This information is shared with a cult member who has voluntarily agreed to participate and learn.

I personally have used this approach since 1979 as a former Unification Church member who experienced deprogramming in 1976. I felt a strong desire to help people programmed by destructive cult mind control but was dissatisfied by both deprogramming theory and methodology. In this chapter I wish to describe how my personal exit-counseling approach has developed into what I now refer to as strategic intervention therapy and focus on its advantages over forcible deprogramming. I wish to emphasize that my own point of reference is based on my own observations, impressions, and direct experiences with thousands of people in the past sixteen years.

At the core of strategic intervention therapy is an eclectic approach to help members of destructive cults, as well as their family and friends, who are "stuck" and unable to move forward to develop more awareness, flexibility, creativity, and better communication skills to live more productive, interdependent lives. The overall objective is to do everything within your power to create the necessary conditions to help the cult member to change and grow rather than merely removing the person from the group. While deprogramming succeeds in helping innumerable people physically leave destructive cults, in my opinion, it falls far short of what could and should take place for healing. People are individuals, and their minds and systems of relationships are incredibly complex. Intervention to achieve mere physical removal from the cult denies that complexity. Indeed, involvement in a destructive cult affects each one in the family system—father, mother, siblings, other relatives, as well as friends. Therefore, a dynamic, process-oriented approach is undeniably critical. Real healing should take place within *all* those involved.

At this point, I would like to define some of the terms as I use them:

Mind Control/Brainwashing

Mind control is a sophisticated set of "influence" processes that include Behavior control, Information control, Thought control, and Emotional control (B.I.T.E.).[1] Under mind control the subject unwittingly cooperates in these processes and typically views the agents of influence as benevolent friends, teachers, or mentors. Some mind control techniques can be used ethically and constructively (behavior modification and hypnosis, for example). If, however, they are used with deception by someone who functions as an outside authority to manipulate and create a new identity and belief structure in the victim who is dependent and controlled, then it is destructive. It is that very destructive use of mind control technology that I discuss as a way of introducing several new key ideas (dual identity model, thought-stopping and phobia indoctrination—see Hassan, 1990:53-75) to enhance our understanding of the destructive cult phenomenon. Please note that people under mind control do not perceive that they have been lied to or that they themselves lie in service of the "greater good." Likewise, they do not understand what mind control is, and therefore they do not perceive themselves as victims.

Brainwashing is a word coined in the 1950s by Edward Hunter and was used to describe the process used by the Chinese Communists. Although researchers (Lifton, Schein, West & Singer) determined that the process did not require the use of physical force in order for it to be effective, the word "brainwashing" has come to be commonly known as a more coercive process in which physical forces, overt threats, sleep deprivation, and torture are sometimes used in the beginning. The subject often views the agents of influence as "the enemy" and typically tries to maintain defensive personal boundaries and may even try to escape. A good example of this process can be seen in the kidnapping, and forced detention and rape, of millionaire heiress Patty Hearst. As she became "Tania," the abuse lessened and she received more positive reinforcement for her new behaviors.

Torture (brainwashing) is commonly used in political settings around the world. It is successful in effecting compliance behavior (false confessions, for example), but it is questionable how "deep" the new identity is when the subject returns to his or her normal cultural environment. The degree of dissonance between real and cult identity and the living environment will determine how fast the cult beliefs and behaviors tend to dissipate.

Destructive Cult/Cults

Destructive cults are pyramid-shaped, authoritarian groups, controlled by someone or some group of people at the top who have absolute power. They always use deception in their recruitment; subjects do *not* know, up front, what the group really is, what the beliefs are, and what is expected of them upon joining. They use mind control (B.I.T.E.) to indoctrinate and maintain their followers.[1] These groups can have one or more operational frameworks: political, "psychotherapy/ educational," commercial, or religious. They range in size from just three people to many millions of people. The practices and behaviors, not the beliefs, characterize a destructive cult.

A **cult** can be any unorthodox group with a prescribed set of beliefs and rituals. Cults can be of any size and any orientation. They may be hierarchical but contain structural "checks and balances" that respect personal freedom and safeguard members from abuse of power. As long as informed consent is consistently used when recruiting members, high pressure "sales" techniques to make an immediate commitment is avoided, information flow is open, and personal autonomy is respected (i.e., people can leave if their conscience so moves them and are not indoctrinated with phobias), then a cult can be considered "good" or benign. Even though I do not agree with most cult groups' beliefs or rituals, I fully support their rights to believe whatever they want to believe. As a civil libertarian, I fully support the rights of people to believe and their rights to disbelieve. There are far more benign cults than destructive cults. My concern is exclusively with destructive cults.

Deprogramming/Exit-counseling/Strategic Intervention Therapy

Deprogramming is the "old school" approach started by Ted Patrick in the early 1970s. The cult member was "snatched" to "break" him or her out of the cult trance through a process of "deprogramming" the mind. The term sounds as if one was dealing with a computer and not with a human being with a unique, separate identity. This approach, despite all efforts to make it as pleasant as possible, was filled with stress, pressure, and anxiety due to its inherently coercive nature. If it wasn't for cult programming and indoctrination, families would never resort to such an extreme measure to help. Although the process has succeeded in liberating hundreds, perhaps thousands of people from destructive cults, its negative after-effect has been felt by many despite their gratefulness to be free. Deprogramming typically operates outside the law unless there is a court ordered conservatorship in effect; the member is held, at least initially, against his or her conscious will. It is the respect and recognition of this conscious will that is the foundation of exit-counseling and strategic intervention therapy.

While it was true that deprogramming was the only method practiced in the 1970s, it has long since declined in frequency. Despite cult propaganda that paints a picture of hundreds of deprogrammers, there was never more than two dozen individuals who were doing deprogramming professionally, and that number has dwindled. This is at least partially due to litigation against deprogrammers by cults whenever a case was unsuccessful.

Exit-counseling refers to the "new school" or approach to helping victims of mind control in destructive cults. It operates within the laws as they exist today, using neither abduction nor coercion to obtain or maintain access with the cult member for a period of time. It is primarily an information-based approach, supplied by the exit-counselor and usually a former member of the particular cult. Most exit-counselors are themselves former cult members. They have little or no formal counseling training yet are able, through their knowledge and experience, to help cult members to have new information and perspective on their involvement. Other than supplying general information to the family, their sole focus is on the cult member, and their hope is that information alone will be enough to make a difference. If the individual decides to exit the cult, he or she is often encouraged to attend a one-to-two week rehabilitation facility, such as Wellspring, in which trained mental health professionals and staffs assist with any formal counseling.

Part of the confusion of terminology between deprogramming and exit-counseling is due, no doubt, to the practice of a few individuals who would operate primarily as exit-counselors. Principally they would do legal, voluntary interventions but would occasionally participate in a case that entailed the use of coercion. However, there is an emerging consensus that to be recognized as an exit-counselor one must *only* perform legal interventions.

Strategic Intervention Therapy is the term I currently use to describe my personal approach to exit-counseling at this point. It is an eclectic approach that draws on a wide variety of orientations. It is a client-centered, more "holistic" approach that looks at people as unique individuals and families as complex dynamic systems. It uses counseling skills and methodology and relies heavily on teaching family members and significant friends how to understand cult mind control and how to communicate more effectively with each other and the cult member. It is a process that *relies on finesse, not force.*

It typically involves a one-to-two day preparation meeting with all key people who are trustworthy, care enough to participate, and want to make a positive contribution. This forms the basis of an on-going "coaching" process of the "team." This is usually done by telephones, fax machines, and mail. The goal is to make everyone active participants in a constructive communication process. Individuals are offered numerous suggestions to enhance and develop rapport with the cult member, such as reading a cult book but only if the person agrees to discuss it chapter by chapter. Depending on the unique situation, I might suggest to specific individuals to try "mini-interventions" that serve to plant seeds of doubt and encourage reflection and analytic thinking. The family maintains contact with me and advises me as to every contact with the cult member, preferably keeping notes as things take place to keep everyone apprised of developments. With this approach, the family is actively improving not only their relationship with the cult member but also their communication skills with respect to one another.

Like exit-counseling, during the formal intervention important information about mind control and the specifics of the cult as well as other cults is given. However, strategic intervention therapy's focus is on people and the process of change and not just information. It is more concerned with people's perceptions, thought processes, emotions, and needs rather than on information that can be obtained through books, literature, or tapes. It is therefore ultimately flexible, and no two interventions are the same. Whatever is needed is what is accommodated. This will be more fully discussed.

Strategic Intervention Therapy differs from deprogramming in a number of important ways.

First, it is completely legal. Unlike deprogramming, there can be no claim whatsoever of abduction and/or false imprisonment. This is important for several reasons, not the least of which is the absence of any legal liability should the person return to the destructive cult. The financial burden and the emotional stress that everyone goes through when this has happened are enormous. What is more important, however, is the psychological and emotional aspect. There is no question that an exit-counseling puts much less stress on the family and is designed to minimize stress for the cult member, creating the foundation for a trust-building, growth experience. It is indeed difficult for family members to conceive of the terror that destructive cults instill in members against deprogramming and the fear and anger experienced by a member when he or she is being abducted and held involuntarily. Clearly, the trauma of deprogramming has a sustained, long term impact in the life of the member. I have been told time after time by former members (although grateful that they are out of the group) that, ten to fifteen years later, their experience during the abduction and deprogramming felt like they were being psychologically raped. This experience was often reported to be more traumatic than anything they had experienced while in the group.

I want to emphasize that I am NOT validating cult propaganda about tales of people being tortured, sleep deprived, or rapes. These actions, of course, do NOT occur. What loving parent willing to sacrifice so much to rescue a loved one would ever allow anything like that to take place? What I am addressing is the definitive psychological advantage strategic intervention therapy has by creating a safe environment in which the cult member feels choice and empowerment, instead of using coercion like involuntary deprogramming. Furthermore, a positive therapeutic exit-counseling experience neutralizes cult propaganda about deprogramming used to keep members in fear of their loved ones, e.g., kidnapping, witch hunts, Nazis, hate groups, suppressive people, etc.

Eventually, I believe cult mind control interventions will become regarded as an intervention approach somewhat similar to modern day alcohol and drug treatments. These interventions are similar in several ways: the family is actively involved; communication of thoughts and feelings are emphasized; and ultimately, the individual must come to terms with the realities of how his or her personality and behaviors have negatively changed, as well as how these behaviors have negatively affected loved ones.

Second, strategic intervention therapy as an approach requires extensive training and preparation with all potential resource people, much more so than is ever done with deprogramming. It relies heavily on information, skill, and counseling techniques to work with family members and friends to encourage them to be active forces **before, during, and after** the intervention. This requires a great deal of preparation, time, effort, and cooperation. Family members and friends are encouraged to become lay experts and learn about mind control and destructive cults (both the one in which their loved one is a member as well as about others.) They are expected to learn communication strategies and techniques that will maximize rapport and trust, gather vital information, and plant seeds that will undermine cult programming. They are expected to use creativity, flexibility, and patience to influence the cult member. Family members and friends are encouraged to watch videotapes, meet with former members, and in some cases, with the proper preparation, attend cult functions, and read cult literature. The family and friends become the focal point of a support system for the individual after the intervention, minimizing (but not eliminating) the need for formal rehabilitation. *Actively training and coaching family members and friends to develop effective communication styles with the cult member is one of the major differences* between strategic intervention therapy and other forms of exit-counseling, especially deprogramming.

Third, correct timing is crucial for a successful intervention. Ideally, an intervention should take place when the cult member is in a disillusioned phase, and/or will be physically away from the cult for several days to minimize reindoctrination. Deprogramming is usually timed to accommodate the schedules of the deprogrammer and members of the family exclusively. I think this is a grave mistake. In addition, I have met people who claim that it is better to do an involuntary intervention within the first few months of involvement rather than actively working with the family while waiting for the right opportunity to intervene. Although each case must be evaluated individually, I strongly believe that there is a danger in doing an intervention too soon. If the person is still in the "honeymoon" phase, for example, efforts should be made to connect with him or her, avoid "loaded words" like brainwashing or cult, and encourage a "cooling off" period for research and reflection. If no window of opportunity can be created, I believe it is usually better to wait until after the person has been in long enough to experience first hand the negative aspects of the group. While I certainly believe that destructive cult membership should be kept to a minimum, this cannot be accomplished at the risk of a precipitous, and potentially damaging, "cure." Unfortunately, family members all too often go into a panic when they learn that a loved one is in a cult, conjuring up images of dead bodies at Jonestown, and consequently they impulsively rush to do an intervention while ill-prepared and ill-advised. People should make major decisions like planning an intervention when they are fully informed and more level-headed. The only time rapid action must be taken is in situations regarding life or death, e.g., a diabetic in a "faith-healing" cult has stopped taking his insulin, or a cult member is being sent to commit a robbery or murder. These situations, however, are relatively rare.

The strategic intervention process begins with the education of family and friends (Hassan, 1990:112-67). My background questionnaire is filled out by all significant people giving their views and feelings in writing. It continues over the course of weeks or months, culminating in an intervention after the foundation has been laid and the timing is right. During this "waiting" period, family members are actively communicating with the cult member, gathering information, planting seeds, offering reality-testing, and building rapport and trust. Ideally, the cult member will signal when the time is right. He or she might even ask for books or articles to read, or names of experts and ex-members to speak with.

Fourth, the actual intervention is done in ways that will maximize respect for the cult member and encourage a sense of validation that he/she is an adult and is ultimately responsible for his/her own decisions. This is significantly different from viewing the person as a programmed robot who must be deprogrammed. The cult member is treated like an individual, not a clone. The approach is thus tailored to fit his/her needs, not those of the counselor or family. Therefore, every exit-counseling is unique. There can be no cookie-cutter approach; the cult member is not restrained and shown the same series of videotapes and written material, day after day, just like every other member deprogrammed from that group. Use of trained counselors at a rehabilitation center is a welcome option, not an requirement.

I believe that a person's true self is not obliterated by cult mind control, even those born into a destructive cult. It is the individual's inner self that always wants to be free, and thus that inner self will guide the counselor and the family. In this context, my role as a strategic intervention therapist is that of a resource person who will facilitate the growth process of the member, the individual, and the family and friends around the member. As such, I do not "take people out of cults," make anyone believe anything, or take away anything that is perceived as valuable, particularly spiritual experiences. Rather I encourage people to get in touch with **their** inner feelings and thoughts, offer information that can provide new perspectives, and guide them so that they can open doors to new alternatives. The individual chooses whether to consider and accept them or not. I take my cues from the people with whom I am working, keeping my own personal beliefs out of the way as much as possible. I usually show very few, if any, videotapes during an intervention, although I always bring them along. Unlike some deprogrammers, I use them as adjuncts to the counseling and do not depend on them to do my work for me. Flexibility in meeting my client's needs and concerns is essential to a successful experience.

Fifth, with strategic intervention therapy actual counseling does take place. There is a significant educational component within strategic intervention therapy, including topics such as mind control, destructive cults, and specific information about the particular group. But there is much more, including one-to-one sessions, couples counseling, counseling sessions between particular family members, as well as family counseling sessions if needed and desired. Often I have seen how the family-centered nature of strategic intervention therapy operating within the crisis provided by cult involvement offers an opportunity for issues of the past to be intentionally surfaced and resolved. Simultaneously communication skills are developed among family members. Brothers and sisters, father and mother talk more openly about themselves and their feelings, reflecting on life choices and how they have grown through them all. This promotes a powerful bond among them, providing a new emotional reference point for future relationships. If the cult member does decide to disaffiliate, a natural support system is in place and feelings of high self esteem are reinforced. Furthermore, by working with the entire family, this also takes the "heat" off the cult member because he or she can see how much everyone is benefitting from the experience. This also helps me as an exit-counselor gain respect and credibility because the person can see that my interest is in helping everyone to change and grow and not merely "putting the group down." The entire experience becomes an opportunity for everyone to change and grow.

Because it is a process-oriented approach without coercion, a cult member may walk out of the intervention and not return. This is a risk. Hopefully, enough rapport and trust will have been established that if this occurs, it will be only a short time before contact is resumed, and constructive reality-testing influence resumed. While it would be unfortunate that the intervention didn't fully succeed at this time, it would not be viewed as a failure. At that moment, the family is encouraged to go forward and not give up, or fall back into destructive communication patterns (e.g., calling the person "a brainwashed zombie" out of anger). There is always more that can be done to follow-up. Family members must remain positive, believing in the person's inner self. They should attend to their and their family needs while continuing to work to enhance communication skills, gather more information about the group, work cooperatively and network, and focus on building their relationship with the member. These efforts are buoyed up by the belief that the person's true self is stronger than mind control and that love is much stronger than the conditional love of cult membership.

Although there is much more to discuss about strategic intervention therapy than can be described here, there are some additional points I would like to make about deprogramming theory and methodology. Most of these points have emerged from extensive interviews with individuals successfully deprogrammed within the past ten years or so. Since I have not participated in deprogramming since 1977, I can only speak about it second-hand.

1. Concerned relatives typically abhor the use of force but view the destructiveness of membership in a destructive cult as something so bad that deprogramming is seen as the lesser of two evils. Therefore, they feel justified in breaking existing laws because the law does not recognize the use of mind control. They want to rescue their loved one and they want to do it now! They feel they cannot go on with their lives until they do an intervention. They will often mortgage their homes, risk legal problems, or cause divisions in the family to help the person they love. They often believe that they will have only one chance to do the rescue, so they had better stack the deck to ensure success.

I do *not* believe people will have only one opportunity for influence provided they use the processes described in this chapter. Involuntary intervention should not be used as a remedial solution but only as a very *last resort!* It disturbs me when I hear anyone recommending a deprogramming, particularly to emotionally distraught people. I have come to realize that those who usually recommend it did a successful deprogramming on a loved one, typically many years earlier. Because it "worked," some people feel strongly committed to defend deprogramming as a process, justifying their own decision and wishing to validate it. I have encountered a few people who recommend it to everyone, regardless of the situation. Perhaps this is where destructive cults get their perspective that such groups as the Cult Awareness Network endorses deprogramming, even though the C.A.N. national board of directors and affiliate heads clearly do not. However, the organization cannot prohibit individuals who have joined C.A.N. (if successful at rescuing a loved one through deprogramming) from speaking their own minds.

2. However, the member's post-deprogramming perspective, in comparison, can range from highly positive to extremely negative. Positive experiences span the entire gamut from "it was the most wonderful, enlightening, healing experience" to "I'm glad I'm out of the cult, but I still am really angry and resentful about what happened." If the experience was very negative, the person typically goes back to the cult, alienates relatives, and occasionally takes legal action against them and the individuals involved. Sometimes the person does not go back to the group but is nevertheless alienated for years from the family. They inevitably ask the family why they had to resort to such coercion. This is one reason why I believe that families should do everything within their power for at least two to three years before even contemplating

doing an involuntary intervention. In my experience, if the family recognizes the cult problem early, the person leaves the group way before this ever needs to be considered. If the person has been in the cult for many years, I still believe in building a support system first, and then doing an intervention. Laying a firm groundwork always pays off. This way if the family eventually opts for an involuntary intervention, they can then look the person in the eyes and recount all the conversations, questions, books, articles, tapes, and negative responses made when still a cult member and says "we tried everything else first!"

3. What aspects of deprogramming facilitated its success in the past? These used to be catalogued, such as: (a) the person is physically away from the group and all ongoing group activity and reinforcement; (b) the person can sleep and eat as much as desired. (Indeed sleep does wonders for brain functioning.); (c) information is given to create new understanding and help elicit inner doubts, critical thoughts, and suppressed feelings; and, (d) deprogrammers, particularly former members, and family members, were experienced as real, caring, spiritual people, undermining phobia indoctrination and cult programming against deprogrammers.

4. Since deprogrammers have limited, if any, counseling training, they have few tools to make realistic assessments of cases and accept them based upon a minimum of information about the member. They often fail to talk with different family members, and thus overlook important information to find out that: (a) mom and dad are having marital difficulties because dad had an affair; (b) younger brother is angry at his sister in the group for revealing a secret he previously told her; (c) there is a cousin who is a member of another cult for many years, and there have been intensive family discussions about how he has become a liar and a thief in order to get money for courses; or (d) the cult member has been writing to her best friend from college about her doubts

and desire to leave the group. They will likely be unaware of an enmeshed family system in which individual boundaries are unclear, people do not function as individual people, and conflict engenders silent withdrawal. They are unable to teach effective communication techniques and strategies without an understanding about family dynamics, extensive formal preparation, and sufficient knowledge about the group. A higher failure rate is inevitable, ultimately causing more harm than good.

5   Unlike the old style of deprogrammer, exit-counselors access and maintain a high level of information about mind control groups and encourage the family to learn about the group, and others, as well. When I receive a call from a distraught relative about a group with which I am not familiar, I research that group to determine whether it truly is destructive before I agree to take the case. *Any group is considered to be "innocent" until proven guilty,* with "guilty" defined according to my criteria of destructive cults. I require that before I schedule a phone consultation, parents and significant relatives and friends read my book *first,* and then cooperatively (sometimes individually) fill out an extensive background information for a case evaluation form for me to review. Then I try to have a phone consultation with all key people, if possible. Simultaneously, I actively research the group seeking articles, legal documents, and former members and may even contact current group members (anonymously, of course) to ascertain whether the group does, in fact, use destructive cult tactics. This process is critical to weed out cases such as that of "Johnny's" parents who believe that Johnny is involved with "unsavory" people, and no longer wishes to go to law school or attend the Catholic Church. Strategic Intervention Therapy is not meant for parents or spouses who want to impose their own values and beliefs on their adult children and make them clones. Also, there are thousands of alternative religions, therapies, political groups, and businesses that are NOT destructive cults. Just

because they are different does not make them automatically bad! Use of hypnosis, meditation, or yoga, for example, does not automatically mean destructive!

6. Deprogrammers tend to use a model of mind control popularized by the best-selling book *Snapping: America's Epidemic of Sudden Personality Change* (Conway & Siegelman, 1978). Conway and Siegelman posit a theory of destructive cult phenomenon using an information processing model. They propose that people are overloaded by a variety of techniques and processes in the recruitment process. Overloaded, their minds "snap," creating a "brain crisis" which renders them vulnerable to programming with beliefs they would not otherwise choose in a normal state of mind. Although this book's weakness is its dismissal of legitimate spirituality, its theory has validity. I view snapping as part of the "unfreezing" phase, aimed at undermining a person's state of psychological equilibrium, as a prelude to indoctrination as described in Chapter Four of my book. Unfortunately, Conway and Siegelman assert that deprogramming is the only process that works to undo mind control. Undoubtedly in the seventies when they wrote the book, it was true. But, despite the more contemporary exit-counseling approach, *Snapping* was still being sold in bookstores as late as 1988 and has influenced a tremendous number of people.

I have worked with countless members whose minds were overloaded and indoctrinated and witnessed "snapping" first hand. I recall my snapping experiences going into the Moonies and during my deprogramming. These were dramatic moments filled with disconnected thoughts and feelings of confusion and elation. Deprogramming by its very nature entails fear and stress engendered by cult phobia programming and definite physical detention. Therefore, with the most sensitive, humanitarian actions given by deprogrammers and family, it still is a source of tremendous stress. Although I do believe the mind can be subjected to overload again and intentionally snapped, I do NOT think it is a healthy, therapeutic goal.

Over the years, my understanding of the "snapping" experience has crystallized. It is something akin to a tearing of the fabric of the mind. Instead of a destructive approach, strategic intervention therapy offers a constructive process, a low stress, step by step development of insights and connections to feelings, a series of "aha!" experiences, culminating in the empowerment of the individual. An analogy can be made that what is desired are four-foot waves at the seashore that a person can safely body surf on, as opposed to a twenty-foot storm surf of deprogramming. Cult programming instills such virulent phobias that leaving the group means automatic destruction (committing suicide, possession of evil spirits, insanity, terminal illness, or betraying God) that it is essential to first build bridges to safety. Phobias must be defined and explained. A discussion must take place about how "other" groups install phobias to control members. The person must first get in touch with his or her *own internal resources,* accessing pre-cult goals, values, beliefs, and personal dreams. All of this should take place before directly discussing "what is wrong with the group."

As a strategic intervention therapist, it is up to my client to choose to disaffiliate or not, and to choose *when* he or she wants to leave the group, thus honoring and respecting their own personal beliefs and value criteria, rather than those held by the family or myself. I want my client to leave the group with head held up high, armed with an understanding of the true nature of the group, mind control, and destructive cult practices. I want each to realize that, contrary to group indoctrination, there *are* legitimate reasons to leave. Most importantly, I want them to own all of their positive growth experiences during their membership but move forward in a much healthier, more integrated life, finding possible paths to fulfill their personal needs and goals.

Many destructive cults are religious in orientation. I must therefore acknowledge spiritual as well as psychological issues as a strategic intervention therapist. I never try to minimize or explain away what people describe to me as spiritual experiences. I may offer alternative ways to interpret experience, but I am always careful to be respectful. I also firmly believe that it is unethical to proselytize to a client. When working with a member of a Bible cult group, it is usually appropriate to have a devout Christian present, particularly someone who is a minister or theologian, who can explain biblical passages and legitimate methods of interpretation. However, if that person pressures the cult member to accept that perspective as the "One and only Truth," there is abuse of authority. Even if the family is very religious, the member may not wish to follow that religious perspective. Therefore, to pressure the member to substitute the family's religious doctrine could become just as manipulating as destructive cult groups. Similarly troublesome are counselors who are so locked into their own belief system that they cannot consider the validity of alternative perspectives. Again, this elitist, "us-versus-them," mentality mirrors those of the cults. Success for them with victims of mind control is predicated on their recruiting new members.

People should not feel so pressured that they have to automatically readopt their family's religion. They should take their time and do research, avoiding the tendency to look for absolute answers taken on "faith." This may avoid precipitous entry into a substitute group. For example, someone from a Catholic background joins a fundamentalist "shepherding" cult (which are usually extremely anti-Catholic) and then upon leaving, decides to join a fundamentalist Protestant church. As part of the Strategic Intervention Therapy healing process, I do encourage former members to first reexamine beliefs and practices of their original faith system. Part of the healing process is to reexamine the beliefs and practices of their spiritual "roots" before joining another orientation. If one is going to reject their heritage, then he or she would benefit from taking the time to learn what is being rejected. Such persons should be encouraged to look at more than one representative or one book, taking as much time as needed, avoiding the emotional needs to immediately find a new group. Spirituality emerges from integrity, and evolves through a process of awareness, knowledge, and experience. Truth is eternal; it will be there tomorrow, next week, and next year— just as the groups, if legitimate, will remain. As such, former members must learn to trust themselves to know what is right for them and when it is right for them. Assessing and reassessing one's own beliefs is part of the human experience. I seek to validate what they have learned from their cult experience, both positive and negative, and guide them to grow from it towards a healthier path.

Summary

Strategic intervention therapy is a process that transcends the limitations of deprogramming, i.e., just "getting the person out of the group." It is a family systems, process-oriented approach through which the individual is empowered by knowledge, communication training, and counseling. It promotes personal integrity, new perspectives, and choice. It is self-contained within the member's family/friend community, and focuses on the development of effective, respectful communication thereby supporting mutual understanding and growth. It is thus sustained far beyond the time frame of the intervention. It is distinguished from deprogramming, as follows: (1) it is completely legal; (2) it requires extensive preparation and communication training; (3) the intervention is planned and executed according to best timing and context for the member; (4) the feelings, thoughts, and individuality of the member are respected, and all those involved feel empowered; (5) actual therapeutic counseling takes place; and (6) it is a much less stressful approach, seeking to effect *change with finesse, not force!* With the strategic intervention therapy approach, one takes the time to get at the root of key issues, and appropriate steps are taken—respecting everyone's feelings and needs but emphasizing good communication, critical thinking, and free will.

Strategic intervention therapy and exit-counseling require a great deal of sensitivity, knowledge, flexibility, and experience. Effective therapists must understand their client's "model of reality," and not be afraid to accompany the client in his or her perspective of reality. Ethical counselors must be self aware and guard against the imposition of their own beliefs and values systems on those of the member. A variety of personality and cult models are used as templates upon which to build an accurate representation of the person. The strategic intervention therapist must understand how belief systems operate, and develop information about three models of identity for the client: the model before joining, the prototypical cult model for that group, and a model for "where the person is now."

Obviously, therapists must have a variety of communication skills, demonstrating sensitivity to subtle non-verbal and verbal cues, explicit as well as implicit, and respond appropriately to them. They must know how to ask questions in a non-threatening manner, and to promote new thought patterns and perspectives. They should know when to talk, when to listen, and when to encourage silence. They should know when to probe and when to let something go. They should avoid making declarative statements about "Truth" and avoid discussions of personal spiritual beliefs that might unethically influence the individual. A therapist is there as a guide for growth, but knows when to step back and observe.

Strategic intervention therapy and more traditional exit-counseling represent a new profession in its infancy stages. Exit-counselors represent a new breed of counselors willing to travel to the client, not expecting the client to come to him or her. This enhances a sense of security as the change-work is anchored to the client's own environment, rather than the therapist's office. Flexibility is "built-in" with breaks dictated by the needs of the client. Change-work, therefore, is not constrained to a 50 minute period or any set time once, twice, or three times a week. During an actual full scale intervention, typically lasting three days, 6-12 hours a day for the therapist, depth and intensity can produce change that ordinarily might take weeks, months, or years to accomplish.

I believe that the experiences of former members provide them with an advantage over other mental health practitioners in helping people come away from mind control groups. This is not to say that mental health professionals cannot make excellent strategic intervention therapists. Former members interested in becoming strategic intervention therapists would benefit from receiving formal counseling training. If possible, acquiring a masters and preferably a doctorate will help achieve respectability and credibility. It is my hope that within the next five years, strategic intervention therapy will be taught systematically, and that it will take its rightful place within the mental health profession.

I end with a note of hope for those who have had a loved one involved with a destructive cult for many years. There *is* hope, even if you attempted a deprogramming and it failed and you have almost no contact. It is NEVER too late to learn how to communicate. As long as the individual is alive, it is NEVER too late to develop positive relationships. Unfortunately, many people have given up out of emotional exhaustion, believing that their loved one has been in too long and could never be happy living in the "real" world. If you are such a person, or know of such a person, I encourage you to talk on the telephone, or better yet, to meet with a former member who has left after 15 to 30 years. It is never too late to take control of your life and opt for freedom!

NOTES

[1]MIND CONTROL

Mind control can be understood in terms of four basic areas:
  <u>B</u> ehavior Control
  <u>I</u> nformation Control
  <u>T</u> hought Control
  <u>E</u> motional Control

Below is a summary of this behavioral control pattern:

1. **Regulation of individual's physical reality**
    a. where and with whom the member lives
    b. what clothes, colors, hairstyles the person wears
    c. what food the person eats
    d. how much sleep the person is able to have
    e. financial dependence
2. **Major time commitment required for indoctrination and group rituals**
3. **Need to ask permission for major decisions**
4. **Rewards and Punishments**
5. **Individualism discouraged/Group think prevails**
6. **Rigid rules and regulations**
7. **Need for obedience and dependency**

Information Control:

1. **Use of deception**
   a. deliberately holding back information
   b. distorting information to make it acceptable
   c. outright lying
2. **Access to non-cult sources of information minimized or discouraged**
   a. newspapers, magazines, t.v., radio
   b. critical information
   c. former members
   d. keep members so busy they don't have time to think
3. **Compartmentalization of information—outsider vs. insider doctrines**
   a. information is not freely accessible
   b. information varies at different levels and missions within pyramid
   c. leadership decides who "needs to know" what
4. **Spying on other members is encouraged**
   a. pairing up with "buddy" system to monitor and control
   b. reporting deviant thoughts, feelings, and actions to leadership
5. **Extensive use of cult-generated information and propaganda**
   a. newsletters, magazines, journals, audiotapes, videotapes, etc.
   b. misquotations, statements taken out of context from non-cult sources
6. **Use of confession**
   a. information about "sins" used to abolish identity boundaries
   b. past "sins" used to manipulate and control—no forgiveness or absolution

Emotional Control:

1. **Manipulate and narrow the range of a person's feelings**
2. **Make the person feel like if there are ever any problems it is always their fault**
3. **Excessive use of guilt**
   a. Identity guilt
      1. who you are (not living up to your potential)
      2. where you came from
      3. your family
      4. your past
      5. your affiliations
      6. your thoughts, feelings, actions
   b. Social guilt
   c. Historical guilt
4. **Excessive use of fear**
   a. fear of thinking independently
   b. fear of the "outside world"
   c. fear of enemies
   d. fear of losing one's "salvation"
   e. fear of natural disasters
5. **Extremes of emotional highs and lows**
6. **Ritual and often public confession of "sins"**
7. **Phobia indoctrination**
   a. no happiness or fulfillment "outside"
   b. terrible consequences will take place if you ever leave
   c. never a legitimate reason to leave

REFERENCES

Conway, Flo and Jim Siegelman, 1978. *Snapping: America's Epidemic of Sudden Personality Change.* Philadelphia: J. B. Lippincott.

Hassan, Steven, 1990. *Combatting Cult Mind Control: The #1 Best-Selling Guide for Protection, Rescue, and Recovery from Destructive Cults.* Rochester, VT: Park Street Press.

Patrick, Ted and Tom Dulack, 1976. *Let Our Children Go!* New York: E. P. Dutton.

MODERN ANTI-CULTISM IN EUROPE

CHAPTER VII

NEW RELIGIOUS MOVEMENTS IN EUROPE: DEVELOPMENTS AND REACTIONS

James T. Richardson and Barend van Driel

INTRODUCTION

According to Schnabel (1983), a large amount of potentially religious creativity in Europe has been channeled into the areas of political policy and theological thinking, seemingly diverting attention from matters dealing with the meaning of life and personal religious experience. This means that there is little impetus for the development of significant religious movements within the European context. Almost all novel religions that have gained a foothold in Europe during the past century have arrived from the U.S.A. Religions like Pentacostalism, Jehovah Witnesses, Seventh Day Adventists, and Mormons are good examples of this migration of religious ideas and practices to Europe.

Contemporary new religious movements (or "NRMs" as they will be referred to here) are no exception to this pattern. In the 1960s and 1970s, a rapid growth in the interest and participation in novel marginal religious movements, often with an Eastern orientation, occurred in the U.S.A., but also elsewhere (Wuthnow, 1986; Richardson, 1983). Shortly after these religious movements entered the counter-cultural scene of America, they also started to be introduced to and gained influence in Europe, with most of them flowing from the U.S.A. to Europe, with a distinctively American flavor (Beckford and Levasseur, 1986; Barker, 1989).

The expansion of new religious movements in Europe did not go unnoticed by the general public and news media there; indeed, media coverage followed a pattern somewhat similar to that within the U.S.A. In the latter case, the initial response to NRMs, after being somewhat positive within the context of social and political disruption associated with the Vietnam War, became one of suspicion. Anti-cult groups readily organized themselves to warn the public of the danger they perceived the "cults" to represent (Shupe and Bromley, 1980). Warning signals of this expansion were also emitted by the major U.S. news media, as were endeavors of new religious movements in South America (e.g., *San Francisco Chronicle,* Feb. 18, 1984; *New York Times,* Feb. 16, 1984) and Asia (*San Francisco Chronicle,* March 6, 1984).

Although there are distinct parallels between the situation in the U.S.A. and Europe, movements such as the Unification Church, Hare Krishna, Transcendental Mediation, and Children of God never have had the same impact on Europe's youth as they did on some youth in America. Findings such as those represented by Bird and Reimer (1982) which indicate that 20-30% of the populations of Montreal and San Francisco had been involved in "new religious and/or para-religious" movements (note that their definition is extremely broad) are not found in Europe (also see Wuthnow, 1986). Still, it appears that both in the U.S.A. and Europe NRMs were socially significant and relatively durable social movements with roots in the turbulent decade of the 1960s, movements which attracted a similar following among relatively affluent youth (Beckford and Levasseur, 1986:40). However, in Europe the attraction for NRMs apparently developed within a smaller proportion of available youth (Beckford and Levasseur, 1986:36).

Europe, of course, cannot be viewed as a single entity, even with the contemporary movement toward economic and political integration. The development of movements and the subsequent societal responses differed according to existing religious, cultural, social, historical, political, and judicial transitions in the various European nations (Beckford, 1985). This paper will attempt to shed some light on the relationship between NRMs in the European community and pinpoint major problem areas. Great Britain, Germany, France, and the Netherlands will be of special interest, with comparisons to the U.S.A. situation made where relevant.

First, we will deal with the emergence and development of NRMs in Europe and major socio-cultural factors which influenced this phenomenon. Our basic approach distinguishes itself in that we shall posit that NRMs have been relatively *unsuccessful,* in terms of numbers of participants as well as political power, within the European context. However, it is our contention, partly based on the small number of European adherents, that an examination of the failure of NRMs to become major cultural forces in Europe can be a fruitful endeavor. Our discussion may thus illustrate the point made by Beckford and Levasseur (1986:49) that the significance on NRMs is not in their numbers but in their demonstration of the limits of tolerance in modern European society.

Sections 2 and 3 will cover more practical matters dealing with societal responses to the phenomenon of NRMs. Section 2 will discuss the public response to NRMs in several nations in Europe. Section 3 will briefly examine NRMs within the context of church-state relationships in Europe. Issues dealing with the relationship between NRMs and governmental agencies have become especially salient since the European Parliament adopted a proposal based on a controversial report introduced by Bristol MEP Richard Cottrell (1983) which sought to limit and control the growth of NRMs. The aftermath of this development has raised fundamental questions for the European Community and individual Member States about the place of minority religions. This paper attempts to speak to these issues (see also Richardson, 1993b).

Section 1: New Religious Movements: Success or Failure?

The success of NRMs as a category in Europe has been limited, despite the sometimes exaggerated accounts that can be found in media reports and the over-estimations of membership figures that originate from, and also serve both the purposes of, the so-called "anti-cult" movement and the NRMs themselves. An accurate account of precise numbers is complicated considerably by the fact that some groups such as the Way International do not recognize true "membership," and ignore problems of who in the past have ever taken one mediation course, for instance, but without committing to the sponsoring movement itself. Different approaches result in conflicting tabulations and conflicting conclusions, making it difficult to create a clear-cut line of division in assessing who should and who should not be included in tabulations of the sizes of NRMs (see Barker, 1989, Appendix II, for a full discussion of this issue).

In our opinion the best way to assess the impact of a social movement at any one period of time is to look at the number of active participants. Although the actual impact of a social movement may extend beyond these participants, it is these individuals who largely determine the actual day-to-day functioning of the group. Reliable figures on the size of NRMs can be derived from studies that offer insight into the relative sizes of NRMs in various countries, despite the fact that such data are sometimes incomplete.

Although it has been widely recognized that the phenomenon of NRMs have altered the counter-cultural make-up of Western Europe and continue to have visible impact, Table 1 in Appendix I clearly shows that the level of participation in most NRMs which have attracted attention is quite low. Barker's (1989) careful study of the issue of membership numbers reveals a similar pattern of relatively small membership numbers. Beckford and Levasseur (1986:30) agree with this assessment of numerical strength:

> It seems unlikely . . . that any one of (the NRMs) could truthfully lay claim to more than a few thousand members who were living and working full-time for its benefit in Europe. Moreover, the indications are that the rate of recruitment to full-time membership is declining in most movements.

Recognition of this fact of low and even declining participation leads to the question of why NRMs have not blossomed into movements with large numbers of adherents, a question to which we now turn.

Various scholars have attempted to show that NRMs have proliferated because certain societal conditions came into existence and still exist, which serve as fertile ground for the emergence of NRMs and make them attractive vehicles of individual or societal change for a segment of the educated young. Major individual and socio-cultural variables addressed by authors include, for instance, the continuation of secularization (Wilson, 1976); the search for *Gemeinschaft* or community in an increasingly impersonal and hostile world (Robbins et al., 1978; Kilbourne and Richardson, 1986); the failure of the family in modern society (Nicholi, 1974); the development of widespread higher education, with a focus on science and technology (Wuthnow, 1986); the existence of a ubiquitous cultural and orientational crisis (Eister, 1974); the search for meaning and the sacred (Richardson, 1980; 1985a); the loss of legitimacy of traditional societal institutions (Bellah, 1976); identity confusion (Adams & Fox, 1972); increasing individualism and narcissism (Lasch, 1979); the perceived threat of a highly uncertain future (van Loon, 1981); the acting out of idealism (Kilbourne, 1986; Barker, 1984); and the seeking of amelioration of psychiatric symptoms (Galanter, 1978, 1980; Richardson, 1985c, 1990), among others.

These variables may be partially responsible for the emergence of NRMs, both in Europe and the U.S.A., since significant socio-cultural changes in Western societies are seldom confined to one nation. The question remains why, despite such growth-reinforcing factors, NRMs have had limited success in Europe. Besides a highly general observation that the processes touched upon above differed significantly within the contexts of American and European societies, other factors can be found with more specific explanatory value.

We shall first turn to the realm of religion. Religion is a much more pervasive force in American society than in most European societies, despite the official separation of church and state as embodied in the Constitution of the U.S.A. During the 1984 Republican Convention, President Ronald Reagan remarked, "Without God, democracy will not and cannot long endure. If we ever forget that we're one Nation under God, then we will be a nation gone under."[1]

Numerous studies and polls have shown that Americans tend to believe in God more than Western Europeans and also consider their religious beliefs to be more important to them. In a Gallup poll conducted in 1975, for instance, 94% of Americans said they believed in God or a universal spirit. The figures for Britain, West Germany, France and the Benelux (Belgium, the Netherlands, Luxembourg) were respectively 76%, 72%, 72%, and 78%. More significant perhaps is that a 1976 Gallup poll found that 56% of all Americans viewed their religious beliefs as being very important to them, while for the same four Western European areas the figures were 23%, 17%, 22%, and 26%. These are large differences which strongly support the notion that religion is much more embedded in the average American's view of reality and plays an important part in their everyday lives. That these findings also relate to understanding America's youth is evidenced by a nationwide survey of people 18 to 36 years old by the American Council of Life Insurance, indicating that 78% considered religion to play an important part in their lives (*Los Angeles Times,* November 17, 1983).

What consequences do these findings have for our discussion? Problems and answers to important life issues are often defined in religious terms by Americans. Roger Straus (1976) and others after him (Lofland, 1978; Richardson, 1985a) have shown that many members of NRMs define themselves as religious seekers and adopt a religious problem-solving orientation to life. Religious seekers then engage in an active search for potential alternatives which best fit their religious needs, often embarking on a "conversion career" (Richardson, 1978; 1980) involving several different sets of religious/philosophical ideas and groups. This applies especially to those members for whom beliefs precede participation in a movement (see Lofland & Skonovd, 1981).

We can deduce from the foregoing that Europeans who do not view religion to be such an important part of their lives will be far less inclined to become religious seekers. Among the young in the U.S.A. it is, in many places, culturally acceptable and approved to label oneself a religious seeker and adopt such a perspective on life, even if sometimes the particular vehicle chosen for this personal quest may evoke concern and even controversy. In Europe, where the dedicated religious seeker will be viewed by many, including his/her peers, as being deviant and fanatic, young people seem much less prone to use religion as an avenue for personal expression and identification. Eileen Barker, in describing religious commitment in Great Britain, states (1983:35): "Indeed to talk too much about religious commitment is considered rather bad taste," and in comparing Britain to the U.S.A.: "All this is done in a gentle, taken-for-granted manner which has little of the fiery rhetoric that can be heard from across the Atlantic in the United States. Their (U.S.) religiosity is indeed considered somewhat vulgar." Van der Lans (1981) makes the related point with reference to the Netherlands.

The religious route is thus culturally a less accepted path of knowledge and means to solve the major issues and problems that confront young people in Europe. New religious movements are therefore not as viable an alternative to traditional systems of meaning for the European young as they are for their American peers. They are also seen as being less valid as instruments for societal change and innovation.

Even if religious commitment was equally strong in Western Europe there are further pressures of a religious nature which reduce the attractiveness of NRMs. Schnabel (1982) offers some interesting insights in this regard, suggesting that political ideology and religious conviction have shown much more coherence in the U.S.A. than in Europe. He shows that a strong connection of these elements has been present in all Christian-inspired movements and churches that have found their way to Europe from the U.S.

Religions that combine the elements of political ideology, religious conviction, and morality can become successful in Europe as long as they create only minor disruptions in an individual's everyday life. The Pentecostal movement and Youth for Christ have been reasonably successful, Schnabel notes, while more life-transforming groups such as the Mormon Church, the Jehovah's Witnesses, and the Unification Church are more unattractive religious bodies. Goddijn and van Tillo (1979) found that less than one per cent of the adult Dutch population felt any attraction to the Mormons, Jehovah's Witnesses, or the Unification Church. For the Pentecostal movement, this was 7% and for the Jesus Movement 4%. These figures remained fairly stable when just categories of young people were considered.

The level of desire for religious innovation in the U.S.A. also varies strongly from that in Europe, according to Schnabel. In Europe, religious innovation is sought primarily in a continual process of reinterpretation of the original sources, while, in the U.S.A., innovations are related to the desires and needs of those in the spiritual marketplace. This gives rise to movement organizations which often combine or integrate new religious elements into their belief structures. In the sense that an adaptation to the shifting religious needs takes place, innovations in the U.S.A. are far more pragmatic changes than theological reflections. This, again, has consequences for the attractiveness of NRMs. As discussed earlier, such religious movements do not usually represent culturally acceptable or approved alternatives in Europe.

Movements such as Bhagwan Rajneesh and Transcendental Meditation, which deemphasize their religious character, have been relatively successful in the Netherlands (and elsewhere in Europe), Schnabel points out, while those overtly expressing their religious character have remained limited in size. When a movement stresses a more "high demand" religious nature it loses considerable recruitment capability. This is further illustrated by the almost negligible number of converts to Islam in Western Europe, despite more than a million immigrant workers and their families who openly practice this faith in these societies.

Let us now turn to the more acceptable channels of change for the dissatisfied among Europe's youth, the most important of which is perhaps the political realm. In the U.S.A., where two ideologically overlapping political parties dominate the total political spectrum and few political alternatives exist within or outside the political structures, there is usually little opportunity to find political outlets for one's creativity and political or socio-economic dissatisfaction. Consequently, a substantial portion of the eligible U.S. voting population, especially the young, have become estranged from political processes in society. That less than 30% of the eligible voters actually voted (a minimal political activity) in presidential elections over the past decade or so supports this point.

In Europe, the situation is radically different, although there are variations from country to country. Many of Western Europe's upper middle-class youth (the group which generally made up the conversion/recruitment base for new religions in the U.S.A. and Western Europe: see Richardson, et al, 1979; Richardson, 1985a, and c; Beckford and Levasseur, 1986; Wuthnow, 1986) are involved in marginal political parties and organizations. In the Netherlands, for instance, there are more than ten political parties in Parliament, including several religious parties on both sides of the political spectrum. Outside the political establishment there is also considerable political activity among the young, and political protest is engaged in on a regular basis in the various European societies.

Some traditional religious bodies are deeply involved in political protest movements and are sometimes the organizing force behind them. Traditional (liberal) churches, for instance, play an important role in the broad-based European peace movement in which many critical and dissatisfied young people participate. In this manner, traditional religions can remain viable instruments of defining social problems and promoting societal criticism and change in a way not perceived in America.

Another fundamental difference between the European and American situations can be found on a more psychological level. The psychological need to improve one's (spiritual and/or psychological) well-being and to experiment in this area traditionally seems to be stronger in most Americans. The attractiveness of a self-focused cultural climate in America is not so surprising, considering the heavy emphasis U.S. culture places on individualism and individualistic causality.[2]   In recent decades this has even reached narcissistic proportions, according to Lasch (1979), who refers to contemporary American culture as "the culture of narcissism."

Furthermore, American society is characterized by more social and geographic mobility by its members than is the case in Europe (e.g., American college students often move hundreds or thousands of miles away to attend school.) These processes disrupt countless social ties and relationships and can create a social vacuum forcing individuals to make it on their own, often far away from the security of friends and relatives. In some instances, NRMs fill this vacuum and serve a functional social purpose (see Kilbourne and Richardson, 1984, for a discussion of functions served by NRMs for participants). Experimentation in individual (religious) experiences within a secure social setting, and the trying out of various "trips" that fulfill individual needs, seem to fit better into American than European society (Richardson and Davis, 1983; Robbins and Bromley, 1992).

The hippie movement, which represented a shift in focus away from revolutionary structural and institutional change to self-oriented change, attracted considerably more adherents in the U.S.A. (especially California) than elsewhere. In this counter-cultural tradition NRMs picked up where the hippie era left off. The NRMs, too, are more attuned to the subculture of U.S. youth, including its religious and individualistic dimensions (Richardson, Kilbourne, and van Driel, 1988).

Section 2: Public Responses

An untrained observer of new religious movements would probably conclude that the response to beliefs and activities of new religious movements has been almost uniformly negative both in the U.S.A. (as well as Canada) and Europe (see van Driel and Richardson, 1988a, 1988b; van Driel and van Belzen, 1990). The most striking developments have been the establishment of anti-cult campaigns propelled by concerned parents and ex-members, allegations of manipulation and "brainwashing," and a general public suspicion of groups perceived to be weird, extreme, exotic, and sometimes dangerous (see Shupe & Bromley, 1980; Bromley & Richardson, 1983). Indeed, to a certain extent this negative perspective characterized all the nations discussed here. But beyond these superficial similarities there are distinct and profound differences between these societies.

An overall trend of negative responses to new religious movements is easily recognizable. In some nations the response occurred significantly later than in others, mainly due to the fact that new religious movements developed there comparatively late. Only within the last two decades has anti-cult sentiment emerged in nations such as Spain and Italy, which are located at the periphery of industrialized Western Europe.[3] Due to the constant interaction, however, between each unique society and the new religious movements attempting to gain a foothold there, this negative response has assumed a quite different character in different places (see Beckford, 1985).

It is our intention in this section to point out the major ways in which the "cult" problem" has been identified and defined in Great Britain, France, the Netherlands, and Germany. First, we shall briefly describe several European documents that contain relevant information on the subject of NRMs.

EUROPEAN DOCUMENTS

The European Convention on Human Rights and Fundamental Freedoms, which dates back to 1953, contains a series of provisions concerning fundamental rights and freedoms that can be regarded as supplementary to the laws of the nations that have ratified it (including the four nations under examination) (Peaslee, 1974a; Richardson, 1993b). The two main paragraphs relating to the freedom of religion read as follows:

Article 9, paragraph 1:   Everyone has the right to freedom of thought, conscience, and religion, this right includes freedom to change his religion or belief, and freedom, either alone or in community with others and in public or private to manifest his religion or belief in teaching, practice, worship, and observance.

Article 9, paragraph 2:   Freedom to manifest one's religion or beliefs shall be subject only to such limitations as are prescribed by law and are necessary in a democratic society in the interests of public safety, for the protection of public order, health or morals, or for the protection of the rights and freedoms of others.

One important segment of Article 9 is the passage pertaining to the protection of health, and the limitations it places on religious freedom. Clear over-rulings of religious considerations in favor of health have occurred in cases such as the refusal by some orthodox Protestant groups in the Netherlands to let their members be vaccinated against polio. In this incident the Dutch Supreme Court judged that, in accordance with Article 9 of the European Convention, "the government has the right to enforce obligations upon its citizens to protect their health, without offering exemption on the basis of their belief system" (judgment discussed in Schnabel, 1982:330). The Supreme Court, in actuality, takes the stance that belief systems may not interfere with the protection of an individual's health because the community will, in the end, be responsible for treating and financing the resultant illnesses.

Utilization of the passage of Article 9 on health, public order, and morality offers possibilities to combat alleged mental health abuses by NRMs, but its widespread application has not occurred and seems doubtful for the future. This passage and decisions justified in the manner of the Dutch Supreme Court may leave room for the introduction of conservatorship laws such as have been used in some states of the U.S.A. to gain legal control of some individual participants in NRMs (Bromley, 1983; LeMoult, 1983). There has been some discussion on this topic in Europe. Article 9 also reinforces a government's right to warn against or spread information about religious beliefs and practices that the government considers to be damaging for an individual's health or environment. The West German government has exercised this right to a considerable degree, as will be discussed.

The European Convention documents a further nuance of religious freedom that is aimed at both protecting the freedom of individual citizens and society as a whole against the influence of religion and also protecting the freedom of religion *per se* (Schnabel, 1982). Religion, in this document, is conceived as a value in the life of an *individual*, but not necessarily a value for the society as a while. In such a conception the European Convention thus reflects a view of religion as being a strictly individual concern which takes place in a private setting. This corresponds with the analyses of many social scientists who conclude that this has become the dominant meaning of religion in modern Western societies (e.g., Wilson, 1976; Berger, 1967; Luckmann, 1967; Hunter, 1983).

Society can therefore legitimately challenge the influence of religion and religious institutions in a wide array of public spheres of life. The individualization and privatization of religion almost automatically places it in a transcendental perspective, according to Schnabel (1982). He contends that the European Convention might be introducing a new stage in the domestication of religion: religion must bow to the secular values of modern society where protection of health has become the chief concern. It appears that health has been bestowed with the aura of religiosity in our modern era. The question, however, is to what extent this also applies in the U.S.A., where religion seems to be a more profound cultural phenomenon.

Government agencies seeking to resist the growth of NRMs can also turn to Article 48 of the European Economic Community Treaty that allows the possibility to restrict the free passage of a national from one Member State to another Member State (Peaslee, 1974b). The restriction on freedom of movement between Member States is contained in the following provision (Art. 48.3): "It shall entail the right (to travel between member states), subject to limitations justified on grounds of public policy, public security, or public health . . ." (Peaslee, 1974b:473). In this line, the English minister of public health, in 1968, introduced a measure that allowed immigration authorities to refuse resident visas to foreign Scientology members (Barker, 1984). In 1974, a Dutch woman was also refused entry to the U.K., a decision which was upheld by the European context. Perhaps the most important development in relation to NRMs has been the 1984 passage of a resolution put to the European Parliament which took an overtly repudiatory stance toward NRMs. In June of 1982, the Parliament sent a draft resolution, initiated by several members in response to alleged abuses by the Unification Church, to the Committee for Youth, Culture, Education, Information, and Sport. The resolution was created in September of 1982, and the British conservative MEP, R. Cottrell, was appointed as rapporteur. After barely three months of investigation into the phenomenon, Cottrell's draft report was presented to the committee in charge (Cottrell, 1983).

Cottrell's document echoes claims made by anti-cultists, and it is evident that very few social scientists were consulted. The document showed a dearth of objective research results, precluding consideration of information which would offer a more than superficial examination of the controversies surrounding NRMs. The core of the document consists of a rough summary of accusations toward NRMs. Cottrell's position is illustrated lucidly by the following remarks in his conclusion: "To describe the majority of cults as inspired by genuine humanitarianism is facile: some may very well be deeply and insidiously dangerous." A revised version of Cottrell's report was adopted in the Spring of 1984, amidst strong protests from some traditional religious groups and from some NRMs, and was submitted to the European Commission of Human Rights, where it was acted upon in 1989 (Beckford and Levasseur, 1986:48-49; Richardson, 1993b).

The Cottrell resolution proposes the development of uniform charity laws (reflecting concerns in England), assistance of information between member states relating to various violations of their laws, an "assessment" of NRMs according to several criteria, and the development of communication networks to search for missing persons (see Subcommissie Sekten, 1984). The contents and proposals of the report have been criticized from many quarters, including the British Council of Churches and its French counterpart. In a 1984 government report (to be discussed in more detail) released at approximately the same time in the Netherlands, Cottrell's report is heavily criticized and the hope is conveyed that the report shall "rapidly sink into the quicksand upon which it is built."

The long term ramifications of the European Parliament's decision are, as yet, still vague (see Richardson, 1993b). It could stimulate anti-cult activities, reconfirm existing negative impressions of NRMs, and reinforce policymaking aimed at combatting NRMs. This is perhaps especially the case in West Germany where governmental involvement in the "cult problem" has become an essential element in the anti-cult cause. In the Netherlands, on the other hand, its own governmental report was markedly more significant in dealing with the problems associated with NRMs.

Great Britain

Since the time of the Reformation, Britain has officially been a Protestant country in which the Church of England has played a dominant role in its position as England's official church. This is still somewhat the case in contemporary Britain, but religious activity by citizens is on the wane in the era of secular society.

We stated earlier that 76% of the British believed in God or a universal spirit. Religion is for most of these people a highly personal affair and has lost a great deal of its social dimension. Only 18% of the adult population are members of a church and even less, 11%, attend church on a regular basis. Due to decreasing participation in religious institutions, a climate has now arisen that treats overzealous religious behavior as deviant and undesirable. Religious leaders with an aggressive approach are met with a great deal of distrust and face almost certain rejection.

On the other hand, throughout history, movements of dissent have constantly arisen to claim their place in English society despite the strong opposition by the Church of England and other established institutions (Barker, 1983). Some have now been totally accepted and have become "bona fide religions," such as the Quakers and the Baptists. This has led to a situation of pluralism and tolerance in the area of religion, fitting well into the general mold of British society in which most institutions are decentralized and pluralistic.

Britain is a plural society, but its tolerance of minority groups has been questioned (Barker, 1984). Bagley (1973), in a comparison between the Netherlands and Britain, discovered widespread prejudices in Britain towards minority ethnic groups whether they tended to conform to the dominant society or not. According to him, the roots of British prejudice are located in the inherently racist aspects of British colonial policy. In a large scale study of Britain social attitudes released in early 1984, there was a striking amount of agreement among the public that Britain is a prejudiced country (see *Washington Post,* May 30, 1984). One-third described themselves as prejudiced against other races. Whether this intolerance is an underlying personality trait, or is an attitude restricted to the area of skin color, is uncertain. If it does reflect an underlying rigid world view, significant prejudice towards NRMs in British society might also be expected.

Both developments described above are important in understanding the response that new religious movements evoked in Britain. Pluralism and tolerance led the focus of attention away from any concerns about societal and/or cultural implications, but a general suspicion of high levels of religiosity led to an application of labels of deviance to those who expressed their religion overtly, an approach Beckford (1983a and b, 1985) has termed "Anglo-Saxon." Accounts of problems related to new religious movements concentrate on the psychological processes which take place before, during, and after membership, instead of on societal level consequences of involvement.

Many persons reason that because it is not normal for a young educated person to join an extreme, irrational "cult" something wrong has happened. Therefore, the field of abnormal psychology is thought to offer the best perspective from which to view the phenomena of new religious movements. The troublemaker and villain, as can be deduced from anti-cult literature is, of course, the "manipulative cult" that attempts to corrupt the minds of the unwary young.

In the "Anglo-Saxon" approach, as outlined above, the victims of the cults are first and foremost affected individuals and their families, not the society at large. Others feel that they themselves are not affected, justifying the attitude that it is essentially the problem of the alleged victims. Others must deal with their own problems. Psychologization of the "cult problem" has also led to treatment of the cult phenomena as an isolated problem area. Few discussions relating to broader, social, political, and religious issues have become salient, and links to other problems involving Britain's youth are rarely made when the "cult problem" is debated. Therefore, new religious movements have failed to become a major social problem with far-reaching consequences in the eyes of the general public. Consequently, the opposition new religious movements have faced has had an *ad hoc,* pragmatic nature.

There is little formal involvement in the ongoing debate by established organizations such as the trade unions and the mainstream churches. Response, if made, typically is quite reserved. Civil rights pressure groups have also refrained from getting involved, whereas in the U.S.A., for instance, groups like the American Civil Liberties Union have become staunch supporters of new religious movements in court and elsewhere when their fundamental rights were at stake. One of the reasons for this stance is that deprogramming is rare in Britain. It is important to note that the medical profession has also remained on the sidelines, preventing the cult problem from being overly medicalized. During the famous *Daily Mail* libel trial (to be discussed later) the major witness for the defense, psychiatrist Margaret Singer, was flown over from the U.S.A. to testify against the Unification Church suggesting a dearth of available experts from the medical field at that time in Britain.

Despite an ubiquitous negativism surrounding new religious movements, the only serious criticism and opposition in England has stemmed from the media and a few anti-cult groups. The media have helped shape and strengthen the pervasive anticult mood as in other countries (Beckford, 1985; van Driel and Richardson, 1988a and b), but British media differ to the extent that they treat new religious movements individually and not as a large social phenomenon. The Unification Church especially has been the object of scrutiny, often being brandished as a threat to the British way of life. The limited number of members of new religious movements and their marginal impact hardly justifies the amount of attention devoted to new religious movements by the media, but this does not seem to matter.

FAIR, a parents' movement and Deo Gloria Trust, a movement with a distinctly Christian base, are the two most influential anticult groups. FAIR has good contacts with other anti-cult organizations throughout the world and carries a considerable amount of international news material and information in its newsletter. Neither group has been able to influence governmental policymaking to much of an extent, however. Instead, each has pressed for the enforcement of existing legislation and shifted efforts to counseling activities and the distribution of information on the various new religious movements.

Several battles have been fought in court, the most influential and internationally reported case being the lengthy libel suit brought against the *Daily Mail* by the Unification Church. The *Mail* had published a series of articles about the Unification Church which were extremely derogatory and involved, among other things, allegations of "brainwashing" of recruits by the UC. The widely reported jury's decision in 1981 was a stunning victory for anti-cultists and was immediately viewed as a warning signal to the Unification Church throughout the rest of Europe. German Parliament members even queried the German government about ways to incorporate the London High Court decision into its own policies (Deutsche Bundestag, 1982). It is clear that the widely publicized court decision in the *Daily Mail* case played a significant role in later discussions of the Unification Church and other NRMs in the European Parliament.

France

France's religious tradition is characterized by the monopolistic position of the French Catholic Church, with 89-94% of the population holding at least nominal membership. Catholicism is identified as the essence of French national culture. Opposition to its hegemony and the concomitant fissures have not led to a general acknowledgement of France being a plural society with diverse traditions and lifestyles. In this regard, France differs significantly from the other nations we are discussing, especially Britain and the Netherlands.

Many still perceive France to be a unique organic whole which has had to contend with threats to its internal stability. Traditionally, the major threat to the "natural order of things" was judged to emanate from encroaching Protestantism and the so-called "classical sects." New religious movements have been placed in this same category of organizations which threaten the national interest.

Beckford (1985) has referred to the French attitude toward NRMs as an "organicist" response, quite distinctive from the "Anglo-Saxon" emphasis on issues concerning individual well-being and psychological manipulation. He also notes (Beckford and Levasseur, 1986:45) that the official governmental response to NRMs had been virtually nil until 1982, when a new Socialist government took power and, in response to mounting pressure from the public, authorized a parliamentary inquiry into problems posed by sects in France. This "Vivien Report" (named after its author), released in 1985, contained a number of recommendations designed to clarify the position of sects in France, most of which demonstrate the "organic" of concern about NRMs (see detailed discussion in Beckford and Levasseur, 1986:45-46).

In France, fear of an attack aimed against the foundations of society has usually led to an emphasis on ideological totalitarianism, subversion, and conspiracy when discussing groups defined as threatening to society. Media comparisons between the ideologies of Adolf Hitler and Reverend Sun Myung Moon evidence this approach (Beckford, 1981), for example. The drawing of such parallels by anti-cultists was designed to create extremely negative associations, of course. Allegations against NRMs, seen in this perspective, are far more serious than in other Western European nations.

By defining the cult problem in the above terms, anti-cultists have been able to gain broad-based support. The Catholic Church has sided with the major anti-cult organization, ADFI (Association for the

Defense of the Family and the Individual), as has the media. ADFI, essentially a parents' organization, receives subsidies and support directly from the state, though it has experienced little success in determining government policies.

Legal channels of social control have had some effect. In a 1970 judgment, Scientology founder L. Ron Hubbard was sentenced, in his absence, to four years in prison and a fine of approximately $2,000 on account of the unauthorized practicing of the medical profession (Deutsche Bundestag, 1979). In an attempt to control NRMs further, judicial channels have been used as well. Sympathizers with the anti-cultists have pressed for measures against the "psychic conditioning" of adherents. With support from ADFI, Morin (1979) proposed to create a law punishing the use of "mental violence." However, it is doubtful if such a law can be passed because of difficulties in the interpretation of this concept (Subcommissie Sekten, 1984).

Recently in France a new tactic has developed toward selected NRMs (Richardson, 1993a). Accusations of child abuse, including sexual abuse, in The Family (formerly known as the Children of God) by former members and others led to police raids against two Family communes and noncommunal members. A number of adults were arrested and large numbers of children were taken into custody. This issue is unresolved at this time, but seems to show that at least some groups such as the Family are viewed by authorities as enough of a threat to French society to justify strong action. Basing the action on concern for children seems to fit an international pattern of such accusations being used as a device for social control of such groups (Richardson, 1993a). This recent action also may relate to the earlier Vivien Report, which contained a major recommendation that the rights of individual children be supported, even against parental rights, and that childrens' right to proper schooling also be asserted by the state. Whether there is any direct connection between what has happened and the Vivien Report remains to be seen.

The Netherlands

Traditionally, the configuration of Dutch Society has been defined by the twin edifices of pluralism and "pillarization." Pluralism evidences itself clearly in the areas of politics and religion, where compromise has been the key word. Neither Protestantism nor Catholicism have been able to totally dominate religious thinking, or earn the label "state religion," as is the case in France and Britain. Freedom of religion is a central concept in the Dutch constitution and in society's institutions.

Pillarization, as it occurs in the Netherlands and in Belgium, refers to the institutionalization of a structure in which each belief system has constructed its own extensive network of social organizations. Its roots can be traced to intense conflicts between religious groups in the past. In order to mitigate the destructive and disruptive consequences of conflict, the system of pillarization emerged (Bagley, 1973). In the areas of education, media, and social welfare this process has determined the shape of society. Pillarization based on religious denomination, as was originally the case, has gradually faded in the wake of secularization.

Secularization has deeply affected Dutch society as it has others. Religion now occupies a relatively marginal position in the everyday lives of most individuals and is valued as a personal matter. Only about a third of the Dutch population regularly attends church, with religious commitment strongest among the older generations. The group of persons claiming no denominational membership now constitutes the largest single category in the Netherlands (41% according to Schnabel [1982]).

Another historical well-recognized dimension of Dutch culture is its tolerance towards minorities and minority viewpoints. Bagley (1973:244) commented that despite the extreme segmentation of Dutch life caused by pillarization, social conflict is notably absent. He concluded that Dutch society is significantly less prejudiced than British society and that "tolerance of diversity has been a feature of Dutch society which institutionalized harmonious relationships between very diverse ideological groups." Intolerance of deviance is a feature of Dutch society where established patterns of social behavior are threatened. Bagley claimed (1973:20), "Non-conformity is tolerated as long as it does not interfere with the prevailing social order. At points where the norm of orderliness is violated, the tolerance of the social system ends." In Bagley's study, for instance, his Dutch sample discriminated significantly more against hippies than against blacks. Although more recent developments have illuminated the limitations of Dutch tolerance,[4] the general attitude when assessing *religious* convictions appears to remain one of tolerance and caution.

The overall Dutch response to the advent of NRMs can be categorized as "Anglo-Saxon," using Beckford's (1985) scheme. Issues pertaining to brainwashing manipulation and individual vulnerability have been of paramount importance in the discussion about NRMs. As is the case in the U.S.A. and Britain, concerns about the social or cultural implications of NRMs have been relegated to the background. Discussions in the Netherlands have lacked the intensity and fierceness common to discussions in other countries, which have focused on the negative aspects of NRMs (van der Lans & Derks, 1982; van Driel and van Belzen, 1990). The news media, as elsewhere, adopted a generally negative stance toward NRMs, but other group problems such as unemployment, vandalism, rising racism, squatting, and drug abuse were deemed far more imperative problems by the media and the society at large.

Conversion of some famous Dutch personalities to the Bhagwan religion in the late 1970s and early 1980s further served to reduce feelings of hostility. One of the Netherlands' most popular and widely read psychiatrists (Jan Foudraine), as well as two popular entertainers (Ramses Shaffy and Albert Mol) became followers of the Rajneesh Bhagwan. Such developments vastly increased the Bhagwan movement's value in society news and gossip columns.

Established institutions have shown hesitance in getting involved in the debate about NRMs. The Protestant and Catholic Churches have eschewed the subject, as has the medical profession. Judicial battles in the courts have also been limited in scope, as opponents of NRMs have little to gain by initiating a trial. When religious elements become salient in a case, involvement of concerns pertaining to religious freedom occurs. Civil courts are hesitant to take action in such cases, especially because in most instances it is difficult for anti-cultists to obtain hard evidence supporting their allegations.

Anti-cultism in the Netherlands has been spearheaded by the parents' organization, SO, which totaled approximately 100 members in the 1980s. Their efforts and those by other anti-cultists were repeatedly confounded by unresponsive authorities and a disinterested society. The Dutch government report, published in the spring of 1984 (to be discussed in the next section) undercut many anti-cultists' efforts.

Actually, the efforts of anti-cultists in the Netherlands to constrain the growth of NRMs have been repeatedly counter-productive. The major media account of NRMs was a series of programs broadcast between September of 1980 and March of 1981, hosted by a dogmatically inclined fundamentalist minister. While diligently denouncing "abusive cults" he discredited his own cause by invoking a large portion of Christian moralism into his programs, and by attempting to convert the audience to his brand of Christianity at the end of each program. It reminded some of an old-fashioned witchhunt. Instead of invoking distrust and fear among the audience, as was intended, the series offered some free promotional opportunities for NRMs.

Most recently, a highly publicized event captured the attention of the Dutch public when the premises of a Tai-Chi group (branded a "cult" by the media) in Amsterdam were raided by the police. The action, which was filmed by the media, was undertaken due to allegations and rumors that the children of group members were suffering from extreme neglect. As Derks and van der Lans (1982) document, the media, which covered the daily developments diligently, gradually shifted from a highly critical view of the group to a critical view of the raid as more information surfaced. Later, it was revealed that all the children were in excellent physical and mental health, which led to a dropping of charges against the group.

Germany[5]

The religious landscape in what used to be West Germany has remained relatively calm, uneventful, and in balance in recent decades. Protestantism is anchored in a strong Lutheran tradition which remains the dominating religious denomination. Protestants still outnumber Catholics by a ratio of 55:45 during a period of encroaching secularization. Christian values continue to permeate all spheres of life, but in recent years only about 37% of Catholics and 9% of Protestants claimed to attend church regularly. Outside of these two monoliths, marginal sectarian religions have gained only a limited following, even though Mormons, Jehovah's Witnesses, and the Pentecostal movement proselytize vigorously.

A critical difference between the Netherlands (and to a lesser extent, the U.S.A., Britain, and France) and its German neighbor is the important role that the government and the churches and their affiliated organizations (those principally concerned with social work and mental health) play in resisting NRMs (or "new youth religions," as they are referred to in Germany) and in the rehabilitation of ex-members back into West German society. Although research (Sieber, 1980; Kuner, 1979,1983) has shown that the problems related to NRMs were blown out of proportion, the West German government has concerned itself with this phenomenon a great deal. Suffice it to say here that research and a general lack of complaints failed to support anti-cult warnings and has not deterred the West German government and churches from adapting an extremely hostile approach to the NRMs. Various official and semi-official organizations have been established or supported to confront the NRMs.

Hardin (1983) attributes the excessive negativism of the German public to at least three factors: (1) research from other countries is only selectively used, (2) sociological research on NRMs has been minimal in West Germany, and (3) the vested interest of established groups in society that have easy access to the media. Because social scientists have avoided the topic, there is an abundance of pseudo-scientific analyses which propagate the ideas of anti-cultists. All this implies a dearth of objective, quality information.

The best known authority in West Germany is Rev. F. W. Haack, who has been on the editorial board of the European journal on NRMs, *Update.* One book he did on NRMs has sold over 500,000 copies. Rev. Haack's position on the issue of NRMs can be deduced from his comments in a 1981 publication entitled, "Judicial Problems in Connection with the So-Called New Youth Religions." Haack says (Engstfeld et al., 1981:31), "Without a doubt, we can state that NRMs pose a threat to the individual and society." He then proceeds to cite the reputable church-jurist and leader of the Church-law institution of Evangelical Churches in West Germany, Axel von Campenhausen, who points to the destructive character of NRMs and urges the government to take action. Haack voices his agreement and even adds a little spice by commenting that such groups constitute a threat to democracy and are out to destroy it. Position-taking in this fashion bears a strong resemblance to the concerns expressed by French anti-cultists. The reason for such condemnations and the involvement of a wide variety of religious, political, consumer protection, and other bodies is based on several different concerns.

Since World War II, German society has become highly suspicious of extreme ideologies and has incorporated several safeguards to counter their influence, particularly where young people are concerned. Most safeguards are located at the government level. Teachers who belonged to the Communist Party, for instance, could be kept out of the schools by means of "Berufs-verbote," a law adopted some 25 years ago which limits the access of communists to governmental jobs. In the past, student rebellions and demonstrations, political terrorism, squatters, and NRMs have also been defined as extremist ideologies from which the young need to be protected.

Roots of various forms of youth disaffection have been sought in one basic explanatory model. This model, officially accepted by government agencies, has treated radical involvement in marginal social movements, whether it be political terrorism or NRMs, as a behavioral aberration with its roots in a general flight from reality. Stressing the "flight from reality" explanation creates a link between terrorism and NRMs, awakening the anxieties of the general population that still has the Baader-Meinhof period of terrorism fresh in its memory. Anxieties reinforced by accruing evidence offered through the media, the government, the churches, and experts such as Rev. Haack, have propelled the phenomenon of NRMs into national attention and defined it as a serious social problem.

Distrust of NRMs has other causes as well. For many German parents, their child's participation in a NRM can have long-term consequences for them. They always remain partially legally responsible for the welfare of their children, even after they have reached adulthood, and under certain circumstances they can be compelled by the government to provide financial support for their children (e.g., if they decided to continue their studies after leaving a NRM). Reluctance by parents to tolerate involvement with NRMs is quite widespread as a result of this type of social arrangement.

Beliefs that NRMs are undermining basic societal institutions have also become salient, as they have in France. By dislodging young people from their educational and career trajectories (in a culture that highly values careerism) NRMs are perceived as removing them from a network of mutual responsibilities. The nation's social welfare system depends on the contributions by the young to keep it economically intact. Some fear that the welfare system could falter should too many young people turn their backs on society and join NRMs. This problem has gained in importance as people have become aware of the developing distorted population pyramid. An impending steady decline of the former West Germany's population in future decades will leave fewer young people to support a relatively large mass of dependent retirees.

The population decline also coincides with what is seen as an infiltration of culturally alien elements into German society. Not only by NRMs but primarily by immigrants who, on the average, have more children than the German families. A fear is rising that Germany will no longer retain its German culture if present trends continue. Thus, the tolerance of Germans towards alien elements and alternative lifestyles has been tested in recent years and the wave of violence against migrants shows the results.

Nevertheless, the anti-cult movement in West Germany is fairly small, but this is compensated by its effectiveness and power. Its power is derived from influential individuals who have been able to persuade established institutions to take a firm position on NRMs. It has been perhaps the German Lutheran Church, in coordination with its "Sekten-beauftragten" (clergy commission to study NRMs) that has offered the most organized formal response to NRMs in Europe. This nature of anti-cultism in West Germany has been accurately described by Shupe et al. (1983:185) who conclude that "in contrast to the United States the parents' organization, insofar as they exist other than on paper, serve more as legitimation for the actions of several key individuals than that they reflect any widespread parental unrest." These key individuals are often clergy, like Rev. Haack, active within the Protestant Church, with longstanding experience dealing with local and federal officials. At present, though, far-reaching policy guidelines only loom on the horizon.

Section 3: New Religious Movements in the Church-State Context

Conflicts between NRMs and their opponents have involved a variegated cross-section of society: churches, lawyers, judges, social scientists, clinicians, the media, clergy, civil rights organizations, ex-members, and parents among others. For the most part, governments in the U.S.A. and Europe initially kept their distance from the new phenomenon, partially to avoid getting stuck in a situation that could be viewed as state interference in religious affairs. The relationship between church and state in the Western world has always been a tense one, full of friction points.

Under mounting pressure by concerned parents, anti-cultists, the media, and court decisions, governmental agencies at all levels in the U.S.A. have been gradually drawn into the intense debate about NRMs and related topics, such as mental health and religious freedom. Perhaps most important is the pressure originating from the multitude of court battles which demand interpretations of the law and the constitution. Decisions like those involving large awards of civil damages to former participants (Anthony, 1990; Richardson, 1991), the conviction of the Reverend Moon of tax evasion charges (Richardson, 1992), the *Daily Mail* libel trial outcome, development of concern about possible child abuse in some of the new religions (Richardson, 1993a), and the recent tragedy in Waco, Texas (Lewis, 1993) buttress the claims of anti-cultists that governments need to intervene in order to curb the tide of "destructive cults." Anti-cultists also dispute the rights and privileges claimed by NRMs that the state offers to "bona fide" religions (e.g., tax exemption). Inquiries have been repeatedly demanded to investigate the official status of NRMs both in the U.S.A. and Europe. On the other hand, the occasional convictions of deprogrammers and parents who kidnap their children in order to resocialize them also puts pressure on governments to attend to these concerns.

If NRMs were to represent a temporary phenomenon, governments might perhaps refrain from immediate action. Now that it appears that the NRM phenomenon will be a relatively long-term even if numerically limited one, and that the endeavors of anti-cultists will continue, it is increasingly unlikely that governments can eschew the subject. Many governments have undertaken some initial investigations into the activities of NRMs or are planning to do so (see Shupe and Bromley, 1980; Beckford, 1985; Richardson, 1993b).

Official investigations into the belief systems or activities of marginal religions automatically take issue with church-state relations. Any position taken concerning minority religious groups has consequences for that nation's interpretation of its laws and principles, and the manner in which all minority groups are treated. Of course, an existing position or change in that position is influenced by various pressures emanating from the existing societal climate with regard to NRMs, and, in its turn, position taking influences and modifies that climate. Government involvement does not occur in a vacuum: movements themselves are sensitive to official measures and opinions. Their attitudes, practices, openness versus closeness, etc. will, to an extent, be determined by the policies that affect them (Richardson, 1985b).

In this section, we briefly but specifically discuss the attitudes and policies of the governments of the four selected countries towards NRMs. Our argument shall be embedded in the context of church-state relationships in those countries.

GREAT BRITAIN

The psychologization of the "cult-problem" in Britain, as discussed in Section 2, has deterred the government from paying much attention to NRMs. Church-state relations have been of minor concern where NRMs are involved, although some governmental decisions in the past did have negative implications for NRMs.

Former Minister of Health Kenneth Robinson viewed Scientology to be a socially destructive organization, and in 1968 he subsequently refused foreign student admission to the U.K., if their sole intention was to study at Hubbard College, a Scientology school. Work permits were also refused to foreigners intending to work at Scientology establishments. The data on which Robinson based his decision were inconclusive and meager, and, in 1980, his policies were overturned, apparently because some in the government thought the policy indefensible. Another significant incident occurred in 1978 when the Reverend Sun Myung Moon was denied a temporary stay in Britain. Yet, on the whole, British government agencies' policies toward NRMs have been in a relative inchoate stage of development (Barker, 1984).

At present there is no official governmental policy on NRMs and there seems to be little pressure from the British public to change this situation, with the exception of strong animus shown toward the Unification Church in the aftermath of the *Daily Mail* trial. Religious matters are, in essence, viewed as a private matter not to be tampered with by the government. This is indicative of the development of a modernity which includes as essential a sharp division between public and private spheres of life (Hunter, 1983).

According to Barker (1983), religious movements in Britain are potentially vulnerable to persecution in the courts because of a lack of a British first amendment, as it exists in America, which guarantees fundamental rights and freedoms. British courts are therefore in the position to arbitrarily judge cases in conformity to norms and values which they regard to be correct and generally acceptable.

We should reiterate that it was the *Daily Mail* decision that caused the more major developments in this area. Pressure on the Charity Commission and the Inland Revenue Department has led to a push for radical changes in legislation to accommodate the charges of anti-cultists. Specifically, strong efforts have been made to take away the status of the U.C. as a charity. However, the government has not succumbed to the pressure so far, even in the face of attacks from MPs who have aligned themselves with anti-cultists in the U.K.

FRANCE

The government has been reluctant to take an official position on the matter of NRMs because of the fundamental freedom at stake. Under anti-cultist's pressure, the justice committee of the Assemblee National appointed a subcommittee (mission d' information) in December of 1978 to study NRMs. The subcommittee failed to survive the 1981 elections and the issue was dropped.

In the early 1980s, the vice-chairman of the Assemblee National wrote a report for Premier Mauroy that advised improved education of the public and the establishment of special persons or committees which could serve as mediators between parents and NRMs. The government reviewed the report and its proposals but took little action. However, the Vivien report was sanctioned shortly afterward, and was eventually made public in 1985. Its recommendations have not become law, but they may have served as a partial justification for recent governmental action concerning NRMs.

The more recent actions against The Family, in which well-coordinated raids apprehended a large number of adults and children after accusation of child abuse surfaced, suggests that segments of the government might become more involved with NRMs. There have been hints that high ranking French justice officials sanctioned the raids, and that the government is supportive of the effort to exercise control over this controversial minority religion. Time will tell if this is an isolated incident or represents a fundamental shift of policy.

THE NETHERLANDS

The manner in which the relationship between church and state has developed in the Netherlands has prompted the establishment of a cautious approach by the Dutch government toward NRMs. The 1848 constitution, for instance, confirmed the freedom of each citizen, as guaranteed in the 1815 constitution, to profess one's religion and bestow equal protection to *all* churches (Schnabel, 1982). Although there is no state church in the Netherlands, nevertheless the government should not be regarded as a neutral party in its handling of religious affairs. When claims are made about an alleged encroachment upon the freedom of religion, the government is quite hesitant to take a position. On the other hand, where the interests of established religious communities can be advanced, the government, on the whole, behaves in a fashion supportive of traditional religions.

Religious bodies are considered to be different from non-religious organizations and are treated accordingly, with various advantages being enjoyed by accepted religious bodies. Though there is no definition of "religious community" in any Dutch law, practical guidelines have been set out in the past to distinguish what should not be labeled a religious community (see e.g., Supreme Court description in Schnabel, 1982:321). Accordingly, any group that considers itself to be a religious community can register as such, although registration *per se* does not guarantee any formal rights or privileges. By the 1980s, Scientology, the Divine Light Mission, and the Bhagwan movement were officially registered as religious communities.

NRMs have disrupted the normal church-state relations in The Netherlands, however. A major concern shared by many, including on the government level, is that abuse of religious freedom and damage to health may result from the activities of NRMs. According to Schnabel (1982), a redefining of church-state relations, now in an unsteady and uncertain stage, is long overdue because the constitution and the law on religious communities were instituted in the nineteenth century, a period when almost the entire population belonged to a Judeo-Christian community. Religious beliefs and behavior have changed considerably since then, accompanied by development of more pluralism in the Netherlands.

Despite a hesitant attitude, the government has made several inquiries into the phenomenon of NRMs. There has been an active group of concerned parents, constituting a nascent anti-cult movement, which has continually engaged in seeking support for their cause in the media and in various governmental agencies. The Dutch Inspector of Mental Health, whose powers are defined in the law on public health, has been the target of much of that pressure, and not entirely without results.

In 1979, the research department of the National Center for Health sought contact with numerous organizations in the area of mental health, the justice department, and service industries to ascertain how frequently they were confronted with complaints about NRMs. Complaints were discovered to be rare, with most originating from the parents of members. Then in January of 1981, the Chief Inspector of Mental Health launched a government-related project. A questionnaire pertaining to "sect-related" problems was sent to ambulant and clinical facilities in The Netherlands dealing with mental health. There was a considerable amount of resistance on the part of the queried institutions to cooperate, leading to an effective response rate of only 31%. The results, covering the period 1978-1980, indicated clearly that there were relatively few instances of contact with (ex-) cult members. A total of 32 cases were reported by 139 institutions. Generally speaking, the belief was conveyed that the mental health of the ex-member was not a problematic issue. As a matter of fact, there were several institutions (14) that had experienced problems related to commitments of individuals from other more traditional religious communities.

In June of 1980, the Permanent Commission for Public Health instructed a subcommittee to conduct an in-depth inquiry into the activities of NRMs in The Netherlands. The results (Subcommissie Sekten, 1984), released four years later, represent a landmark study of a quality seldom achieved by government studies. The report, over 320 pages long, carefully weighed all the evidence from numerous sources, on different sides of the issue, including a large bulk of social-scientific evidence from throughout the Western world. A well-balanced, in-depth account of the problems associated with NRMs and concomitant policy guidelines was the end result.

Conclusions of the study coincide with what most social scientists have repeatedly stated and depart drastically from the accusations profusely put forth by anti-cultists. The initial reason for conducting the study, the supposed danger to the mental well-being of NRMs, is even critically reflected upon: "in the light of the results obtained, our efforts might have been better spent on another subject" (p. 315).

What are these results? We shall explain these by presenting the conclusions most relevant to the controversies surrounding NRMs. The report states: "Our findings should leave little doubt about the fact that, generally speaking, the use of techniques aimed at manipulation and coercive persuasion by NRMs, during the recruitment of new members, is not a relevant issue" (p. 217), and "It should be added that the conditions, which Lifton calls ideological totalism, were by no means fulfilled by any of the groups we examined" (p. 218). Anti-cultists claims are directly addressed and dismissed somewhat later in the report: "So we can ascertain that there is insufficient reason to assume that NRMs use techniques of manipulation and indoctrination during recruitment that would undermine a potential member's freedom of choice. With this, the fundamental for an appeal for measures to protect an individual's freedom of decision disappears" (p. 220).

Accusations by anti-cultists are dismissed one by one. The epilogue and summary, printed in English, begins with the following statement: "In general, NRMs are no real threat to mental health" (p. 314), and adds: "The allegations that NRMs use coercion when recruiting and then subject members to forms of conditioning has not been confirmed by our study. As a rule, membership of a NRM is the outcome of a carefully weighed choice" (p. 317).

The contents and conclusion of the Dutch government report are a far cry from those of the Cottrell report, compiled for the European Parliament. Whereas the Cottrell report emphasized the negative aspect of NRMs, the Dutch report downplayed them. Each comes to diametrically opposed conclusions. Cottrell concedes that there are evident dangers involved and that measure need to be advanced to obviate the dangers. The Dutch report, on the other hand,. denies the existence of serious problems and dissuades the development of support for counter-measures.

It appears that the net result of the extensive Dutch report has been the reduction of anxieties of those worried by NRMs, and a lessening of the friction between NRMs and the Dutch society at large. A more balanced, objective, and in-depth approach to NRMs was made possible by the report. Not so with the Cottrell resolution, which strengthened the already dominant climate of distrust and hostility found in the U.K. Mitigation of problems related to NRMs seems elusively distant if the ideas contained in that resolution are accepted and the proposals implemented, as seems to be happening in some European countries and in the community institutions (Richardson, 1993b).

GERMANY

As mentioned earlier, the anti-cult movement in the former West Germany has been given impetus by the established churches and the government. Governmental agencies have released several documents portraying NRMs as severe health hazards, outlining possible channels of governmental action (Shupe et al., 1983). We shall turn to these in a moment.

After World War II, a new West German constitution was constructed containing provisions requiring the government to comment on movements and trends that negatively influenced German families. This burdensome task was delegated primarily to the Ministry for Youth, Family, and Health, which has more recently become the major spokesman for the government on issues relating to NRMs. These issues have also been attended to and deliberated in Parliament.

In an official 1979 government response to parliamentary questions posed about NRMs, the deeper causes of conversion to deviant perspectives are touched upon (Deutcher Bundestag, 1979). Dissension from traditional social institutions is seen, above all, as the result of a general flight from reality combined with societal rejection. Other factors of importance are considered to be existential uncertainty, anxiety towards the future, the incapacity to deal with pressure to achieve, and the failure to resolve mental and social conflicts adequately. The deeper roots, according to the government, lie in deficient socialization processes leading to identity confusion.

The answers submitted to the Parliament reflect a clear bias permeated by anti-cult ideology. An American anticult psychiatrist's ideas are employed (as the only professional mentioned) in several instances to describe the recruitment methods of NRMs and the concomitant consequences for a member's personality development. Various governmental studies (e.g., Foster Report in England, Australian Parliament Report, and U.S. Congress Reports) and court decisions (e.g., French conviction of L. R. Hubbard and a 1978 report from the state of New York on the Children of God) are discussed to show that there is an international consensus on the overly apparent dangers of NRMs. Only studies and decisions are mentioned that condemn NRMs (often in strong terms).

In 1980 the Ministry for Youth, Family, and Health released a twenty-three page document entitled, "Jugendreligionen in der

Bundesrepublik Deutschland" (new religious movements in West Germany). It addressed the phenomenon of NRMs and eventual courses of action by the German government. The Ministry's role in the conflict between the government and NRMs is circumscribed in the document's preface: "The Minister for Youth, Family, and Health has, in accordance with the provisions of the constitution, the duty to warn about dangers which threaten young people—there is an anchored-down protection herein of Youth and Family" (p. 3). An argument outside of the religious domain is thus used to justify involvement.

Contained in the report are explicit warnings regarding the practices of several NRMs. Again, the flight from reality paradigm is accentuated: "The federal government considers the turning to NRMs to be a form of this flight from reality" (p. 5). Furthermore, one gets the impression, when reading this and the earlier document, that we are dealing with young people who could not cope with the pressures and realities of everyday life, and have consequently suffered a mental despair, only to be snatched up by manipulative cults.

In sharp contrast to the Dutch government report which rejects the validity of arguments that NRMs pose a serious threat to the mental health of their members, the German government espouses a deep concern for the mental welfare of members. The 1980 document states that those who are engaged in the therapeutic treatment of "sect-damaged" individuals have shown that only those persons with a strong ego can leave a group without injury. Often psycho-therapeutic, psychiatric, or medical aid is necessary, the document claims. The line of thinking here coincides with that of the Cottrell report.

Although the German government, in its report, concludes that a general prohibition of NRMs is not realizable, it does vow to disseminate information on NRMs and continue to place their activities under surveillance in order to judge the validity of complaints made that such groups violate German law. In an attempt to avoid the issue of religious freedom, the government has concentrated on other channels of operation: criminal law, civil law, and tax law. In this area, the various non-religious organizations associated with NRMs are especially vulnerable.

In 1982 the federal government again officially responded to questions pertaining to NRMs (Deutscher Bundestag, 1982). On this occasion the response was somewhat low key, perhaps due to a period of several years characterized by the absence of serious incidents involving NRMs. The confidence in the potential destructive aspects of NRMs for one's personality appears again, but it seems weakened. Instead of stating in 1980 that in many cases post-cult help is needed, the government claims: "In sporadic cases, serious crises of mental damage are the result (of 'cult' membership)" (p. 4). The Cottrell report and its aftermath (Richardson, 1993b) could serve to reinforce anxieties and hostility toward NRMs.

Some federal states in the former West Germany have been even more negative about NRMs than the German federal government. The state of Rheinland-Pfalz, in its 1980 report on the "so-called new youth-religions," carries the title: "Youth in Destructive Religious Groups." This staunch rejection clearly has a lot to do with the close relationship between religion (not so much church) and state in the federal states that boast a CDU/CSU (Christian Democratic) absolute majority. Both Protestants and Catholics have opposed NRMs and pressured the politicians in the (conservative) Christian CDU/CSU parties to confront this issue and take a stance. The CSU has adopted a position that attacks NRMs and asks governments to approach NRMs aggressively.

Conclusions

New religious movements in Western Europe and America, although serving similar clientele, have developed considerably differently. Different historical and societal conditions have meant that NRMs within the European context have been somewhat less significant as cultural phenomena, although they are not without interest to social scientists, policymakers, and others.

The reactions of the public and governments within the selected European nations examined herein has differed markedly, with the Netherlands taking the more tolerant view so far, followed by England, France, and Germany in that rough order. After some earlier efforts to exert more control, English authorities seem to have generally "taken a walk." French authorities may be developing a more aggressive policy toward NRMs, if recent actions concerning the Family of Love are an indication. However, that episode is too recent to assess properly. In Germany there has been a more pervasive attitude of control shown toward NRMs, although the demands of German unification have forced such concerns into the background for the time being. What will happen in the future is uncertain.

Superimposed on the individual nations' policies now, of course, is the overwhelming impetus toward European unification. Thus there may well be significant cross-national policies developed concerning NRMs. The Cottrell Report was an opening gambit in this area, but it has been followed by other significant developments (Richardson, 1993b). Only time will tell how these broad European concerns interact with the policies and practices of the individual nations. However, it is worth noting that two major powers in the European unification effort, Germany and France, seem to be quite receptive to a more negative posture toward minority religions, a situation that should give pause for thought to those who favor more flexibility and freedom for NRMs.

NOTES

1. Remarks made on August 23, 1984 during campaign speech at a "Prayer Breakfast" in Dallas, Texas attended by 19,000 people, most of them fundamentalist and conservative ministers.

2. The "American Dream," of course, is about the enterprising individual who casts off his social shackles and in his own manner rises to individual greatness and prosperity. See Richardson, Kilbourne, and van Driel (1988) for a discussion of the way this focus on individualism has related to the rise of NRMs.

3. This lends further evidence to the observation that it is the disaffected youth of highly industrialized societies that constitute the major target populations of new religious movements.

4. The influx of foreign minority groups launched a racist party into Parliament over a decade ago and evoked widespread negative sentiment towards ethnic minorities. Also, empirical studies by Boverkerk (1978) uncovered overt ethnic hostilities among the Dutch public and cast doubt on Bagley's findings.

5. This discussion will focus on what used to be West Germany, in part because of the limited history of the unified country and also because of less available information about NRMs in what used to be East Germany.

TABLE 1. Number of Active Members in New Religious Movements in Sweden, West Germany, France, Britain, the Netherlands and the U.S.A.

	Sweden Pop. 8,310,000	West Germany Pop. 61,700,000	France Pop. 54,200,000	Britain Pop. 56,100,000	The Netherlands Pop. 14,300,000	U.S.A. Pop. 226,504,825
Divine Light Mission	250[a]	500-600[b]		150[f]	150[g]	1000[f]
International Society for Krishna Consciousness	50[a]	80-100[b]		<500[f]	25[g]	4000-5000[i]
Transcendental Meditation (no. of teachers)		1000[b]		Approx. <200[f]	240[g]	
Bhagwan	64[a]	900[d]		Approx. 200[f]	2000[g]	
Ananda Marga	35[a]	200[d]		30[f]	30[g]	2000[i]
Unification Church		500[b]		<700[f]	80[g]	2000-7000[i]
Scientology Church		300-400[d]	1000[e]	500[f]	80[g]	
Children of God		*[b]		<1000[f]	*[g]	Approx. 200[i]
TOTAL			**30,000[c]**		**300-900[h]**	

* Nears zero
a. Nordquist, 1982
b. Mildenberger, in Schnabel, 1982
c. Deutscher Bundestag, 1979
d. Deutscher Bundestag, 1982
e. Cottrell Report, 1983
f. Barker, 1983, 1989
g. Schnabel, 1982
h. This figure includes UC, HK, Scientology, C of G, and DLM
i. Richardson, 1983

REFERENCES

Adams, R. L. and Fox, R. J., 1972. "Mainlining Jesus: The New Trip," *Society,* vol. 9(4), pp. 50-56.

Anthony, D., 1991. "Religious Movements and Brainwashing Litigation: Evaluating Key Testimony," in T. Robbins and D. Anthony, eds., *In God We Trust,* 2nd ed. New Brunswick NJ: Transaction Books, pp. 295-344.

Bagley, C., 1973. *The Dutch Plural Society: A Comparative Study in Race Relations.* Oxford University Press.

Barker, E., 1983. "New Religious Movements in Britain: The Context and the Membership," *Social Compass,* vol. 30(1), pp. 22-48.

------, 1984a. "The British Right to Discriminate," *Society,* vol. 21(4), pp. 35-41.

------, 1984b. *The Making of a Moonie.* Oxford: Basil Blackwell.

------, 1989. *New Religious Movements: A Practical Introduction.* London: Her Majesty's Stationary Office.

Beckford, J. A., 1981. "Cults, Controversy, and Control: A Comparative Analysis of the Problems Posed by New Religious Movements in the Federal Republic of Germany and France," *Sociological Analysis,* vol. 43(3), pp. 249-264.

------, 1983a. "The Public Response to the New Religious Movements in Britain," *Social Compass,* vol. 30(1), pp. 49-62.

------, 1983b. "The Cult Problem in Five Countries: The Social Construction of Religious Controversy," in E. Barker, ed., *Of Gods and Men.* Macon GA: Mercer University Press, pp. 195-214.

------. 1985. *Cult Controversies.* London: Tavistock.

Bedford, J. and Levasseur, M., 1986. "New Religious Movements in Western Europe," in J. Beckford, ed., *New Religious Movements and Rapid Social Change.* London: Sage, pp. 29-54.

Bellah, R., 1976. "The New Religious Consciousness and the Crisis of Modernity," in C. Glock and R. Bellah, eds., *The New Religious Consciousness.* Berkeley: University of California Press, pp. 333-352.

Bird, F. and Reimer, B., 1982. "Participation Rates in New Religious Movements," *Journal for the Scientific Study of Religion,* vol. 21(1), pp. 1-14.

Bovenkerk, F., 1978. *Omdat zij anders zijn: Patronen van Rassendiscriminatie in Nederland.* Boom: Meppel.

Bromley, D., 1983. "Conservatorships and Deprogramming: Legal and Political Aspects," in D. Bromley and J. Richardson, eds., *The Brainwashing/Deprogramming Controversy.* New York: Edwin Mellen, pp. 267-293.

Bromley, D. and Richardson, J., 1983. *The Brainwashing/Deprogramming Controversy.* New York: Edwin Mellen Press.

Bundesminster for Jugend, Familie und Gesundheit, 1980. *Jugendrelilgionen in der Bundesrepublik Deutschland.* Bonn.

Cottrell, R., 1983. "The Influence of the New Religious Movements Within the European Community." Draft Working Document prepared for the European Parliament Committee on Youth, Culture, Education, Information, and Sport.

Derks, F., and Lans, J. van der, 1982. "The Abortive Birth of a Destructive Cult" Unpublished paper, Nijmegen, The Netherlands.

Deutscher Bundestag, 1979. *Neuere Glaubend und Weltanschauungsgemeinshaften (sogennannte Jugendsekten).* Antwort der Bundesregierung, Bonn.

Eister, A. W., 1974. "Culture Crises and New Religious Movements: A Paradigmatic Statement of a Theory of Cults," in I. Zaretsky and M. Leone, eds., *Religious Movements in Contemporary America.* Princeton NJ: Princeton University Press.

Galanter, M., 1978. "The Relief Effect: A Sociobiological Model for Neurotic Distress and Large Group Therapy," *American Journal of Psychiatry,* vol. 135, pp. 588-591.

------, 1980. "Psychological Induction into a Large Group: Findings from a Modern Religious Sect," *American Journal of Psychiatry,* vol. 137. pp. 1574-1579.

Goddijn, W., and Van Tillo, G., eds., 1979. *Opnieuw: God in Nederland (Onderzoek naar godsdienst en kerkelijkheiingested in opdracht van KRO en weekblad De Tijd).* Amsterdam: De Tijd.

Hardin, B., 1983. "Aspects des Nouveau Mouvements Religieux en Allemange Federal," *Social Compass,* vol. 30(1), pp. 13-32.

Hunter, J. D., 1983. "The New Religions: Demodernization and the Protest Against Modernity," in B. Wilson, ed., *The Social Impact of New Religious Movements.* New York: Rose of Sharon Press, pp. 1-19.

Kilbourne, B., 1986. "Equity of Exploitation: The Case of the Unification Church," *Review of Religious Research,* 28(2), pp. 143-150.

Kilbourne, B. and Richardson, J., 1984. "Psychotherapy and New Religions in a Pluralistic Society," *American Psychologist,* vol. 39(3), pp. 237-251.

------, 1986. "Communalization of Religious Experience," *Journal of Community Psychology,* vol. 14, pp. 206-212.

Kuner, W., 1979. *You Gotta be a Baby Oder Happiness Flutsch. Eine Untersuching zu Character, Genese und Sozialen Ursachen einer den Sogenannten 'Jugendrelihionen', Zugeordneten Sozialen Beewegung der Kinder Gottes (Familie der Liebe).* Tubingen: Unveroffentlichte MA-Arbeit.

------, 1983. "New Religious Movements and Mental Health," in E. Barker, ed., *Of Gods and Men.* Macon GA: Mercer University Press, pp. 255-263.

Lans, J. van der, 1981. *Volgelingen v.d. Goeroe.* Utrecht: Ambo.

Lans, J. van der, and Derks, F., 1982. "Reakties in Nederland," *Jeugd en Samenleving* 3, pp. 213-216.

Lasch, C., 1979. *The Culture of Narcissism.* London: Abacus.

LeMoult, J., 1983. "Deprogramming Members of Religious Sects," in D. Bromley and J. Richardson, eds., *The Brainwashing/ Deprogramming Controversy.* New York: Edwin Mellen, pp. 234-257.

Lewis, J., 1993. *From the Ashes: Making Sense of Waco.* Savage, MD: Rowman and Littlefield Publishers.

Lofland, J., 1978. *Doomsday Cult* (Revised Edition). New York: Irvington.

Lofland, J. and Kkonvod, N., 1981. "Conversion Motifs," *Journal for the Scientific Study of Religion,* vol. 20(4), pp. 373-385.

Loon, T. V., 1981. "De Nieuwe Onmaatschappelijken: Jongvolwassenen als een Sociaal Verschijnsel." Unpublished doctoral dissertation: University of Nijmegen.

Los Angeles Times, 1983. November 17, 1983.

Luckmann, T., 1967. *The Invisible Religion.* New York: The MacMillan Company.

Morin, J. P., 1979. "Le Viol Physchique: Un Projet de Definition Juridique," *Revue d'etudes et d'informations de la Gendarmerie Nationale,* 120, p. 33.

Newsweek, 1979. "Europe's Rising Cults," May 7, 1979, pp. 100-101.

New York Times, 1972. February 24, 1972, pp. 2, 4.

New York Times, 1984. "Uruguay is Fertile Soil for Moon Church Money," Feb. 16, 1984, p. 3.

Nicholi, A., 1974. "A New Dimension of the Youth Culture," American Journal of Psychiatry, vol. 13(4), pp. 396-401.

Nordquist, T., 1982. "New Religious Movements in Sweden," in E. Barker, ed., New Religious Movements: A Perspective for Understanding Society. New York: Edwin Mellen, pp. 173-180.

Peasle, A. J., ed., 1974a. "Convention for the Protection of Human Rights and Fundamental Freedoms," in International Governmental Organizations Constitutional Documents, Part I. The Hague: Martinus Nijhoff, pp. 354-373.

------, 1974b. "Treaty Establishing the European Economic Community," in International Governmental Organizations Constitutional Documents, Part I. The Hague: Martinus Nijhoff, pp. 457-543.

Psychology Today, 1983. "Moonset in Brazil," April, 1983, p. 86.

Richardson, J., 1978. Conversion Careers. Beverly Hills CA: Sage.

------, 1980. "Conversion Careers," Society, vol. 17(3), pp. 47-50.

------, 1983. "New Religious Movements in the United States: A Review," Social Compass, vol. 30(1), pp. 85-110.

------, 1984. "Conversion to New Religions: Secularization of Reenchantment?," in P. Hammond, ed., The Sacred in a Post-Secular Age. Berkeley CA: University of California Press, pp. 14-121.

------, 1985a. "The Active vs. Passive Convert: Paradigm Conflict in Conversion/Recruitment Research," Journal for the Scientific Study of Religion, vol. 24(2), pp. 163-179.

------, 1985b. "The 'Deformation' of New Religious Groups: Impacts of Societal and Organization Factors," in T. Robbins, ed., Cults, Culture, and the Law. Chico CA: Scholars Press, pp. 163-175.

------, 1985c. "Psychological and Psychiatric Studies of Participation in New Religions," in L. Brown, ed., New Perspectives in Psychology of Religion. Pergamon Press, pp. 209-223.

------, 1990. "Clinical and Personality Assessment of Participants in Minority Religions." Paper presented at conference on "Psychopathology and Religion," Institute for the Study of Religion, Jagiellonian University, Cracow, Poland.

------, 1991. "Cult/Brainwashing Cases and Freedom of Religion," *Journal of Church and State,* vol. 33, pp. 55-74.

------, 1992. "Public Opinion and the Tax Evasion Trial of Reverend Moon," *Behavioral Sciences and the Law,* vol. 10, pp. 53-63.

------, 1993a. "Child Abuse Accusations and Social Control of New Religions." Paper presented at biannual meeting of the International Society for the Sociology of Religion, Budapest.

------, 1993b. "New Religions, the New Europe, and the United States: A Comparative Convergence of Control." Paper presented at conference on "New Religions and the New Europe," London School of Economics.

Richardson, J. and Davis, R., 1983. "Experiential Fundamentalism: Revisions of Orthodoxy in the Jesus Movement," *Journal of the American Academy of Religion,* vol. LI(3), pp. 397-425.

Richardson, J., Kilbourne, B., and van Driel, B., 1987. "Alternative Religions and Economic Individualism," in M. Lynn, ed., *Research in the Social Sciences of Religion.* JAI Press.

Richardson, J., Stewart, M. and Simmonds, R., 1979. *Organized Miracles.* New Brunswick NJ: Transaction Books.

Robbins T., Anthony, D., and Richardson, J., 1978. "Theory and Research on Today's 'New Religions'." *Sociological Analysis,* vol. 39(2), pp. 95-122.

Robbins, T. and Bromley D., 1992. "Social Experimentation and the Significance of American New Religions," *Research in the Social Scientific Study of Religion,* vol. 4, pp. 1-28, JAI Press.

San Francisco Chronicle, 1984. "Moon's Church Pours Millions Into Uruguay," Feb. 18, 1984, p. 10.

------, 1984. "Indonesians Quiz Two in Sex Cult," March 6, 1984, p. 4.

Schnabel, P., 1982. *Tussen Stigma en Charisma: Niewe Religieuze Bewegingen en Geestelijke Volksgezondheid.* Deventer: van Loghum Slaterus.

Shupe, Anson, and Bromley, D., 1980. *The New Vigilantes.* Beverly Hills CA: Sage.

Shupe, A., Hardin, B., and Bromley, D., 1983. "A Comparison of Anti-cult Movements in the United States and West Germany," in E. Barker, ed., *Of Gods and Men.* Macon GA: Mercer University Press, pp. 177-193.

Sieber, G. M., 1980. *Jugendsekten: Zur Evaluierung des Beratung-und Rehabilitionsbedarfs Betroffener.* Munchen: Poko-Institut.

Straus, R., 1976. "Changing Oneself: Seekers and the Creative Transformation of Life Experience," in J. Lofland, ed., *Doing Social Life.* New York: Wiley, pp. 252-272.

Subcommissie Sektn, 1984. *Onderzoek Betreffende Sekten.* Den Haag.

Time, 1984. "Cuckoo Cult," May 7, 1984, p. 44.

Update, 1984. June, 1984, pp. 15-16.

U.S. News and World Report, 1983, December 12, 1983, p. 22.

------, 1984, January 12, 1984, p. 22.

------, 1984. April 30, 1984, pp. 82-83.

van Driel, B. and van Belzen, J., 1990. "The Downfall of Rajneeshpuram in the Print Media: A Cross-National Study," *Journal for the Scientific Study of Religion,* vol. 29(1), pp. 76-90.

van Driel, B. and Richardson, J., 1988a. "Cult vs. Sect: Research Note on the Characterization of New Religions in the American Print Media," *Sociological Analysis,* vol. 49(2), pp. 171-183.

------, 1988b. "Print Media Coverage of New Religious Movements," *Journal of Communication,* vol. 38, pp. 377-61.

Washington Post, 1984. "Britons See Themselves as Prejudiced, Class-bound," May 30, 1984, pp. A21-A22.

Wilson, B., 1976. *Contemporary Transformation of Religion,* Oxford: Oxford University Press.

Wurfbain, J.S., 1981. "Godsdienstige Seketen vanuit een Juridisch Iig Bckeken." Unpublished doctoral paper presented at the University of Nijmegen.

Wuthnow, R., 1986. "Religious Movements and Counter Movements in North America," in J. Beckford, ed., *New Religious Movements and Rapid Social Change.* London: Sage, pp. 1-28.

CHAPTER VIII

ANTI-CULT AND COUNTER-CULT MOVEMENTS IN ITALY

Massimo Introvigne

The media in Italy has called attention to the existence of movements against so-called religious "cults." Although these movements are not particularly prominent, they do offer an interesting perspective on Italy's reaction to minority or alternative religious movements. The first part of this paper will discuss anti-cult and counter-cult movements in Italy, starting from a description of the Italian religious background. The second part offers a theoretical model introducing a typology of different possible anti-cult and counter-cult movements. The typology will be applied in the third part to the anti-cult and counter-cult movements presently active in Italy. Finally, the fourth part will discuss the chances of success for the movements against the "cults" in Italy.

THE ITALIAN BACKGROUND

Religions in Italy

Until recently, religious pluralism has been practically unknown in Italy. Even at present more than 90% of all Italians are baptized in the Roman Catholic Church (Garelli, 1991:63). Different surveys agree that roughly one third of all Italians (around 30-31%) are considered active Roman Catholics and attend church with some regularity (Garelli, 1991:58). Although this figure demonstrates that active Roman Catholics are a minority in Italy, it compares favorably with other EEC countries with a strong Catholic tradition, like France (where active Catholics are around 12%) and Spain (Fondazione Agnelli, 1991). The recent history of the Roman Catholic Church in Italy can only be understood against the background of its relationship with the State. The unification of Italy was accomplished by a minority deeply imbued with the ideas of the Enlightenment, which was actively opposed by the Church. After Italy was unified in 1861 under the Savoy Dynasty, and Rome (then capital of the Papal States) was conquered by the Italian army in 1870, the Church regarded the newly founded Kingdom of Italy as an enemy. Kings were routinely excommunicated, and Roman Catholics were forbidden (under the rule of *non expedit,* "it is not appropriate") from voting and being candidates for public office. Thus, Italy became a strange democracy in which only a tiny minority voted or ran for public office. Notwithstanding the conflict with the State, the Church remained quite strong, but among lower classes it was soon challenged by the spectacular success of a new enemy of the liberal State, Marxist socialism. Middle-class fear of rising socialism was not the last reason for the success of Mussolini's fascism, who seized power in 1922. Although Mussolini was originally anti-clerical (in his youth he had authored pornographic novels which graphically depicted Roman Catholic Cardinals making love with young girls), he included in his program the solution of the "Catholic question" and entered with Pope Pius XI into the Treaty of the Lateran in 1929. Under the Treaty, the Church recognized the Italian State, and the Italian State in turn recognized the Vatican and agreed to assume a number of undertakings toward the Church which would be guaranteed by international (not domestic) law. Although the Treaty was renegotiated and modified in 1984, and is now less favorable to the Church, it is still in force today.

After the demise of fascism, Catholics were free to participate in elections, and in the first democratic elections of 1948 the Christian Democrat Party—with substantial Church (and U.S.A.) backing—won an absolute majority against the communist-socialist coalition. The Christian Democrat Party (Democrazia Cristiana) has been the main partner of all government coalitions in Italy from 1948 to date. Although the Democrazia Cristiana has been often dominated by liberal Catholics and at times has been in trouble with the Church, it has been consistently supported by Bishops in all general elections. According to recent sociological surveys 91% of the Christian Democrat voters are active Roman Catholics (Garelli, 1991:100). Roman Catholicism has continued to be strong in the middle and lower-middle class, whereas the social elite who supported the prefascist anti-clerical State has remained largely alienated from the Church. The lower classes of society have for years adopted communism as a substitute for religion.

Even after the collapse of Eastern communism in 1989-1990, the two Italian communist parties (the hard line Rifondaziona Comunista and the more moderate Partito Democratico della Sinistra) could still count on roughly one fourth of the Italian votes (Christian Democrats poll one-third), although corruption, scandals, and the emergence of new political parties (particularly the so-called "leagues"—"Leghe"— expressing a regional nationalism in the North) may significantly change the political geography in years to come.

Against this background, the presence of non-Catholic religions in Italy has always been almost insignificant. Less than 2%, and possibly less than 1% of the Italian population follows a religion other than Roman Catholicism (Garelle, 1991; Fondazione Agnelli, 1992). Roughly half of the non-Catholics are either Moslem or Jewish. Mainline Protestantism is represented for the most part by Waldensians, pre-Reformation Protestants who were persecuted in their native France and eventually settled in the valleys of North-Western Piedmont. In recent years, they have reached a working agreement with the Methodists. Other mainline Protestant denominations—Anglicans, Lutherans, Baptists—only count a few thousand followers in Italy. Efforts carried out under the Savoy Dynasty in the nineteenth century to "import" Protestantism into Italy to counter the influence of the Roman Church were largely unsuccessful, although occasionally prominent figures emerge in academia, politics, or science who are of Protestant background. Anti-clerical liberalism in Italy found its religious expression in Freemasonry, although the largest Italian masonic body ("Grande Oriente"), long excluded from mainline international Freemasonry for its extreme anti-clericalism, was readmitted into communion with the United Grand Lodge of England in 1972 and started downplaying its once typical anti-clerical theme. The Roman Catholic Church still does not allow its members to join Freemasonry. (Although the new Canon Law Code of 1983 no longer mentions membership in Freemasonry as a ground for excommunication, a declaration by the Congregation for the Doctrine of Faith, published the same day the new Canon Law Code came into force, confirmed that Freemasons are to be excluded from Catholic sacraments.)

"New Religions" in Italy

The word "cult"—that literally translates as "culto"—in its current English meaning is unknown in Italy outside of the anti-cult subculture.

The term that is generally used, and regarded as derogatory, is "sect" ("setta"). Traditionally, "sect" in the language of the Roman Catholic Church and in the Italian language denoted any religious denomination or group other than the Roman Catholic Church (see Palazzini, 1968). It is now generally agreed, even in the media, that Judaism, Islam, and some mainline Protestant bodies, including the Waldensians, are not "sects," but in popular language one still hears "Protestant sects" mentioned as such. A survey carried out in the Turin area in 1990 showed that the general public is completely unfamiliar with the words "cults," "new religions," and "new religious movements"; it is, on the other hand, more familiar with the term "sects." Some 80% of those interviewed thought that "sect" was something "bad" or "negative," and 80% mentioned Jehovah's Witnesses as one "sect" they were familiar with; another 14% indicated the Mormons and 1% mentioned Scientology (Introvigne and Ambrosio, 1990). In general literature—and even in some scholarly historical or sociological literature—there is no difference, in Italy, between nineteenth-century "sects" such as the Jehovah's Witnesses or the Mormons and twentieth-century new religious movements such as Scientology or the Unification Church. This distinction has been introduced only recently in some scholarly literature but has not been generally accepted even by academics. The Roman Catholic Church is now realizing that "sect" is a derogatory word and proposes to substitute it with "new religious movements." In recent documents, Catholic authorities have however proposed a large typology of "new religious movements," including "new religious movements of Protestant origin" (non-mainline Protestantism, particularly Evangelical and Pentecostal) and "new religious movements of Christian background" but whose inclusion in Christianity is doubtful, such as Jehovah's Witnesses and the Mormons (Arinze, 1991; see Introvigne, 1991).

The press liberally mentions that there are in Italy 600 "sects" (a word that serves in the Italian media all the purposes served in English by the word "cults"), and the Center for Studies on New Religions (CESNUR) is aware of at least 500 groups. However, the media often fails to explain that most of these groups have less than one hundred members. The only "sect" with a very significant success in Italy is Jehovah's Witnesses. In 1992 it counted 196,013 members active in witnessing and 362,167 participants to its yearly celebration of the Lord's Supper (*La Torre di Guardia*, 1993). Assemblies of God, the largest Pentecostal group (now not unanimously regarded as a "sect" and sometimes included in the mainline), has roughly 100,000 members, concentrated in Southern Italy and particularly in Sicily. Mormons number two stakes and 16,000 members (*Deseret News,* 1993). For all the other groups, statistics are normally controversial (see Barker, 1992) but very few of them have more than 1,000 committed or "real" members. Although thousands of people have attended a Scientology or a Transcendental Meditation course, less than 1,000 stay in touch regularly with each movement. There are less than 500 followers of the Unification Church (Introvigne, 1987; Ambrosio, 1987) and there have never been more than 600. The largest new religious movements—with a national following of around 1,000—appear to be Sahaya Yoga, the Sathya Sai Baba movement (whose Italian leader is Antonio Craxi, brother of the former Prime Minister and leader of the Socialist Party, Bettino Craxi), Rajneeshees, Universal Life (followers of the German prophetess Gabriele Wittek), Scientology, Hare Krishna, and the Japanese new religions Soka Gakkai and Sukyo Mahikari. At least one Italian communal group is also worth mentioning (and has been particularly targeted by anti-cult activities): Damanhur, a magic-esoterical community of 300 members (600 including the satellite communities), established by the Italian guru Oberto Airaudi in the hills near Turin in 1971. A large number of esoterical-New Age groups exist, but none of them is particularly prominent and, as in other countries, New Age is more interesting as a network and a milieu. Rumors of large widespread Satanic activities have been circulated from time to time by the press, particularly about the city of Turin, but they are largely urban legends, although four small Satanic churches do exist in Turin, Bologna, and Rome, each one with a few dozens of members (see Introvigne, 1990).

The picture would not be complete without recognizing that, although new religious *movements* have been relatively unsuccessful in Italy (with the exception of Jehovah's Witnesses, if we decide to call them a "new" movement), new religious *beliefs* have gained much more widespread acceptance. Reliable surveys indicate that more than 30% of the Italians (Garelli, 1990:72) and more than 30% of the young people in the high schools (CESNUR, 1993) believe in reincarnation, notwithstanding efforts by the Roman Catholic Church to point out that this belief is not compatible with Roman Catholicism (Commissione Teologica Internazionale, 1992).

ANTI-CULT AND COUNTER-CULT
MOVEMENTS: A THEORETICAL MODEL

A large body of sociological literature exists concerning the so-called "anti-cult movement," both in the United States and internationally. Most students of the anti-cult movement agree that this movement consists of at least two separate and conflicting sub-movements, one secular and the other sectarian. The *secular* anti-cult movement insists on strong legal and police measures to undermine the "cults," which they view as delusions perpetrated by unscrupulous characters—gurus, preachers, and self-styled prophets—who exploit the weak, the young, and the gullible for power and money. The key feature—and the standard slogan—of the secular anti-cult movement is that it only discusses deeds, not creeds. It is not interested in whether any particular religious persuasion is true or false; it claims to be only interested in *behavior* which it regards as harmful to individuals, families, or the society at large. The secular anti-cult movement wants to free people *from* "cults;" it does not presume to tell them what religious or philosophical ideas they should join once they have left the "cult." A fraction of the mental health profession has added fuel to the fire of the secular anti-cult movement by advancing the controversial theory of "brainwashing." Pop psychology has contributed the still more dubious theory that "subliminal messages" are hidden everywhere, from rock music to apparently innocent books.

The *religious* anti-cult movement disagrees with almost every priority espoused by its secular counterpart, and—as I have suggested (see Introvigne, 1993)—should perhaps instead be called a "*counter*-cult movement." Its proponents maintain that the borders between belief and behavior are less clearly marked than the anti-cult movement would prefer to believe. Counter-cultists insist that false belief—or heresy—breaks the law of God, and this is at least as dangerous as any behavior contrary to the laws of men (see Aagaard, 1991). A "cult," from this point of view, is not primarily a money-making enterprise but is defined as a heresy. One problem with this perspective, of course, is that each religious persuasion has its own definition of heresy and hence of "cult," and counter-cult movements of Protestant and Catholic origin are surely different in many respects. Another difference between the counter-cult movement and the secular anti-cult movement is that counter-cultists are obviously not happy when someone simply leaves the "cult" unless he or she is converted to the "true" faith.

A sub-typology may be introduced by distinguishing between a rationalist and a post-rationalist brand of both anti-cult and counter-cult movements. Why do "cults" continue to grow? Explanations may be quite different. In the "rationalist" phase, the main explanation is that human beings are indeed gullible, and it is a fact of life that they become victims of clever frauds, particularly in religion. Anti-cultists emphasize the secular features of the fraud (e.g., "bogus" miracles) and the counter-cultists its religious elements (e.g., "manipulating" the Scriptures), but the fraud explanation remains prominent. The post-rationalist explanations of why "cults" succeed, on the other hand, invest "cult" leaders with superhuman powers and abilities. For the religious post-rationalist counter-cultists, "cult" leaders are in contact with Satan or the occult. For their secular counterparts of the anti-cult movement, "cultists" have the more-than-human power of "brainwashing" their victims; but, as it has been noted, "brainwashing" in some anti-cult theories appears as something magical, the modern version of the evil eye (Hargrove, 1983:303). The post-rationalist phase of the sectarian counter-cult movement has been reinforced by the "spiritual warfare" theories. The "spiritual warfare" movement, born in the 1970s and 1980s in California Evangelical and Pentecostal circles, gained international prominence in 1986 when the best-selling novel *This Present Darkness,* by Frank Peretti (1986), was published. By 1991, one and a half million copies of the novel had been sold (Guelich, 1991).

Peretti's novel is about a battle fought through exorcisms and prayers by both humans and angels against devils, and against human beings who become "demonized" and promote a wide range of "cultic" ideas and behaviors, including Eastern "cults" and the New Age. After Peretti's success, the idea that "cults" are spread through "demonized" individuals has become common in Evangelical circles and in some Catholic circles heavily influenced by Evangelical and Pentecostal "demonization" theories.

Different possible attitudes about "cults" according to the model are represented in Figure 1.

	Anti-Cult	Counter-Cult
Rationalist	the religious opportunist as fraud	the "heretic" as fraud
Post-Rationalist	brainwashing	demonization in the context of "spiritual welfare"

Figure 1 - Different Explanations of Why "Cults" Succeed

I also believe that the well-known distinction proposed by Stark and Bainbridge (1986) between audience cults, client cults, and cult movements may be relevant for both anti-cult and counter-cult movements. Some crusaders against the "cults" only seek an *audience:* they write books, occasionally appear on television, but do not care to organize their followers. Others seek *clients,* offering a wide range of counseling services for a fee, from the extreme "deprogramming" to the more gentle "exit counseling." Finally, leaders of the crusade against the "cults" may decide to organize social *movements* with a newsletter, a hierarchy, or a close-knit system of beliefs and attitudes. Particularly when the movement against the "cults" belongs to the post-rationalist group it may exhibit the same features it attributes to "cults": "Many of the same arguments used against new religions can be plausibly made against the ACM [anti-cult movements] as well" (Kilbourne and Richardson, 1986:265). Some movements against the "cults" exhibit, in fact, a set of beliefs—primarily the belief in a widespread and mysterious "cult conspiracy"—that does not appear to be shared by the society at large. When members of these movements against the "cults" start regulating their life based on this set of beliefs they become a marginal group, devoted to and identified by persuasions regarded by the majority as bizarre and even deviant; they become—in their own sense of the word—"cults."

A SURVEY OF SOME ITALIAN MOVEMENTS

Rationalist Anti-Cult Movements

The basic paradigm of the rationalist anti-cult movement is fraud, perpetrated by religious opportunists in order to make money at the expense of the gullible. The most typical rationalist anti-cult movements are those of the "professional skeptics" whose aim is to "debunk" the claims made for religious miracles and psychic phenomena. Although the existence of professional skeptics is at least as old as psychical research and spiritualism (stage magicians, for example, took pleasure early in the nineteenth century in showing that they were able to replicate the phenomena of the spiritualist mediums), currently the most influential group of skeptics in the international anti-cult scene is the U.S.A.-based Committee for the Scientific Investigation of Claims of the Paranormal (CSICOP), publisher of the widely read magazine *Skeptical Inquirer* (see Melton, Clark and Kelly, 1991:105-114). In Italy an organization very similar has been established under the name of CICAP (Comitato Italiano de Controllo delle Affermazioni sul Paranormale, or Italian Committee to Control the Claims of the Paranormal). Although administratively independent, CICAP emphasizes its connection with CSICOP. The main spokesman for CICAP is TV journalist Piero Angela, who has for years written books and produced TV shows against the paranormal. He has been successful in enlisting the aid of popular writers, such as the comic novelist (and amateur philosophy historian) Luciano De Crescenzo, and of famous scientists, such as Italian Nobel Price laureates Carlo Rubbia and Rita Levi Montalcini, as well as astrophysical Margherita Hack (who was already well-known as a spokesperson for secular humanism). Imitating the *modus operandi* of CSICOP, its Italian counterpart has also obtained the help of stage magicians such as Victor Balli, who claims to have replicated more than one thousand phenomena usually presented as miracles or evidence for the supernatural by religious movements and psychic groups. CICAP has also tried to create a media event by offering a prize of $100,000 to anyone who may offer unimpeachable evidence of a "genuine" paranormal or miraculous event. It has been said that in the United States "as a popular movement and antiparanormal lobbying group, CSICOP has been a spectacular success" (Melton, Clark and Kelly, 1991:114). Compared to CSICOP, CICAP has been only a minor success but its yearly conference routinely attracts media attention and it has produced more than a hundred news clippings. Piero Angela remains a popular professional skeptic, but he was well-known for his TV programs even before founding CICAP.

We could select the treatment of "miracles" of Sathya Sai Baba—who enjoys considerable fame and notoriety in Italy—to illustrate the different attitude of different Italian movements against the "cults." CICAP has discussed the "miracles" of Sathya Sai Baba in a couple of its yearly conferences and has concluded that they are frauds. It has been stressed that there is nothing particularly "strange" in Sathya Sai Baba's miracles: a skilled stage magician would be able to replicate most of them, and there is no serious evidence for the others. They regard as gullible those scholars who have accepted some of the most strange facts of the guru from Puttaparthi as genuine (see, for example, Haraldsson, 1988), but in general these critics are not interested in an in-depth discussion of scholarly literature on the SAI Baba movement. In fact, CICAP has failed to produce any relevant scholarly literature. They think that it is more useful to publicize the names of the famous scientists in their Board to impress the popular media and rescue, if not the souls, then the pocketbooks of Italians "threatened" by the new religious movements and the paranormal. Recently CICAP—in an obvious illustration of the differences between anti-cult and counter-cult movements—has moved to attack the Evangelical and Catholic groups that see the influence of the Devil behind the new religious movements and some psychic phenomena of the New Age.

One of the groups crusading only against one specific religious movement could also be classified among the rationalist anti-cult movements. It is the Centro Studi sul Mormonismo (Center for Studies on Mormonism), established in 1992 in Siracusa, Sicily, by Sergio Caldarella. It would seem that this anti-Mormon group exhibits some features of the counter-cult movements. Caldarella writes mostly in Catholic magazines (see Caldarella, 1992) and tries to influence Catholic counter-cult groups such as GRIS. He also calls the American post-rationalist counter-cult writer Ed Decker (who certainly believes that Mormonism is the brain-child of the Devil) "one of the greatest world scholars of Mormonism" (Caldarella, n.d.:23). However, Caldarella is not himself a Roman Catholic; he is a liberal Jew who spent some years among the Mormons (now he claims only to study them). He is convinced that Joseph Smith was a fraud and that the main aim of Mormonism is making money. Caldarella claims that in Mormonism "88 out of 138 revelations" have "something to do with money," and that "Money is the true god of the Mormons" (Caldarella, n.d.:23). He even goes as far as to mention Arthur Conan Doyle's anti-Mormon novel (and his first novel with Sherlock Holmes) *A Study in Scarlet* as reliable evidence of the "criminal" nature of Mormonism and the State of Utah at large (Caldarella, n.d.:24). We could conclude that with Caldarella's Center—so far, largely a one-man show—we are confronted again with a secular anti-cult (rather than a religious counter-cult) movement, still of the "rationalist" group because the metaphor of brainwashing is almost never used.

The distinction between the different anti-cult and counter-cult attitudes is objective, not subjective. Thus, it may happen that Roman Catholic priests exhibit an anti-cult rather than a counter-cult attitude. This seems to be the case with Pier Angelo Gramaglia, a Catholic priest and professor of patrology in the Turin Seminary, who operates at the level of an audience anti-cult since he has not joined any of the organizations against the "cults" nor has he organized the readers of his books into a movement. Gramaglia makes it clear that he does *not* write against the "cults" to defend the Catholic faith; his enemy is rather the "sectarian struggle against rationalism, historical criticism, and the use of a scientific method in Biblical exegesis" (Gramaglia, 1992:4). From this position he attacks a considerable array of "cults" and "sects," from Mormons (Gramaglia, 1985) to the New Age (Gramaglia, 1992b). His vitriolic style—more often than not degenerating into insult—has compelled him to offer his most recent books as privately published. While, for some time, he found a public amused by his tirades against Jehovah's Witnesses or the Mormons, the number of his readers appear to be declining, and his frequent use in his name-calling of four-letter words and sexual insults has scandalized many fellow clergymen. One could imagine that Gramaglia is a very conservative Catholic priest, but he is, on the contrary, extremely liberal. He follows his own brand of liberation theology and sees in the "cults" an expression of anti-communism and of a reactionary attitude against science and the political left. Fanatically anti-American, Gramaglia sees social sciences (particularly produced in the United States) as objective allies of the "cults;" he has singled out particularly—in addition to this writer—sociologists Anson Shupe, David G. Bromley, and Eileen Barker as examples of the evils of sociology (Gramaglia, 1992:3, 100, 104). Gramaglia, as mentioned earlier, is a lonely and declining figure with little influence in the Italian anti-cult movement, and still less in the Catholic Church. He has attacked what he calls "Wojtylism" and popular Catholic forms of devotion to the Virgin Mary (Gramaglia, 1985b) as strongly as he attacks the "cults," and has called the present Pope a "demagogue" (Gramaglia, 1989:6). Gramaglia deserves mention here for the use the anti-cult (rather than the counter-cult) movement has made of some of his early books, and also because his case shows that occasionally Catholics are part of rationalist anti-cultism rather than of the more familiar Christian counter-cult movement.

Post-Rationalist Anti-cult Movements

Post-rationalist anti-cult movements are still secular rather than sectarian, but rely almost exclusively on brainwashing as a preferred explanation for the success of "cults." Particularly when their leaders are not mental health professionals, they tend to look at brainwashing as something mysterious and magical and, to some extent, parallel the attitude of post-rationalist counter-cultists who attribute the spread of "cults" to the Devil. It often happens that Italian movements against the cults heavily depend on an American counterpart. As CICAP depends on CSICOP, the only national post-rationalist anti-cult movement, ARIS (Associazione per la Ricerca e l'Informazione sulle Sette, or "Association for Research and Information on Cults") would probably not exist without inspiration and materials from CAN (Cult Awareness Network) and the American Family Foundation. ARIS was legally incorporated in 1987 by Ennio Malatesta, a Milan businessman whose wife and daughters had left home to join Scientology. (The wife, Maria Merlo, maintains that the real reason she left her husband was that she was mistreated and even beaten by him for reasons originally unconnected with Scientology.)

The name ARIS was obviously patterned after the already existing GRIS. However, while GRIS is a Catholic organization, ARIS emphasizes that it is "a secular group, in contact with similar organizations in Europe and the United States," that avoids to pass judgment on "matters of doctrine or theology" (ARIS, 1992:4). "Cults," for ARIS, are a "serious problem of mental health" due to the "sophisticated techniques of mind control" used by the new religious movements. These techniques are typically described as almost magical: "they are capable of working on *anyone,* even on those who may think they are immune" (ARIS, 1992:1). "Very few people," if any, join a "cult" voluntarily; "normally, joining a cult means only that a mind control operation has been successful" (ARIS, 1991:3). The literature of ARIS—consisting only of small flyers and pamphlets—is not remarkable, since it only repeats or translates material from American groups such as CAN and the AFF. The history of ARIS is, on the other hand, more interesting. The primary purpose which led Malatesta to establish ARIS was fighting Scientology. The vast majority of the first members were relatives of members of Scientology. ARIS obtained its most famous coup when, due in part to its activities and lobbying, District Attorney Ms. Guicla Mulliri of Milan in 1988, with a record 1,218-pages order of indictment, brought to trial a number of leading Italian Scientologists and ordered a number of Scientology branches throughout Italy provisionally closed. Malatesta trumpeted this success in Italy and in the world, became a media character and the guest on popular TV shows, and membership of ARIS rose—according to him—to 300 (other sources indicate that there were never more than 50 active members at any time).

ARIS went public in favor of deprogramming and invited deprogrammers such as Martin Faiers and Ted Patrick to Italy. A first deprogramming of a female Hare Krishna devotee (not organized by ARIS) had been comparatively successful: the deprogrammed girl testified in favor of the deprogrammers (including Martin Faiers) and the parents, who were found not guilty at trial. A second case of attempted deprogramming, where the victim had escaped, also failed to produce a conviction of Faiers. However, ARIS propaganda for deprogramming was received very coldly by the Catholic Church, and failed attempts to deprogram respectively another Krishna devotee and a female Scientologist created trouble for Martin Faiers in the Italian-speaking part of Switzerland (he was ultimately found guilty by the Court of Lugano) and for Ted Patrick in Monza. ARIS was named as heavily involved in the failed deprogramming attempt in Monza, but no charges were ever filed by the prosecutor, who seemed to regard Scientology as more dangerous than ARIS.

More important, disaster struck ARIS when in July 1991 a decision was rendered in the Milan trial against Scientologists. Not only ARIS was refused the position of a co-plaintiff in the trial, but the Court ruled that Scientology's activities per se are not illegal in Italy and overruled almost all the findings of the District Attorney Ms. Mulliri. Although the judges stated the opinion that they felt no sympathy for Scientology, and found some Scientologists individually guilty of minor offenses, they ruled that the very existence of Scientology and its typical activities are protected in Italy by freedom of religion and thought (Tribunale di Milano, 1991). The decision (appealed by both the District Attorney and the Scientologists) also acknowledged that many allegations of ARIS were simply not true.

ARIS was on the verge of collapse but was rescued by its very active group in the Venetian region (semi-autonomous and called ARIS-Veneto) who had decided to concentrate its operations not only against Scientology and other new religious movements but particularly against Jehovah's Witnesses. The president of ARIS-Veneto, Arturo Vascon, had written in 1984 a vitriolic book against Jehovah's Witnesses (Vascon, 1984). A Catholic attorney, Luciano Faraon, emerged as a prominent figure of ARIS-Veneto and was able to establish good relations with Catholic counter-cult groups (such as CIRS) and with local parish priests who had particular problems with Jehovah's Witnesses. ARIS and ARIS-Veneto still exist, although they are now hardly noticed by the media and their membership has declined. ARIS, in fact, managed to survive by significantly altering its targets and taking into account that the only really successful "alternative" religious movement in Italy is Jehovah's Witnesses. They have applied the rhetoric of brainwashing and mind control to Jehovah's Witnesses, but the use for a crusade against the Witnesses (obviously more popular in Italian Catholic circles) of material prepared in the U.S. against more recent new religious movements has not always been easy.

The Studio dei Culti Emergenti ("Study of Emerging Cults"), based in Rome, was created in 1984 by the attorney and professor of law at Camerino University Michele C. Del Re. Del Re was originally the principal lawyer working for ARIS, but abandoned Malatesta's organization when the latter became too openly involved with deprogramming. He also considered Mr. Malatesta personally as unmanageable. Del Re has published a scholarly book (Del Re, 1982) and a number of papers in legal journals (see, for example, Del Re, 1988b; Del Re, 1991) on problems of criminal law connected with what he calls "emerging cults" ("culti emergenti"). He also authored a popular book on "cults" in 1988 (Del Re, 1988). After the break with ARIS, Del Re's activity has been circumscribed to research and lobbying for an anti-cult law, while its organization has researched some small groups active in Italy.

Del Re was also a major participant in a conference that took place in 1989 in Forte dei Marmi, Tuscany, on mind control, organized by a group of mental health professionals (see Di Fiorino, 1990; Di Fiorino and Saviotti, 1991). The problem discussed in these scholarly debates is "plagio," a crime mentioned by article 603 of the Italian Criminal Code. According to American anti-cultist Michael D. Langone, the Italian word "plagio" has no "exact English equivalent" . . . "the closest thing in U.S. law to plagio is probably the concept of 'undue influence,' which is much more nuanced and flexible in its application than plagio, and is applicable in civil, not criminal, law" (Langone, 1992:10). In fact, "plagio" was often used by courts and popular press alike as synonymous for "brainwashing" or "mind control." Langone's review of the first volume of the proceedings of the conference held in Forte dei Marmi fails to clearly understand how the Italian legal system works. In fact, two different institutions have seen their name ambiguously translated as "Supreme Court." The first is the Court of Cassation ("Corte di Cassazione") that is, indeed, supreme as a Court of last resort in the interpretation of points of law. The second is the Constitutional Court ("Corte Costituzionale"), the only body which has the power to strike existing laws as being against the Constitution. It appears, thus, that the functions of the U.S. Supreme Court are carried out in Italy by two different bodies. While the decisions of the Court of Cassation could be and are reversed, the decisions of the Constitutional Court are irrevocable and perpetual, and the only way of changing them would be through an amendment to the Constitution voted by two thirds of the members of the Italian Parliament. The latter event never happened in Italian history.

On June 8, 1981 (Corte Constituzionale 1981) the Constitutional Court declared article 603 of the Criminal Code contrary to the Constitution and, as a consequence, eliminated it from Italian law. The constitutional decision of 1981 has had a crucial weight in the acquittal of Scientologists in Milan, and had been quoted in previous "cult" Court cases. The literature on "plagio" and on the 1981 decision in Italy is very large, and a review is outside our purposes here. All proposals for a law against the "cults"—such as those by Del Re—find as an obstacle very difficult to overcome the irrevocable Constitutional Court decision of 1981. Del Re has suggested a law forbidding the use of "psychagogic techniques" by any group. However, any such proposal has little chance of being approved in Italy, since the ruling of 1981 was based, first, on the idea that mental health sciences do not support the conclusion that it is possible to acquire complete control of the mind of another person without physical coercion (the latter being punished, of course, by other laws), and, second, that any attempt to define "plagio" or "brainwashing" in the law or by authors is so vague that the resulting formulations are threatening to the constitutionally protected freedoms of thought and religion. It thus appears that the Italian Constitutional Court had already decided in 1981—based on a debate completely unrelated to minority religions—most of the issues involved in the brainwashing controversy; and it had decided them contrary to the anti-cult movement. This fact notwithstanding, "plagio" remains a popular word in Italian anti-cult literature, and the purpose of post-rationalist anti-cult movements—that base their activities on the hypothesis of brainwashing—appears to be to revive something similar to the now defunct article 603 of the Criminal Code.

Rationalist Counter-Cult Movements

It might seem paradoxical to label North American Christian counter-cultist Walter Martin (1928-1989) as "rationalist." However, "rationalist" means in this context that "cults" are explained by Martin mostly through empirical elements (including false theology and heresy) rather than by relying principally or exclusively on the Devil's activities. "Rationalist" counter-cultists, as faithful and normally conservative Christians, of course believe in the personal existence of the Devil, and they do not deny that the Devil is pleased because of the success of the "cults." On the other hand, they think that an excessive interest in the Devil is unhealthy and typical of the "cults" themselves, and thus seek first alternative explanations.

As mentioned earlier, Italian Protestantism represents a small minority. Protestants, however, have been aware of new religious movements since the first attempts by Mormons and other groups to proselytize among Waldensians in the nineteenth century. Although no longer the prime targets of proselytization, Waldensians have published books criticizing Jehovah's Witnesses (see Castiglione, 1981: a scholarly but hostile book by a sociologist) and the Mormons (Rostan, 1974). Actually, the counter-cult movement more similar to its American counterpart is Exodos, an "Evangelical center for research and information on religious sects," established in Turin in 1988. Although mostly devoted to spreading Evangelical booklets against Jehovah's Witnesses, it has also translated from English and German books and articles (including some by Walter Martin) against the Mormons, the Worldwide Church of God, and the New Age. Compared with other Christian counter-cult publications, Exodus's literature is typically "rationalist" and tries to explain the growth of the "cults" (in Italy, particularly of Jehovah's Witnesses) with secular and rational arguments. In fact, three main reasons are indicated for the growth of Jehovah's Witnesses: the strength and centralization of their organization; the totalitarian discipline and obedience; the appeal of a group where "each individual finds its value and role emphasized even if he or she is not really very important in the [Watch Tower] society" (Exodus, 1989). Exodus does not exclude a dialogue with certain new religious movements and recognizes that they may include "many people sincere and open," although it makes clear that the ultimate aim of the dialogue is to persuade the "cultist" to leave the movement and return to the Evangelical truth (Exodus, 1988).

The largest Catholic counter-cult movement also corresponds to what I have called the "rationalist" model. GRIS (Gruppo di ricerca e di informazione sulle Sette or "Group for Research and Information on Sects") was organized by Monsignor Giovanni Marinelli, a professor in the Seminary of Ferrara, who had experiences with "sects" as a parish priest in Comacchio (Ferrara) and later met in 1981 don Ernesto Zucchini, a priest from the Diocesis of Massa who had already written against Jehovah's Witnesses. In 1983 Marinelli and Zucchini organized a national conference on Jehovah's Witnesses in Massa, followed the same year by another in Naples. After these conferences the GRIS organization was founded and a letter announcing it was sent to all Catholic bishops in Italy. Further national conferences were held in San Benedetto del Tronto (1984), Bologna (1985), and Verona (1986). On February 8, 1987 GRIS was incorporated in Bologna, a diocese whose Archbishop, Biacomo Cardinal Biffi, has been the main support among Italian bishops of GRIS. In this city a part-time staff works on behalf of GRIS (see Marinelli, 1987).

GRIS has been comparatively successful and has more than 1,000 members in Italy, although its yearly business meetings normally attract from 100 to 200 and its conferences from 150 to 300. As its by-laws clarify, GRIS's aim is not to create its own network but to use the already existing network of Catholic dioceses. Its goal is to be either established or recognized by the local bishop in each diocese. In 1990 GRIS was officially recognized by CEI, the Italian Conference of Catholic Bishops. This, of course, does not mean that any and all statements by GRIS reflect the opinion of either the entirety or majority of the Italian bishops. In fact, GRIS is large enough to represent different segments of Italian Roman Catholicism, with different local and personal attitudes, either general or with respect to new religious movements. Although Monsignor Giovanni Marinelli, who has been continuously president of GRIS since its foundation, is primarily an expert on Jehovah's Witnesses (see Marinelli, 1988)—and Jehovah's Witnesses are still the first concern of the movement—GRIS has dealt with a variety of religious, occult, and philosophical groups ranging from Scientology to Freemasonry, from Mormonism to Theosophy. It includes both parish priests, former members of new religious movements who have converted to the Catholic Church, and a few scholars.

GRIS has been successful in securing the cooperation of respected scholars with priests and religious activists whose concerns are mostly pastoral, as evidenced in its journal *Sette e Religioni,* published since 1991 (another more popular newsletter, *Movimenti religiosi alternative,* appears as a supplement to the Catholic magazine *Presenza Cristiana*). What has proved more difficult for GRIS is to accommodate the different attitudes towards new religious movements in one organization. These attitudes range from some who are more open to dialogue, or to a cold scholarly evaluation of new religious movements to others who are more activist along lines typical of counter-cult movements in general. Typical of these problems is the fact that an issue of *Sette e Religioni* of 1992 devoted to Satanism translated two articles written respectively by Michael D. Langone and by Anson Shupe *(Sette e Religioni,* 1992), two papers with opposite views of the Satanism scare in the United States. The fact that within GRIS there are debates is not surprising, if one considers in general the wide range of different theological, political, and strategic attitudes found among Italian Catholics.

One of the main themes of contrast is whether some cooperation should be established with secular anti-cult organizations like ARIS. Jehovah's Witnesses have accused GRIS of cooperating with ARIS (Associazione Europea dei Testimoni di Geova, 1990:85), but this is not generally true at a national level. GRIS, with its privileged relationship with the Italian Catholic Bishops Conference, is a typical Catholic counter-cult organization whose aims are ultimately different from those of secular anti-cult organizations like ARIS. It is, however, true that some local chapters of GRIS, particularly in the Venetian region, have friendly and regular relations with ARIS-Veneto through one of the leaders of the latter organization, the lawyer Luciano Faraon (who is a

Roman Catholic and a member, although not an officer, of GRIS). This is particularly true of CIRS (Centro Informazione e Ricerca sulle Sette, or "Center for Information and Research on Sects"), operating in the diocese of Treviso (Veneto). Members of CIRS—a Catholic organization that operates in connection with local diocesan structures—are invited to become members of GRIS, but CIRS remains a semi-autonomous organization with its own newsletter called *L'ora della Parola*. Generally speaking, the bylaws of GRIS provide that each diocesan chapter, when established by the Bishop, has a double relation with the local Bishop and with the national headquarters of GRIS. It may thus happen that different local chapters of GRIS adopt different styles and strategies. This has, at times, proven effective, since the autonomy of the local structures minimize the risk that the difference among the local chapters may cause the collapse of the entire structure. Generally speaking, GRIS is the only organization against the "cults" which has had some impact in Italy. A survey of its literature (see GRIS, 1986; GRIS, 1987; GRIS, 1989; GRIS, 1991) shows, however, that different opinions continue to coexist, a factor, as mentioned earlier, which is both a strength and a weakness in the movement.

Post-Rationalist Counter-Cult Movements

I have proposed to call the Christian groups whose explanation of the "cultic" phenomena heavily involves the Devil the post-rationalist counter-cult movements. These kind of movements are not well established in Italy. Some examples, however, exist. In Protestant circles a well-known, if controversial, organization is the Coordinamento Nazionale Fuorisciti dai Testimoni di Geova (National Committee of Former Jehovah's Witnesses), established in 1988 by Adriano Fontani and by other ex-Witnesses who do *not* want to join the Roman Catholic Church. Fontani is particularly critical of GRIS and warns former Jehovah's Witnesses that, in joining GRIS, they will easily find themselves changed from "slaves of the Watch Tower" to "slaves of the Pope" (Fontani, 1991:45). His group is also critical, although more mildly, of Protestant "rationalist" organizations like Exodus, since they adopt a different explanation of the Jehovah's Witnesses and "cults" in general. From his past experience as a Jehovah's Witness, Fontani maintains a conspirational view of history as a Satanic conspiracy against the Kingdom of God. Although some individual Catholics—like Saint Francis or, today, Mother Teresa—deserve respect, the Catholic

Church as an organization is part of an antibiblical conspiracy. Having left the Watch Tower Society, Fontani is now convinced that Jehovah's Witnesses themselves are part of the conspiracy, and that they use mysterious techniques of "plagio" and brainwashing (Fontani, 1991:49) to "enslave" their followers and "destroy their families." Even among former Jehovah's Witnesses who have elected not to return to the Catholic fold, many are critical of Fontani's extreme positions and prefer to describe themselves only as undecided "seekers for the truth," avoiding any demonic or conspirationist view of both the Roman Catholic Church and the Watch Tower Society.

In Catholic circles, post-rationalist counter-cultism of the "spiritual welfare" kind is normally discouraged. It surfaces, however, from time to time, in counter-cult authors—members of, or influenced by, the Catholic Charismatic Renewal—that in turn is obviously influenced by trends prevailing in English-speaking Pentecostalism where "spiritual warfare" and "demonization" theories have been widely discussed and partially accepted (see Guelich, 1991; Pratt, 1991). Tarcisio Mezzetti, an influential lay leader of the Catholic Charismatic Renewal, has lectured extensively against "cults," the occult, and the New Age introducing many "spiritual warfare" themes (see Mezzetti, n.d.). Another Catholic author who relies on demonic explanations of new religious movements is Armando Pavese of Alessandria, a specialist of parapsychology. In 1992 he devoted a book to Sathya Sai Baba (Pavese, 1992), where he suggests that Sai Baba's "miracles" may be "real" but produced by the Devil and that the Indian guru may be "a form of anti-Christ" (Pavese, 1992:205). Pavese has been accepted as an expert on Sathya Sai Baba by GRIS and has lectured for the latter organization. GRIS' campaign against Sathya Sai Baba has been instrumental in convincing the Roman Catholic Church to stop the activities of Mario Mazzoleni, a Catholic priest from Bergamo who had accepted Sai Baba as a divine incarnation and had lectured expressing his belief in Sai Baba and in reincarnation (see Mazzoleni, 1991). Mazzoleni was formally excommunicated in 1992, a rare measure today in the Roman Catholic Church when adopted against identified individuals.

IN SEARCH OF THE HIDDEN PARTNER

It has been suggested in sociological literature that new religious movements are most successful when they spread along existing social networks rather than create their own (and new) networks (e.g., Snot et al., 1980; Stark and Bainbridge, 1980). The same may well be true for movements *against* the "cults," particularly in countries like Italy where individualism is probably less rampant than in other regions and social networks are indeed very important. The movements that have tried to create their own social networks—like CICAP among skeptics and ARIS among the parents and relatives of "cult" members—have experienced very limited success. They have had some media attention but have never achieved substantial membership. Although ARIS may have been instrumental in the judicial prosecution of Scientology, this prosecution has, so far, not achieved the results expected by the anti-cult movement, and its ultimate destiny now seems to be largely independent from the activities of anti-cult groups. The growth or decline of nineteenth-century sects or of new religious movements in Italy has not been affected by the activities of the movements who have opposed them, even if the latter have been successful in forging (or, rather, reinforcing) the negative attitude of the Italian press against any religious phenomenon outside the mainstream (see Ambrosio, 1987b).

The movements against the "cults" have, thus, sought their success by looking for a "hidden partner," and entering one of the two main subcultural meta-networks existing in Italy: the Communist Party with its auxiliary organizations and press, and the Catholic Church. ARIS flirted for some time with individual Communist members of Parliament, and the former Communist Party for a time took seriously the idea of a special law against the "cults." The international events of 1989-1990 turned the attention of the Party and of its successors to other problems, and the involvement of the former Communist metanetwork in anti-cult crusades now appears dubious at best, although individual representatives of the Democrat Party of Left (the main heir to the former Communist Party) still exhibit anti-cult feelings from time to time. What remains—for any movement campaigning against the "cults"—is an alliance with the Roman Catholic Church. If our model distinguishing between anti-cult and counter-cult movements is correct, it is unlikely that *anti*-cult groups will be able to form stable alliances with the Catholic Church. Alliances and cooperations could work at a local level (as it happens between CIRS and ARIS-Veneto), but any larger or national coalition seems destined to fail.

Post-rationalist, and entirely "demonic" interpretation of cults also find ultimately no support in the official documents on the issue from the Vatican and the Roman Catholic Church (see Saliba, 1992). The Catholic Church seems ready to cooperate only with "rationalist" counter-cult movements, and in fact GRIS (although the importance of its official status should not be exaggerated) is, to some extent, part of the Church's effort in dealing with sects and new religious movements. However, the most recent documents from the Holy See (see Arinze, 1991) suggest also "dialogue" and explicitly state that "one, however, should not engage in a blanket condemnation or generalization by applying to all the new religious movements the more negative attitudes of some. Nor should the new religious movements be judged incapable of evolution in the positive sense" (Arinze, 1991:9). And, according to the same document, the attitude of the Catholic Church with respect to new religious movements and sects "should not be an attack": "It should not be negative against their members, although the Church might have to defend herself against the new religious movements that attack her unjustly. It should rather be based on light and love" (Arinze, 1991:29). It has been suggested that, notwithstanding these statements, even the latest document by Cardinal Arinze "has been influenced by anti-cult propaganda" (Saliba, 1992:31). This may perhaps be true with respect to some very specific point, but the general attitude of the document is certainly not "anti-cult." It should also be emphasized that many comments are only based on the summary published both in Italian and in English by the *Osservatore Romano* and other publications, while the full and longer text of the document has not been published in English so far, although it is available to the general public from the Pontifical Council for Inter-Religious Dialogue. (It has been published in a full version, in Italian, as an Appendix to Introvigne, 1993.)

Both anti-cult and counter-cult movements in Italy will only succeed if they work with a hidden partner in control of large existing social networks. Although past hopes were placed in the Communist Party, today the only available hidden partner would be the Roman Catholic Church. The Church has a tradition of being very cautious in its approach to controversial subjects. Although Italian bishops have given their blessing to GRIS, church networks (and GRIS itself at local levels) remain controlled by the bishops rather than by counter-cult leaders, and bishops look to the magisterium for directions on new or not well-known subjects such as the new religious movements. The Vatican Magisterium, in turn, is taking into account the writings and suggestions of theologians and scholars rather than counter-cult leaders, who are often ignored when documents are prepared and consulting groups formed (Saliba, 1992). A possible conclusion is that, while the Catholic Church in Italy may occasionally support local and even national counter-cult (but probably not anti-cult) activities, it will not ultimately play the role of the hidden partner for any large counter-cult crusade. The Church's approach to the problem of sects and new religious movements is much more articulated, cautious, and sophisticated. Absent this hidden partner, anti-cult and counter-cult movements in Italy may continue to exist, organize conferences, and attract interest from the media, but will probably not significantly affect the future of new religious movements. Campaigns and activities directly promoted or managed by the Catholic Church or the bishops may, on the other hand, be much more influential and effective, but the Church will probably proceed cautiously and not use a typical counter-cult (and much less anti-cult) language or style, and will probably not make extensive use of existing counter-cult movements.

REFERENCES

Aagaard, Johannes, 1991. "A Christian Encounter with New Religious Movements and New Age," *Update & Dialog* I, 1:19-23.

Ambrosio, Gianni, 1987. "I Nuovi Movimenti Religiosi in Italia," appendix (pp. 145-176) to Jean-François Mayer, *Le nuove sette,* Italian translation, Genova: Marietti.

------, 1987b. "Neue religiose Bewegungen in Italien," in Johannes Neumann and Michael W. Fischer, eds., *Toleranz und Repression: Zur Lage Religiöser Minderheiten in Modernen Gesellschaften,* Frankfurt and New York: Campus Verlag, pp. 313-335.

Arinze, Francis Cardinal, 1991. *The Challenge of the Sects or New Religious Movements: A Pastoral Approach,* Vatican City: Pontifical Council for Inter-Religious Dialogue.

Aris, 1992, *Nuovi Culti* (flyer).

Associazione Europea dei Testimoni di Geova per la Tutela Della Liberta Religiosa, 1990. *Intolleranza religiosa alle soglie del Duemila,* Roma: Fusa Editrice.

Barker, Eileen, 1992. *I Nuovi Movimenti Religiosi. Un'introduzione practice,* in Massimo Introvigne, ed., Milano: Mondadori.

Caldarella, Sergio, 1992. "Mormoni: Qualche Errore di Troppo," *Cammino,* 26.1.

------, n.d. "Pragmatismo e Mormonismo," in Paolo Blandini, ed., *Mormoni in Cammino,* Caltanissetta: The Author, pp. 22-23.

Castiglione, Miriam, 1981. *I Testimoni di Geova: Ideologia Religiosa e Consenso Sociale. Una Analisi Storico-sociologica Della "Nuova" religiosità in Italia.* Caltanissetta: The Author.

Commissione Teologica Internazionale, 1992. "Alcune Questioni Attuali Riguardanti L'escatikigua," *La Civiltà Cattolica* 143 (3401), pp. 458-494.

Corte Costituzionale, 1981. Decision 8.6, *Giustizia Penale* 1, p. 226.

Cesnur, 1993. "Primi Risultati di Un'indagine Sulla Credenza Nella Reincarnazione," Turin: Cesnur (roneot.).

Del Re, Michele C., 1982. *Culti Emergenti e Diritto Penale.* Napoli: Jovene.

------, 1988. *Nuovi Idoli, Nuovi Dei.* Roma: Gremese.

------, 1988b. "Nuovi Culti: Problemi Penalistici," *Temi Romani* I:348.

------, 1991. "Plagio Criminoso e Lecita Persuasione Nei Culti Emergenti," in *Studi in Memoria di Pietro Nuvolone,* vol. II, Milani: Giuffré, pp. 69-94.

Deseret News, 1993. *Church Almanac 1993-1994.* Salt Lake City: Deseret News.

Di Fiorino, Mario (ed.), 1990. *La Persuasione Socialmenta Accettata, il Plagio e il Lavaggio del Cervello* Vol. I. Forte dei Marmi (Lucca): Psichiatria e Territorio.l

Di Fiorino, Mario and F. M. Saviotti (eds.), 1991. *La Persuasione Socialmente Accettata, il Plagio e il Lavaggio del Cervello* Vol. II. Forte dei Marmi (Lucca): Psichiatria e Territorio.

Exodus, 1988. *Exodus Perché?* . . . (flyer).

Exodus, 1989. "La Forza Dinamica Dell'eresia," *Exodus* II, 4:9-15.

Fondazione, Agnelli, 1991. *La Religione Degli Europei.* Torino: Edizioni Della Fondazione Giovanni Agnelli.

Fontani, Adriano, 1991. "Una Sfido Nuova: Proposta per una Rielaborazione Serene e Costruttiva Della Propria fede (Gv. 1.10:Ef. 4, 14) in Achille Aveta, ed., *Atti Convegno Nazionale di Studi su Bibbia, Società e Geovismo.* Napoli: Tipografia Russo, pp. 39-81.

Garelli, Franco, 1991. *Religione e Chiesa in Italia.* Bologna: I. Mulino.

Gramaglia, Pier Angelo, 1985. *Confronto con i Mormoni.* Casale Monferrato (Alessandria): Piemme.

------, 1985b. *Verso un "Rilancio" Mariano? Voci D'Oltreterra.* Torino: Claudiana.

------, 1989. *G. I. Gurdjieff e la Quarta Via.* Savigliano: Tipografia Saviglianese.

------, 1992. *Scientology e Unification Church.* Giaveno: The Author.

------, 1992b. *New Age: Teorie e Prassi.* Giaveno: The Author.

Gris, 1986. *Cristo Nostro Dio e Nostra Speranza: I Cristiani di Fronte ai Testimoni di Geova.* Leumann (Torino): Elle Di Ci.

Gris, 1987. *I Nuovi Movimenti Religiosi non Cattolici in Italia. L'Ecclesiologia Della Chiesa e Delle Sette.* Leumann (Torino): Elle Di Ci.

Gris, 1989. *Maria Madre di Dio e Madre Della Chiesa. I Cattolici e i Testimoni di Geova.* Leumann (Torino): Elle Di Ci.

Gris, 1991. *Il Destino Dell'uomo Secondo i Cattolici e Secondo le Sette.* Leumann (Torino): Elle Di Ci.

Guelich, Robert A., 1991. "Spiritual Warfare: Jesus, Paul and Peretti," *Pneuma: The Journal of the Society for Pentecostal Studies* 13, 1:33-64.

Haraldsson, Erlendur, 1988. *Modern Miracles: An Investigative Report on Psychic Phenomena Associated with Sathya Sai Baba.* New York: Fawcett Columbine.

Hargrove, Barbara, 1983. "Social Sources and Consequences of the Brainwashing Controversy," in David G. Bromley and James T. Richardson, eds., *The Brainwashing/Deprogramming Controversy: Sociological, Psychological, Legal, and Historical Perspectives.* New York: Edwin Mellen, pp. 299-308.

Introvigne, Massimo, 1987. *Il Reverendo Moon e la Chiesa dell'Unificazione.* Leumann (Torino): Elle Di Ci.

------, 1990. *Il Cappello del Mago. I Nuovi Movimenti Magici Dallo Spiritismo al Satanismo.* Milano: Sugar Co.

------, 1992. "Nel Paese del Punto Esclamativo: 'Sette,' "Culti,' 'Pseudo-religioni' o 'nuove religioni'?," *Studia Missionalia* 41:1-26.

------, 1993. *La Questione Della Nuova Religiosità.* Piacenza: Cristianità,

------ and Gianni Ambrosio, 1990. "New Religious Movements in Italy." Paper presented at the international conference *New Religious Movements: The European Situation,* organized by the Center for Studies on New Religions (CESNUR) and the Swiss National Fund for Scientific Research, Lugano (Switzerland), 20-21 April 1990.

Kilbourne, Brock K. and James T. Richardson, 1986. "Cultphobia," *Thought* 61:258-261.

Langone, Michael D., 1992. "'Plagio'—Undue Influence Addressed in Italy," *The Cult Observer* 9, 8:8-10.

La Torre di Guardia, 1993. Italian edition, Jan. 1, 1993.

Marinelli, Giovanni, 1988. *I Testimoni di Geova: Storia–Dottrina–Problemi–Prassi,* 3rd. ed. Ferrara: The Author.

Mazzoleni, Don Mario, 1991. *Un Sacerdote Incontra Sai Baba.* Milano: Armenia Editore.

Melton, J. Gordon, Jerome Clark, and Aidan A. Kelly, 1991. *New Age Almanac.* Detroit: Visible Ink Press.

Mezzetti, Tarcisio, n.d. " . . . 'Bel è Coperto di Confusione' . . ." (Ger 50.2), in *I Quaderni di "Venite e Vedrete."* n.p., n.d., pp. 1-16.

Palazzini, Pietro, ed., 1968. *Dictionarium Morale et Canonicum.* Roma: Officium Libri Catholici.

Pavese, Annando, 1992. *Sai Baba. Anatomia del "nuovo Cristo" e dei Suoi Miracoli Attraverso la Psicologia del Profondo, la Parapsicologia e la Fede Cristiana.* Casale Monferrato (Alessandria): Piemme.

Peretti, Frank, 1986. *This Present Darkness.* Ventura (CA): Regal.

Pratt, Thomas D., 1991. "The Need to Dialogue: A Review of the Debate on Signs, Wonders, Miracles, and Spiritual Warfare in the Literature of the Third Wave Movement," *Pneuma: The Journal of the Society for Pentecostal Studies* 13, 1:7-32.

Rostan, Ermanno, 1974. *Chi Sono i Mormoni.* Torino: Claudiana.

Saliba, John A., S. J., 1992. "Vatican Response to the New Religious Movements," *Theological Studies* 53:3-39.

Sette e Religioni, 1992. Special issue "Il Satanismo" (II, 5).

Snow, David A., Louis A Zurcher, and Sheldon Ekland-Olson, 1980. "Social Networks and Social Movements: A Microstructural Approach to Differential Recruitment." *American Journal of Sociology* 45:787-801.

Stark, Rodney and William Sims Bainbridge, 1980. "Networks of Faith: Interpersonal Bonds and Recruitment to Cults and Sects," *American Journal of Sociology* 75.6:1376-1395.

Tribunale di Milano, 1991. Decision *In re Scientology* of July 2, 1991 (unpublished).

Vascon, Arturo, 1984. *Camomilla di Brooklyn. Testimone Quanto Basta dei Testimoni di Geova.* Marghera (Venezia): Tipo-Litografia Pistellato.

CHAPTER IX

OFFICIAL CATHOLIC RESPONSES TO THE NEW RELIGIONS

John A. Saliba

The presence of new religious movements (NRMs) in the West has elicited not only social and legal reactions, but also religious and theological responses to their ideologies and lifestyles. Evangelical and fundamentalist Christian churches have been the first to formulate apologetical arguments that rebut the teachings and criticize the practices of sects and cults and specify why they cannot be harmonized with Christian doctrine and morality.[1] In spite of the fact that several of the new movements, particularly those of Christian origin, have often directed their attacks against traditional forms of Christianity, little official response was forthcoming from the major Christian churches and denominations.

The official Catholic response to the NRMs has been rather slow and began to take shape by the mid-1980s. The reasons for this rather late start in examining a spiritual revival that has been having some repercussions on Catholic life are several. Since the Second Vatican Council the Catholic Church has been faced with both internal and external problems which account, in part, for the apparent lethargy in taking seriously the new religions, especially those of Eastern origin. During the 1970s and early 1980s the Catholic hierarchy was preoccupied with the activities of several movements which were affecting the lives of many Catholics.

The first type of movement arose from within Catholic ranks. Negative reactions against the changes introduced by the Second Vatican Council led to the emergence of Catholic traditional (Dinges 1983, 1991) and conservative (Hitchcock, 1991) movements. The Pius X Institute is one of the more prominent examples of Catholic Traditionalism. Led by the late renegade Archbishop Lefebvre, this institute eventually became a schismatic church, in spite of the many efforts made to prevent it from secession.[2] The presence of a strong current of Catholic conservatism is detectable, for example, in the emergence of visionaries whose practices and teachings call for a theological evaluation. Veronica Lueken, who claims to have repeated visitations from the Virgin Mary, is typical of a visionary movement that has attracted a large following. Her experiences, which developed into the devotion to "Our Lady of the Roses,"[3] appeared more dangerous and threatening then the claims and activities of many of the new religious movements.

Other conservative Catholic movements or organizations, such as Opus Dei, which received official recognition well before the rise of the NRMs, have been included by some Catholics with the "dangerous cults" (Coulter, 1984). The controversy about Opus Dei is reflected in Catholic literature[4] and in the reaction of some parents whose children have become members.[5] The debate has not abated in spite of the fact that, over a decade ago, the institute was accorded special status by the Holy See (Sacred Congregation of Bishops, 1982).

A second type of movement received its initial inspiration from outside traditional Catholic sources. The most prominent of these was the Catholic Charismatic Movement which swept throughout the Catholic world during the late 1960s and early 1970s. While this movement never existed separately from, or in serious conflict with, official Catholic teaching and practice, it aroused the concern of many bishops. Official documents on the Charismatic movement date from 1969 (McDonnell 1980, vol. 1, pp. 209-210) and continue to appear through the 1970s and 1980s (McDonnell, 1980; 1989).

A third type of movement was the revival of fundamentalist and Pentecostal churches, many of which directed their conversion efforts towards Catholics. Although these churches and their propaganda methods are not new, they seem to have intensified over the last few decades. The successful missionary endeavors of Protestant groups have been a cause of concern expressed in many Church documents. In Latin America these sects are viewed as a more serious threat to Catholicism (Deiros, 1991) than all the NRMs put together (cf. Gaxiola-Gaxiola, 1991, pp. 123-127).

Finally, one should note that the Catholic hierarchy has had to deal with various movements that apparently challenged traditional theology and practice. Liberation theology (Hennelly, 1986) and the revolt of Catholic women against church doctrine and liturgical practice (Stan,

1988) are but two examples of some of the conflicts that seemed more disruptive than any danger that might come from new religions.

THE VATICAN REPORT:
THE BEGINNINGS OF A CATHOLIC RESPONSE

The 1986 *Vatican Report on Sects and New Religious Movements* (1986) is a unique document for several reasons. It is the result of the cooperation of four different Vatican offices. Unlike many Vatican documents, it does not claim to be an authoritative statement on doctrinal issues. Moreover, it not only contains scholarly reflections on the NRMs, but also includes some popular and negative views that have been repeatedly expressed in the public media.

The *Vatican Report* is divided into three major parts.[6] The first introduces the reader to the phenomenon of cults and sects, drawing attention to the pastoral problems that their evangelizing efforts have created. Various causes that might have triggered the modern phenomenon of NRMs are mentioned.

The second dwells on the reasons why these movements have come into being and flourished. Nine universal human needs and aspirations are described: (1) the quest for belonging; (2) the search for answers; (3) the search for wholeness; (4) the search for cultural identity; (5) the need to be recognized; (6) the search for transcendence; (7) the need for spiritual guidance; (8) the need for vision; and (9) the need for participation and involvement. Sects and cults, according to the *Vatican Report*, appear to be satisfying some genuine religious desires, even though the forceful recruitment programs of some groups might account, in part, for their success.

The third sketches the pastoral challenge the NRMs present. The *Vatican Report* argues that the way to stop defections to the cults is to pay more attention to the religious and spiritual aspirations of the young adults who form the majority of cult recruits. It is suggested that Catholic parishes can offset the attraction of the NRMs by providing the faithful with better opportunities for: (1) building community; (2) continuing their religious education; (3) catering to a personal and holistic approach; (4) providing the means to cultural identity; (5) enhancing prayer and liturgical life; and (6) encouraging people to become involved in the church through participation and leadership.

The *Vatican Report* makes no attempt to evaluate the new religions from a theological perspective, to pass judgment on those Catholics who abandon their faith to dedicate themselves to a new religious belief system and lifestyle, or to specify the relationship that the Church could establish with the novel faiths. Acknowledging that the cult issue is global and complex, the *Vatican Report* admits that more research and study are necessary before any definite proposals can be made and an official Catholic response formulated.

One of the main features of the *Vatican Report* is the adoption of a language and attitude that are more in harmony with the principles of interreligious dialogue and with the approach formulated by the Second Vatican Council (Abbott 1966, pp. 660-668). Hoeckman (1987:136), in a lengthy explanation of the *Vatican Report*, which he himself largely put together, explains that the document does not intend to speculate on "what future anti-sect or anti-cult strategies can be worked out," but rather the pastoral issues and challenges that face Catholic parishes. Consequently, the report draws attention to the Church's need for self-examination and spiritual and ecclesiastical renewal. Further, Hoeckman (1987:137-138) maintains that the *Vatican Report* does not aspire to solve the great debates about the nature of the cults and their activities or to provide a "cult catechism" with handy answers for all the questions about sects and cults. And while he believes that official dialogue with the new religions is not yet possible, he does not rule out its possibility. He certainly does not envisage the Catholic Church engaging in diatribes, accusations, and belligerent crusades.

THE WORK OF F.I.U.C.

A study of the religious movements, commissioned by the Vatican to the International Federation of Catholic Universities (F.I.U.C.), began in earnest in the late 1980s. Between 1991 and 1993 four international conferences were held in which many scholars[7] were invited to participate. These meetings were regionally organized and took place respectively in Omaha, U.S.A. (May, 1991), Vienna, Austria (October, 1991), Quito, Ecuador (June, 1992), and Manila, Philippines (February, 1993). They reflected not only the universal concern regarding the rise of the NRMs in general, but also the particular problems faced by different countries and/or continents. Although the papers presented at these meetings differ both in the data they examine and in the interpretations they propose, they all share some basic attitudes and approaches to the new religious phenomena of the late twentieth century. The F.I.U.C. project is now officially over. The papers presented at the various conferences are in the process of being edited for publication with a short conclusive report to the Vatican, a report which will play a key role in the formulation of an official Catholic response.

Three major features mark the papers presented at the F.I.U.C. meetings. The first is that they are relatively mild in their approach. This does not mean that the beliefs and practices of the new religions are not criticized or that their often belligerent proselytization methods are not deplored. Rather, the presentations at these gatherings have not picked up the rhetoric of the Anti-Cult Movement nor have they copied the diatribe that has become characteristic of the Christian fundamentalist response to the new movements.

Secondly, like the Vatican document, Catholic scholars prefer to focus on the urgency to educate Catholics in their faith and on the necessity of adapting Christian ministry to the particular needs of those who might be attracted to the new religious movements. The argument underlying this approach suggests that many Catholics join new religions not simply because they are heavily (and maybe deceptively) recruited. Other factors, such as a lack of mature Christian education and a lack of pastoral care and sensitivity, play a key role in their decisions to abandon their faith and join a relatively new religion.

Thirdly, Catholic examination of the NRMs is directed both towards ways of evangelizing those who are likely to be attracted to them and towards means of helping those Catholics who are subjected to anti-Catholic propaganda. This attitude is especially apparent in discussions on the religious situations in the former U.S.S.R. and in Latin America. Many traditional sects and new religions have embarked on a campaign to gain converts in the previously communist-dominated countries, where people are less likely to have received a solid religious education. In South America, the newer Pentecostal sects often disseminate anti-Catholic propaganda that, though probably attracting only those who are already alienated or whose Catholic education is minimal, calls into question both religious freedom and interreligious dialogue. But even in these conditions, the Catholic approach is not likely to adopt the forceful proselytization techniques that are characteristic of some religious groups. Such methods are deemed to infringe on religious freedom that was explicitly endorsed by Vatican Council II (cf. Abbott,

1966:675-696) and to go counter to the progress made in the dialogue between churches and religions over the last several decades.

The works of several Catholic scholars, such as Michael Fuss, Massimo Introvigne, and Franc Rodè, all of whom have been involved in the F.I.U.C. study, deserve mention because they are likely to influence future official Catholic documents on the NRMs. In spite of their differences, these authors adopt an understanding of, and approach to, the NRMs that maintains the spirit of Vatican II's declaration on non-Christian religions and is in line with the main trends elaborated in the *Vatican Report*.

Michael Fuss, who has been in charge of the F.I.U.C. research almost since its inception, recently published an essay in which he specified the kind of pastoral and theological challenge posed by the presence of so many religious groups (Fuss, 1992). He maintains that their presence is characterized by a return to a "subjective religiosity" which has nine distinguishing features: (1) the lack of interest in religious truth; (2) the importance given to instant salvation; (3) a dissatisfaction with doctrines and institutions; (4) an orientation towards magic; (5) the fascination with the forces of nature without any personal relationship with God; (6) a total view of reality that includes both humans and the cosmos; (7) a neutral religious experience that encompasses all religions; (8) religious autonomy; and (9) the need of a balanced and mature religiosity to eliminate demonic fear inherent in the cosmos.

Fuss offers several critical reflections on the basic themes stressed in the NRMs. He thinks that one of their major deficiencies is that many of them are not searching for the truth. By this Fuss is probably referring to the individualistic tendency that leads a person to determine her or his own belief system without any accountability to a community of faith. People, observes Fuss, are inclined to embrace different beliefs only insofar as they contribute to their own vitality and usefulness (p. 300). They further reject any kind of ecclesiastical structure, insisting on absolute freedom in belief (p. 304). He finds the common belief in reincarnation faulty from a Christian standpoint, because it leaves no room for a merciful and forgiving God and for a savior (p. 311).

In spite of his negative theological assessments, his approach to the new religious movements is not one of condemnation and refutation. He does not indulge in heated polemics and blanket accusations, nor does he seek hostile confrontations. On the contrary, he points out that the Catholic Church must enter into a relationship with all cultural phenomena and that in dealing with the NRMs one must start with the principles of interreligious dialogue (p. 295). He contends that, notwithstanding the weaknesses of the NRMs, the Church must make a "preferential option for dialogue" (p. 310), the aim of which should be the construction of a Church which is both accepting and acting in the service of the world.

Introvigne has played a leading role in formulating Catholic opinion on the NRMs both through his voluminous writings (see Introvigne 1989, 1990, 1991, 1992, 1993) and especially through the work of CESNUR, a center for the study of new religions located in Turin. It would be difficult to find a Catholic scholar whose knowledge of NRMs is more broad and thorough than Introvigne's. He (1992) has proposed a theological scheme for classifying NRMs, a scheme which was adopted by Bishop Casale (1993) in a recent pastoral letter.

Like many other Catholic scholars, Introvigne observes that there are difficulties in carrying on a dialogue with many of the new religions. He has articulated this in some detail with respect to three established sects, namely, Jehovah's Witnesses, the Church of Jesus Christ of Latter Day Saints (Mormons), and the Seventh-Day Adventists. In a paper presented to the F.I.U.C. meeting in Vienna (Introvigne, 1991), he drew up a strategy for dialogue in three dimensions, namely, (1) the structural (which includes the theological and psychological aspects), (2) the vertical (which consists of the various sections of the church or religion, that is, the establishment, the intellectuals, the community, and the fringe), and (3) the horizontal (which covers the various kinds of dialogical exchanges, namely, the ecumenical, the interreligious, the cultural, and the human. Introvigne does not think that dialogue with the three religious groups he examined is possible on all levels. He suggests that "human dialogue" might be possible with all the three religions. In this kind of dialogue people who find it difficult to agree even on basic human values "could at least interact on the basis of mutual respect in order to gain a better understanding" (Introvigne, 1991, p. 6). His scheme could possibly be modified to cover new religions in general. In spite of his conviction that dialogue is difficult and sometimes impossible, Introvigne does not indulge in the kind of negative and belligerent reactions that have so often characterized Christian responses to the new religions.

Franc Rodè (1993), who delivered a background paper to the participants at the F.I.U.C. meeting in Quito, has largely in mind the phenomenal increase in the membership of Pentecostal churches in Latin America. He cites many pastoral letters from the Bishops of various countries in Latin America in support of the view that sects are a serious pastoral solicitude and that Catholics should respond by stressing religious education and nourishing popular religious devotions. Although he berates the sects and cults for their unhealthy (pathological) religious excitement, their lack of respect for personal human liberty, and disregard for the truth, he follows the *Vatican Report* in stressing the pastoral work that the Catholic Church is called upon to do. Among the pastoral options he mentions are (1) a stress on the essential content of the Catholic faith, (2) the revitalization of Catholic parishes into communities by developing new structures (p. 267), and (3) the enhancement of liturgical celebrations (p. 268).

Like many other Catholic scholars, Rodè thinks that dialogue with the sects is difficult, if not altogether impossible. The reasons he gives are: (1) the sects themselves refuse dialogue; (2) they are too hostile to the Catholic Church; and (3) they constantly attack the core of its teaching. Such arguments are certainly applicable to some of the Pentecostal Churches that have gained ground in South America over the last few decades.[8] Rode further notes that "sects and new religious groups appear necessarily as foreign, alien to the spiritual world of the Latin American continent" (p. 268). This is a surprising statement that is easily open to the accusation of ethnocentrism. Rodè, apparently, fails to realize that the Christian Church was once itself foreign to the spiritual world of the ancient Romans and Greeks and that the Catholic Church itself was entirely alien to the religious beliefs and practices of the natives of South America before the Spanish conquest.

Although some of the statements made by Rodè appear negative, there is little, if anything, in his paper that does not conform to the *Vatican Report*'s main thrust. His arguments must be seen in the context of the unique situation in Latin America, a situation that may call for a different response from that developed to deal with the NRMs in North America and Western Europe. It is unlikely that Rodè would favor the fundamentalist response to the new religions. Nor is he likely to condone some of the more popular accusations against their members. He quotes (p. 268) Saint Augustine's saying, "Odi errores, ama errantes" ("Hate errors, but love those who go astray"). Though somewhat paternalistic, this statement might indicate that Rodè is aware that stemming the tide of Catholics joining Pentecostal sects is not achieved by adopting their belligerent conversion techniques and by aggravating the conflict.

RECENT DOCUMENTS IN
THE WAKE OF THE *VATICAN REPORT*

Since the publication of the *Vatican Report* several official documents on the presence of the new religions have appeared.[9] On the universal level two major events, namely the publication of the *Letter* of the Sacred Congregation for the Doctrine of the Faith (1989) and the deliberations at the Consistory of Cardinals held in April, 1991, explicitly took up the question of the NRMs.

The CDF's Letter on Christian Meditation

The *Letter* on Christian meditation is probably the most important of the Vatican's reactions to the NRMs to date because it is both instructional and directive. Although it does not address the NRMs as such, it evaluates Eastern meditative practices that are central to many new religions, especially those of Eastern origin. While the *Vatican Report* proposes no theological assessment of the beliefs and practices of the new religions, the *Letter* attempts both to explain the nature of Christian prayer and to offer an evaluation of Eastern meditative methods from a Catholic theological standpoint.

Catholic reactions to the *Letter* have been mixed (Saliba 1992:19-28). In spite of its cautious approach and weaknesses, there is no doubt, however, that its contents are not a direct attack against Hindu and/or Buddhist meditative practices, even though these are assigned a secondary and somewhat peripheral role to the traditional forms of Christian prayer and meditation. And though the Letter warns of some of the dangers of Yoga, Zen, and Transcendental Meditation, and questions whether they can be incorporated into Christian practice, it concedes that they have some value (Sec. 28) and could possibly enrich Catholic tradition. In fact, it credits them with two main benefits: (1) they are said to prepare the body for prayer and can thus be compared to some Christian methods (Sec. 26), and (2) they have "valued psychophysical symbolism, often absent in Western forms of prayer" (Sec. 27). Moreover, the *Letter* is also in accord with the spirit of Vatican II's declaration on non-Christian religions (Abbott 1966:660-668).

The Cardinals' Consistory

The need to consider the new religious movements was highlighted by the Fourth Extraordinary Consistory of Cardinals. One session was dedicated to the NRMs, the title of the agenda being "The Proclamation of Christ, the Only Savior, and the Challenge of the Sects." The short Communique[10] issued at the end of the meeting stressed the need for an ongoing religious instruction aimed at helping Catholics "rediscover their identity as well as the riches of their faith in Christ" (Sec. 2). The regional reports presented to the Consistory incorporated many of the ideas and observations from the 1986 *Vatican Report*, such as the need for religious education, the formation of basic eccleastical communities, and the inculturation of Christianity in different cultural settings.

Two lengthy presentations made at the Consistory (Tomko, 1991; Arinze, 1991) might provide some clues as to the main thrust of the forthcoming official Catholic position. The first, by Cardinal Tomko, is more interested in stressing correct beliefs and practices. His speech, entitled "On Relativizing Christ: Sects and the Church," makes little reference to sects, cults, and NRMs. It suggests, however, that their rise and spread is due to the lack of proper instruction in the Catholic faith. According to this Cardinal, doctrinal confusion regarding the content of faith opens the way to the proliferation of sects by jeopardizing the effectiveness of pastoral care and by rendering less convincing the proclamation of Jesus Christ which establishes the Christian community.

Tomko draws attention to one of the pastoral challenges alluded to in the *Vatican Report*, namely "the need for evangelization, catechesis, education, and ongoing formation——biblical, theological, ecumenical—— of the faithful at the level of the local communities, and of the clergy and those involved in formation" (Sec. 3.2). He also emphasizes the unresolved tension that exists between evangelization and dialogue.

A more illuminating address was that of Cardinal Arinze, who heads the Pontifical Council for Interreligious Dialogue. Arinze (1991) both clarifies and amplifies in many respects the approach taken by the *Vatican Report*. Admitting that the majority of NRMs are indeed religious and/or spiritual entities, the Cardinal implicitly recognizes that some form of dialogue with them is, in principle, possible. Moreover, he explicitly rejects a general condemnation of NRMs, a position which is favored, but not clearly enunciated in the *Vatican Report*:

One, however, should not engage in a blanket condemnation or generalization by applying to all the NRMs the more negative attitudes of some. Nor should the NRMs be judged incapable of evolution in the positive sense. (Sec. 9)

And he makes it clear that the Catholic Church is not adopting an anticult response, be it secular or religious. Specifying the Church's response he states that:

It should not be an attack. It should not be negative against their members, although the church might have to defend herself against the NRMs that attack her unjustly. It should rather be based on light and love. (Sec. 29)

Cardinal Arinze's speech includes references to several anticult views on NRMs. He states, for instance, that new religions (1) use methods that violate the principles of religious freedom (Sec. 24); (2) apply forceful proselytization techniques (Sec. 24); (3) cause psychological harm upon unwitting individuals (Sec. 26); and (4) create and/or aggravate many modern social problems (Sec. 27). Arinze's statements are, however, more cautious and avoid generalizations and accusations. They are actually overshadowed by the Cardinal's determination to give priority to the spiritual welfare of Catholics and to the need for reform within the Church itself. He appears to lean heavily towards the view that some drastic structural changes in the church might be necessary if its ministry is to be effective. While still adhering to the traditional distinction between clergy and laity, he suggests that clericalism might lead Catholics to seek religious nourishment in groups where hierarchical distinctions are minimal or nonexistent (Sec 40).

Local Pastoral Letters on the NRMs

On the more local level several official publications that have tried both to survey the new religious scene and to formulate a Catholic response deserve mention. In 1990 Cardinal Danneels, archbishop of Mechlin-Brussels, issued a pastoral letter which, though dedicated primarily to the New Age Movement, makes several statements on the NRMs as a whole. Danneels (1992, pp. 14-15), while referring to the popular accusations, such as manipulation methods and love-bombing, asserts that the "main reason for their success seems to be the fact that our society is increasingly depersonalized" (p. 8). Sects and cults succeed because they respond to genuine human needs and aspirations. They offer spiritual and physical healing, religious experiences, and personal wholeness (p. 10). The response of the church must be, in the Cardinal's opinion, to create warm and healthy communities, to stress the need for religious education, to develop a living liturgy, and to invite people to participation and leadership in Church activities (pp. 16-20). Danneels criticizes the New Age for its egocentric world view and syncretism, but goes on to list the good things it offers, including "a sense of universal brotherhood, peace and harmony," and relaxation techniques, like Yoga, which are beneficial.

A similar approach is adopted by Archbishop McCarthy of Miami in a pastoral instruction on the New Age Movement. McCarthy (1992, p. 334), in a balanced evaluation of the movement, states:

> The New Age Movement espouses many of the ideals of the Church—peace, humanitarianism, respect for the dignity of the person, meditation, and concern for ecology. It embraces, however, many other elements that are altogether incompatible with Christianity and our Catholic faith.

He then adds that this movement has many good features, including its integration of matter and spirit and its stress on mystical experiences, all of which have their counterparts in Christianity.

A much more ambitious pastoral letter was issued by Giuseppe Casale, bishop of Foggia, Italy. Casale (1993) first describes the widespread phenomenon of NRMs and speculates on their sociocultural causes and significance. He then attempts a theological analysis and suggests some pastoral actions that might be taken. The letter, reflecting on doctrinal matters, finds many of the NRMs incompatible with traditional Catholic teaching which, among other beliefs, stresses the personal nature of God and the unique role of Christ. Casale's response is partly apologetic, for he takes time to refute the belief in reincarnation, which has never, in fact, been explicitly condemned. His recommendations are in harmony with the *Vatican Report*. He suggests that the attitude of the Catholic Church should be one of vigilance (p. 85) linked, however, with an openness towards dialogue (p. 86).

It seems to have become common practice to include comments on the new religions whenever the question of religious dialogue is brought up. Thus, for example, in a Vatican dossier on the Catholic Church in Africa, published by the General Secretariat of the Synod of Bishops (1993), one whole chapter is dedicated to "Dialogue and Witness." After discussing dialogue in general and ecumenism, the document proceeds to deal with the question of sects and new religious movements in Africa. Admitting that dialogue with many of these groups is difficult, if not altogether impossible, the document adds (p. 411):

> With some it may not be locally found prudent to engage in formal dialogue. It is, nevertheless, necessary to develop a Christ-like spirit in relation to all, making effort to understand them and to enter into dialogue, while recognizing "false prophets" (Mt. 24:24), pointing out the inconsistences in so many of their answers and promises and in some cases warning of the social and political dangers which some of these sects may pose.

These Church documents, while striving to distinguish between Catholic doctrine and the teachings of the NRMs, never attack the new religions nor pass any judgment on their members. In the spirit of Vatican II's "Declaration on the Relationship of the Church to Non-Christian Religions" (Abbott, 1966:660-668), they recognize that non-Christian religions have many good qualities and, like the 1986 *Vatican Report*, they refrain from aggravating the situation by using inflammatory language and wild accusations. Their approach is in harmony with that of several Catholic scholars (Introvigne, 1991; Saliba, 1982, 1986; Dinges, 1986). Casale (1993) goes as far as to disown the method of deprogramming which several anticult groups advocate. He states unequivocally that deprogramming, when it includes physical coercion "is never acceptable as it is contrary to Catholic morality" (p. 82).

Official documents suggest that matters of orthodoxy and orthopraxis might dominate any Catholic response to the NRMs. If the attitudes and trends expressed in these statements dictate any future official Catholic position, then one can rest assured that the response will not resemble the rhetoric of the anticult movement nor the hysterical condemnations of fundamentalist Christian or Catholic writers. Such an approach is indirectly confirmed in the *New Catholic Catechism* (1993). The catechism is instructional, avoiding polemics with non-Catholics and non-Christians. In a section (p. 231, par. 839) entitled "The Church and non-Christians," it simply reiterates the major principles that Vatican II elaborated in the document on non-Christian religions.

CONCLUSION: WHITHER THE OFFICIAL CATHOLIC RESPONSE?

Official Catholic responses to the New Religious Movements have adhered to the principles of interreligious dialogue and religious freedom sketched by Vatican II about 30 years ago. They have also kept in mind the Church's own mission and the difficult task of reconciling interreligious dialogue and evangelization (Pontifical Council for Interreligious Dialogue and Congregation for the Evangelization of Peoples, 1991). In line with these principles, the official Catholic position on the NRMs appears to be heading in the following direction:

(1) It is concerned with doctrine and with the need for continuing religious education and apologetics when called for.

(2) It is equally pastorally oriented. It stresses the principle that the religious and spiritual aspirations of people must have priority and that, consequently, Church leaders should make the necessary reforms and offer the required services.

(3) It shows willingness to learn from the NRMs, thus openly admitting that they have something positive to offer, notwithstanding their doctrinal and/or moral errors.

(4) Its main goal is to evaluate and discern the NRMs, rather than to condemn them or initiate a crusade against them.

(5) It respects the religious freedom of individuals, even though their choices are deemed doctrinally erroneous and their behavior morally unacceptable.

Official Catholic reactions to the NRMs stand apart both from the anticult movement and from the position adopted by the social sciences. One the one hand, Catholic documents do not condone, much less encourage, the secular counterattacks against the "destructive cults." Further, nowhere in the documents does one find anything resembling the Christian fundamentalist onslaught against sects and new religions. While Satanic intervention in new religious movements is sometimes listed among the many factors leading to the rise and success of new religious movements (see, e.g., Arinze, 1991, p. 608), the main trend of the material surveyed in this essay is to stress the social, cultural, psychological, and spiritual causes. Unlike Christian fundamentalist literature, official Catholic documents do not attribute every human misfortune and deviation from the truth to diabolical intervention. Further, they do not exhibit an apocalyptic fear of the NRMs, nor do they favor a condemnation of all their activities. They do not inspire readers with a crusading spirit. They say nothing to arouse or intensify the readers' negative emotions against the NRMs. The language they use is rather measured and bears no resemblance to the diatribes against all NRMs. On the contrary, the documents urge Catholics to reflect on their own faith and to strive to make it more meaningful and relevant in their lives.

On the other hand, the Catholic official reactions do not adopt the neutral stance of the social sciences, a stance which has often been interpreted as favoring the NRMs. The materials discussed in this essay offer theological evaluations of the new religiosity and manifest a genuine pastoral concern. They are interested in helping those Catholics who are confused by the many religious options that vie for their commitment and devotion and that offer them happiness in this life or in the next and salvation from their spiritual and/or material ailments.

Public responses, official or otherwise, to new religions are important because they influence people's attitudes and channel their activities. They also have an impact on the cults themselves by, for instance, giving them respectability, forcing them to change their evangelization tactics, or increasing interreligious conflict. Because the NRMs and the traditional religions exist in a symbiotic relationship, reactions to the former might contribute, indirectly, to their growth, development, or demise. Moreover, the new religions are likely to have an impact on established traditions, leading them to reexamine and modify their community structures and pastoral programs.

The official Catholic responses to the NRMs are both informative and instructive. They are definitely not dominated by the anticult rhetoric that has influenced some Catholic writers (e.g., DeBold, 1987; LeBar, 1987) and Catholics in general. But whether, and to what degree, the more reflective, balanced, and moderate Church documents will have a measurable impact on Catholic opinion on the NRMs remains to be seen.

NOTES

1. Some typical examples of this response to the new religious movements are Breese (1975), Boa (1979), Martin (1980), Sire (1980), and McDowell and Stewart (1982). Several Christian organizations, such as Christian Apologetics: Resource and Information Service (CARIS), Christian Outreach to the Cults and Occult, Christian Research Institute (CRI), and Institute of Contemporary Christianity were among the earliest groups to criticize the cults from a theological standpoint and to embark on a systematic rebuttal of their tenets.

2. A full history of the Pius X Institute and its road to the final break with Rome has still to be written. See the apostolic letter of John Paul II (1988) which formalized the schism. The essays by Dinges (1988a, 1988b) give a good account of the conflict in its final stages. The problems raised by this movement are, apparently, far from over (see Marra, 1991; Moynihan, 1993).

3. This devotion is also known as "Our Lady of Bayside" (Nobile 1978).

4. One of the most devastating critiques of Opus Dei has been that of Walsh (1989). Needless to say, others (e.g., Giesler, 1988 and McGovern, 1992) have written favorably about the organization.

5. In the United States there are at least two Catholic organizations that came into being precisely to counteract the practices of Opus Dei: (1) Our Lady and St. Joseph in Search of the Lost Child (see Garvey, 1991) and (2) Opus Dei Awareness Network (ODAN). Both groups accuse Opus Dei of using the same methods as most cults to recruit and maintain members.

6. For a full description and in-depth analysis of the *Vatican Report*'s contents and the different kinds of reactions it has elicited, see Saliba (1992).

7. Although most of the participants in these meetings were Catholics, several prominent non-Catholic scholars were also invited to present papers and take part in the discussions.

8. One should note here that Rodè's argument cannot be applied to such groups as the Hare Krishna Movement, the Unification Church, and Scientology who, notwithstanding the bad publicity they have all received in the media, are definitely interested in interreligious dialogue.

9. Casale (1993, p. 103) refers to several documents not quoted in this essay.

10. The Communiquè has been published in *Origins* 20 (April 25, 1991, pp. 746-748).

REFERENCES

Abbott, Walter M., ed., 1966. *The Documents of Vatican II.* New York: Herder and Herder.

Arinze, Francis Cardinal, 1991. "The Challenge of the Sects," *Catholic International* 2: 605-611.

Boa, Kenneth, 1977. *Cults, World Religions, and You.* Wheaton, IL: Victor Books.

Breeze, Dave, 1978. *Know the Marks of Cults.* Wheaton, IL: Victor Books.

Casale, Giuseppe, 1993. *Nova Religiosita e Nuova Evangelizzazione.* Foggia, Italy: Piemme.

Catechism of the Catholic Church (Italian Version). 1993, Vatican City: Libreria Editrice Vaticana.

Coulter, Carol, 1984. *Are Religious Cults Dangerous?* Dublin: Mercier Press.

Danneels, Godfried Cardinal, 1992. *Christ or Aquarius: Exploring the New Age Movement.* Dublin: Veritas.

Debold, Walter, 1987. "The New Cults: A Threat to Unity and Authentic Humanity," *Journal of Dharma* 12: 63-70.

Deiros, Pablo A., 1991. "Protestant Fundamentalism in Latin America," in Martin Marty and S. Appleby, eds., *Fundamentalism Observed.* Chicago: University of Chicago Press, pp. 142-196.

Dinges, William D., 1983. "Catholic Traditionalist Movement," in Joseph H. Fichter, ed., *Alternative to American Mainline Churches.* New York: Rose of Sharon Press, pp. 137-158.

------, 1986. "The Vatican Report on Sects, Cults, and New Religious Movements," *America*, 27 September, pp. 145-147, 154.

------, 1988a. "Lefebvre Abandons Ship: Peter Finally Barks," *Commonweal*, 12 August, pp. 420-421.

------, 1988b. "Quo Vadis, Lefebvre?," *America*, 18 June, pp. 602-606.

------, 1991. "Roman Catholic Traditionalism," in Martin Marty and S. Appleby (eds.), *Fundamentalism Observed.* Chicago: University of Chicago Press, pp. 602-606.

Fuss, Michael, 1992. "Il Fenomeno della Nuova Religiosita in Europa: Una Sfida Pastorale," *Sette e Religioni: Rivista Trimestrale di Cultura Religiosa* 2.2 (April): 295-314.

Garvey, J.J.M., 1991. *Parents' Guide to Opus Dei.* New York: Sicut Dixit Press.

Gaxiola-Gaxiola, Manuel J., 1991. "Latin American Pentecostalism: A Mosaic within a Mosaic," *Pneuma: The Journal of the Society for Pentecostal Studies* 13 (Fall): 107-129.

General Secretariat of the Synod of Bishops, 1993. "The African Church in Dialogue," *Catholic International* 4 (September): 406-419.

Giesler, Michael E., 1988. "Opus Dei and the Sanctification of Work," *Homiletic and Pastoral Review* 88 (February): 28-33.

Hennelly, Alfred T., 1986. "The Red-Hot Issue: Liberation Theology," America, 8 May, pp. 425-428.

Hitchcock, James, 1991. "Catholic Activist Conservatism in the United States," in Martin Marty and S. Appleby (eds.), *Fundamentalism Observed*. Chicago: University of Chicago Press, pp. 101-127.

Hoeckman, Remi. 1987. "The Pastoral Challenge of New Religious Movements," *Origins* 17 (30 July): 136-143.

Introvigne, Massimo, 1989. *Le Nuove Religioni*. Milano, Italy: Sugar Co.

------, 1990. *I Nuovi Culti: Dagli Hare Krishna alla Scientologia*. Milano, Italy: Mondadori.

------, 1991. "The Self-Understanding of Jehovah's Witnesses, Mormons, and Seventh-day Adventists and Their Position with Regard to Religious Pluralism and Dialogue." Paper Presented at the Symposium on *Religious Renewal in Europe: Towards a 'Dialogue' in Truth*, organized by the International Federation of Catholic Universities: Vienna, Austria.

------, 1992. "Nel Paese del Punto Esclamativo: 'Sette,' 'Culti,' 'Psuedo-religioni,' o 'Nuove Religioni'?," *Studia Missionalia* 41: 1-26.

------, 1993. *La Questione della Nuova Religiosita*. Piacenza, Italy: Cristianita.

John Paul II, 1988. "Ecclesia Dei," *Origins* 18 (August 4): 150-152.

LeBar, James, 1989. *Cults, Sects, and the New Age*. Huntington, IN: *Our Sunday Visitor*.

Marra, William A., 1991. "The Priestly Fraternity of St. Peter," *Homiletic and Pastoral Review* 92 (November): 62-66.

Martin, Walter, 1980. *The New Cults*. Santa Ana, CA: Vision House.

McCarthy, Edward A., 1992. "The New Age Movement," *Catholic International* 3.7 (1-14 April): 335-336.

McDonnell, Kilian (ed.), 1980. *Documents on the Charismatic Renewal.* Collegeville, MN: The Liturgical Press, 1991. 3 vols.

------, (ed.), 1989. *Open the Windows: The Popes and the Charismatic Renewal.* South Bend, IN: Greenlawn Press, 1989.

McDowell, Josh, and Don Stewart, 1982. *Handbook of Today's Religions: Understanding the Cults.* San Bernardino, CA: Here's Life Publishers.

McGovern, Thomas, 1992. "Paths to Holiness," *Homiletic and Pastoral Review* 92 (August/September): 11-17.

Moynihan, Robert, 1993. "The Curia's Dilemma," *Inside the Vatican,* August/September, pp. 8-22.

Nobile, Philip, 1978. "Our Lady of Bayside," *New York Magazine,* 11 December, pp. 57-60.

Pontifical Council for Interreligious Dialogue and Congregation for the Evangelization of Peoples, 1991. "Dialogue and Proclamation," *Origins* 21 (July 4): 122-135.

Rode, Franc, 1993. "Sects in Latin America," *Catholic International* 4.6 (June): 264-268.

Sacred Congregation for Bishops, 1983. "Vatican Declaration on Opus Dei," *Origins* 12 (13 January): 310-312.

Sacred Congregation for the Doctrine of the Faith, 1989. "On Christian Meditation," *Origins* 19: 492-498.

Saliba, John A., 1982. "The Christian Church and the New Religious Movements: Towards Theological Understanding," *Theological Studies* 43: 468-485.

------, 1986. "Learning from the New Religious Movements," *Thought* 61: 225-240.

------, 1992. "Vatican Response to the New Religious Movements," *Theological Studies* 53: 3-39.

Sire, James W., 1980. *Scripture Twisting: 20 Ways the Cults Misread the Bible.* Downers Grove, IL: InterVarsity Press.

Stan, Adelle-Marie, 1988. "The Voices of Catholic Dissent," *The Nation,* 9 January, pp. 12-15.

Tomko, Josef Cardinal, 1991. "On Relativizing Christ: Sects and the Church," *Origins* 20 (25 April): 753-754.

"Vatican Report on Sects, Cults, and New Religious Movements," 1986. *Origins* 16 (May 22), 1986: 1-9.

Walsh, Michael, 1989. *The Secret World of Opus Dei.* London: Collier Publishing Company.

CHAPTER X

THE ANTI-CULT MOVEMENT IN THE NETHERLANDS: AN UNSUCCESSFUL AFFAIR

Reender Kranenborg

When in the sixties new religious movements (NRMs) arose in the Western world, it did not take much time before a counter-movement came into being. Concerned people, with different motivations, were organizing themselves to fight the NRMs. This countermovement can be referred to generally as an "anti-cult movement" (ACM). Shupe and Bromley (1980:87-121) have reported that the first parent-organization/ACM in the United States, FREECOG (or Free the Children of God), was established in 1971. In the seventies the North American ACM grew more and more widespread, resulting in a fierce battle between cults and the ACM at local, state, and federal levels. An important aspect in this struggle was deprogramming.

In Europe, the emergence of various ACM groups took more time. In 1974, for example, the public came to hear of "Jugendreligione" (youth religions). Later, in the seventies, many "Elterninitiative's" (or parent organizations—see, e.g., Shupe, Hardin, and Bromley, 1983) were arising in Germany and action was taken against the "destructive sects." In this period we also saw the originating of ACM groups in Great Britain and France (e.g., Beckford, 1983). However, in general the atmosphere in Europe was more moderate than in the U.S.A., and deprogramming never has been popular in Europe.

THE SITUATION IN THE
NETHERLANDS BEFORE 1979

In the Netherlands almost nothing can be found in the seventies which resembles an anti-cult movement. Although the press frequently mentioned "sects" or new religious movements, there was hardly a trace of concern. The word "deprogramming" was unknown. Apart from some minor problems dealing with NRMs, there was no reason to pay special interest to the NRMs. The only important incident worth mentioning is the case of the Church of Scientology. In 1973 a commission was set up by the Ministry of Health to investigate this movement. Scientology took the legality of this commission to court but lost the case in 1975. However, in spite of this, the commission stopped further investigation. This was the only major case with regard to the NRMs in this period which drew attention.[1]

Within the churches there was virtually no immediate reaction to the arrival of new religious movements. Only evangelicals and fundamentalist groups (at that time rather small) wrote and preached against the NRMs. They did not see the NRMs as a danger to Dutch society, but they did detect in these NRMs a kind of faith which was non-Christian and/or even anti-Christian. They considered them as manifestations of the striving of the Devil to manipulate people away from the living God and therefore condemned them as such.

Thus, we have seen that in the Netherlands no parent-organization or anti-cult movement existed before 1979. However, when in November 1978 the terrible communal suicide of the members of the Peoples Temple in Jonestown, Guyana took place, the popular mood changed in Dutch society. At the beginning of 1979 the parent-organization S.O.S. (Samenwerkende Ouders Sekteleden, or Parents of Sect-members Working Together) was founded.

DUTCH SOCIETY:
THE SYSTEM OF SOCIOLOGICAL BLOCKS

This late arising of an ACM parent-organization in the Netherlands is related to the social structure of Dutch society. Furthermore, the fact that this parent-organization did not expand into a real ACM and that ACM ideology did not have much influence on Dutch society can be explained by this structure. This history becomes more interesting when we see that by the beginning of 1991 the S.O.S. ended its activities. Thus, the Netherlands no longer has any ACM parent-organization at all.

In order to understand this collapse of organized anti-cultism, we have to realize that there are three important aspects in Dutch society:

1. The freedom of religion and the separation of church-state. Since the era of Napoleon the principles of freedom of religion and the separation of church-state have been culturally fundamental. In the nineteenth century these principles were developed further, which resulted in the absence of a privileged position for any church in the Netherlands. (Only the Dutch Reformed Church has some small financial privileges. In general churches have some special rights as non-profit organizations.) Every religious group or church has the freedom to organize itself and to do and believe all it wants to do as long as it remains within the boundaries of Dutch law. However, these boundaries are not easily reached. They can only be crossed when a religious group makes financial profits or engages in objectionable practices under cover of religious activities or when it commits offenses against public decency. However, in almost all cases, religious groups in the Netherlands remain within the boundaries of the law and therefore do not cause problems.

2. The system of sociopolitical blocks (the "pillar-system"). In Dutch society one can discern different sociopolitical blocks; that is, a social group which organizes itself on the basis of a block-shared worldview alongside other groups but independent from them. Thus, there are Protestant, Roman Catholic, socialist, and liberal blocks. Inside each block are various parallel institutions; its own schools, universities, trade-unions, churches, and so forth. Each block is a closed society unto itself so that people belonging to a block mostly only meet people of the same group. One element of the block idea is that one recognizes the right of other blocks to exist. In this pluralist arrangement, members have the right to do what they want to do within their own block. Evidently people of the Protestant block do not agree with the ideas within the Roman Catholic group and they will fight and criticize them. Similarly, Roman Catholics will dispute the beliefs held within the Communist block, but the right to exist of rivals and theological/ideological opponents never has been denied.

Of course, it is possible to organize oneself outside the block system but, by doing this, one automatically creates a new block. Many new religious movements which came to the Netherlands were organized outside this system and enjoyed a relative freedom apart from the other blocks. Of course, it happened that people from one block married people from another, which subsequently gave rise to problems.

In most cases, such marriages resulted in ruptures between one of the partners and his/her group. It was not considered good to leave your own group. However, it was not forbidden to join another block, and in the tolerant system of Dutch society it was of course accepted. This principle could also be applied to the NRMs. It was possible for people to leave their group to become a member of another block belonging to a society where different groups or blocks have already lived together for a long time. Thus, the NRMs as innovative groups did not of themselves cause problems in Dutch society.

3. *The general moral ideas.* Even though Dutch society consists of various blocks, there are things people of almost all these groups have in common. Thus, the Dutch do not only enjoy a common history and a language, but they also share moral and social ideas such as the undesirability of killing and stealing, and virtues of honesty, sincerity, the idea of the family as the kernel of society, the authority of the parents and the authorities, and respect for the law. These general social and moral values can be seen as the cement holding relatively homogenous Dutch culture together. It could be expected that NRMs in the 1970s would have conflicts with various of these social and moral ideas, as happened in the U.S.A. There, as we know, parents felt that general ethics were endangered and that it was necessary to fight these "dangerous groups" (Shupe and Bromley, 1983). In the Netherlands things are different because of at least two developments. First of all, we see that the block system implies a kind of relativation of general ethics. For instance, Catholics have different feelings than Protestants regarding their common history; thus, to obey the authorities is good, but within the Protestant block it was clear, that only if they would damage their group, it is possible to disobey the authorities. But general ethics do not have the same color in the different blocks; there are differences in details. This implies that although general ethics were accepted, the validity is not absolute.

In the second place, the 1960s witnessed a major attack on general ethics. Large groups of young people, known as "provos," criticized these general ideas. Thus, the self-evident trust in authorities was unmasked: they were seen as not democratic, so they could be disobeyed. Children chose a different set of values and lifestyles than their parents did and caused conflicts because they did not accept their parents' authority. New ideas on property, sexuality, education, public traffic, and so forth were introduced. General ethics changed considerably as a result of the movement. Provos shocked Dutch society and changed the attitude of many people towards their own block system and towards general ethics. As a consequence, in the Western part of the Netherlands general ethics were very much weakened. This development was accompanied by a growing tolerance to quite different kinds of living and believing.

When new religious movements entered such a mileau it could be expected that there would not be less conflicts over them. Even when this caused problems between parents and children, it was not considered extraordinarily strange or alarming, for since the 1960s such conflicts have been familiar in Dutch society. In short, in the Netherlands there was hardly any reaction to the new religious movements until the Jonestown case.

THE S.O.S. FROM 1979-1984

The Beginning

When the collective suicide of members of the People's Temple in Jonestown became known, the general idea about NRMs changed. People began to wonder if these new groups in our society also could be so dangerous and destructive. Thus, a new critical look was cast on the NRMs. In that situation, parents who had children in selected groups received publicity, and the possible seriousness of their problems was recognized. These parents saw the need for cooperation and investigation, and on July 4, 1979 the S.O.S. was founded. The aims of the new organization were the following:

> The association has as its aim to give help and support to those whose closest relatives have contacts with religious sects and movements, and who are concerned by it to a greater or lesser degree. It tries to realize this aim through assistance from parents to parents—both on a national and an international level—by organizing the reception of ex-members and by all other means which are conducive to this aim.[2]

Here, we can see two aspects of purpose: (a) mutual assistance and (b) the reception (i.e., support) of ex-members. After some time additional goals were introduced: (c) information provided to the schools, (d) publicity in general to warn young people, and (e) requests to the government to investigate these NRMs in case serious intervention measures needed to be taken. These aims were realized in different working-groups: assistance for parents, reception of ex-members, rehabilitation (= deprogramming), information, publicity, documentation, finance, international contacts, and special cases. After several years a special telephone number which was manned continually was put into use.

The S.O.S. as ACM

In spite of the above mentioned activities, the S.O.S. still became no viable ACM. In the early publications of the S.O.S. we do not find the internationally familiar anti-cult ideology of brainwashing, or coercive persuasion. Instead, we find the association expressing its desire to help. However, through international influence (principally from North American groups' publications), the S.O.S. gradually adopted a more recognizable ACM ideology. In December, 1980, representatives of the S.O.S. did not hesitate to sign the anti-cult resolution which was adopted by a congress of international ACM parent-organizations in Paris. The problem of totalitarian tendencies in certain religious and pseudo-religious movements was the subject of this conference. Some 60 people from 14 countries met on behalf of various organizations concerned with the impact of what are often called "New Religious Movements" or "extremist cults," and their effect not only on the youth whom they attract but on the very values of democratic societies. It was noted that these new movements' religious claims often defended them from criticism by a public which believes all religion to be good. In fact, with their elitist and totalitarian claims, some of them (conference participants maintained) were a threat to the freedom. It was argued that religious freedom has traditionally protected the individual from oppressive institutions, but these new movements cynically use the term "religious freedom" to attack the individuals who criticize them. They were accused of destroying normal family relationships for the sake of their own closed communities. They were criticized for encouraging youth to forego free will, suppress conscience, and surrender to a "Fuhrer" authority figure. These groups were alleged to subvert democracy, damage recruits mentally, emotionally, and physically, and pose a problem of transnational dimensions.

After this conference, one can see the S.O.S beginning to develop itself in a more "characteristic" ACM-way. We can illustrate this by quoting some parts of an unauthored circular about the NRMs that made its rounds in 1980:

> Sects know (1) misleading recruitment and manipulation leading to membership. We parents are strongly under the impression that this is happening by a kind of brainwashing technique, which varies from some days to many weeks. Sometimes very short, but mostly longer. (2) This is irrevocably connected with the giving up of studies and work which means that outside the sect there is no more future left. (3) Life in a group or commune, with sometimes a changed use of language. Sect members can be transported abroad, through which they become still more estranged from society. This may end up in total isolation. (4) By meditating in a long and intensive way, many sect members are not capable to work anymore. They become dependent on social security in order to provide for themselves. If they still have a job, their salaries are going to the leader or guru of the group. (5) If they have a breakdown by the circumstances or are not useful anymore to the aims of the sect leaders, they are thrown out. Then, they are and become disoriented and completely penniless. In some cases they are asked to commit suicide.

Still clearer an indication of the growing incorporation of ACM ideology is in an unauthored folder of brochures and handouts which the S.O.S. used after 1981 to warn against the NRMs. We quote some parts of it:

> A sect can be recognized by the following aspects:
> — a leader who claims divinity or a special relation with God;
> — a leader who asks unconditional absolute obedience and who alone is capable to judge the sincerity and the religious intention of the members;
> — controlling or diminishing of contacts with the family; the sect is becoming the new family of the convert;
> — to sect members the aims of the sect are more important than individual cares, interests, studies, or job-ideals;

— sects use sophisticated techniques, which are designed to reach destruction of the ego, conversion, and dependency on the sect;

— members are not fully informed about the faith, the aims, the demands, and the activities of the group until they are won over;

— the sect can hold its members in a state of heightened suggestivity by: changes in the sleeping and dietary patterns, intensive spiritual experiences, continual indoctrination, and controlled group experiences;

— converts can show symptoms of extreme tension and stress, anguish, guilt, lack of humor, decline of communication skills, and a deterioration of the capacity to think in a critical and logical way;

— members are encouraged to see themselves as different from other people; therefore a feeling of isolation and of exclusivity, of being one of the elect, is created.

The S.O.S. saw the following as the results of a stay within a NRM:

A stay within the strict mental and social restrictions of a sect, even only for a short period, can have the following devastating results:

— loss of the free will and control of one's own life;

— diminished capacity to enter into flexible and intimate relations;

— more problems to make decisions;

— problems with delusions, panic, feelings of guilt, identity crises, paranoia, and collapse (in some groups);

— incidental neurotic, psychotic or suicidal tendencies.[3]

How has the reaction towards the S.O.S. been? In the U.S.A. we can see that evangelicals and fundamentalists have been closely connected with various ACM organizations. In some cases this has been so close that the two are almost identical. However, in the Netherlands this never has happened. As we have seen, the evangelicals considered NRMs as dangerous in a theological respect, as a sign of the power of the devil, but they did not concern themselves with the S.O.S. or ACM brainwashing ideology. When publicity generally diminished after 1984 (and Jonestown faded from memory), the evangelicals continued to approach the NRMs in the same way. The churches never reacted in a major way to the S.O.S. They never had many problems with the NRMs, and they did not welcome the work of the government's commission to investigate the NRMs (see below).

Through contacts with international organizations, the S.O.S. was confronted with the question of deprogramming, which turned out to be a dilemma. On one hand, its members saw the legal problems involved in its kidnappings and embedded violence. On the other hand, the method was found sometimes effective, and positive outcomes of deprogramming were known. Therefore, with this ambivalent position the S.O.S. never officially propagated deprogramming. Nevertheless, during the period 1979-1984 the S.O.S. helped parents to find their way to deprogrammers and started a working network of deprogrammings (later called rehabilitation). Outside the S.O.S. the practice of deprogramming was defended by some individuals with whom the S.O.S. was in contact. But examining the whole period, the fact remains that in the Netherlands there have never been many deprogrammings.[4]

Assistance

The S.O.S. has tried to realize its original goals: the mutual assistance of the parents and the reception of ex-members. Throughout the years it has been a place of support for parents who could speak about their problems, and reinforce each other.

As for the latter ex-member issue, in 1980 others than immediate family members had the impression that ex-members were in trouble. Thus, as a result of a meeting of social workers who had some experience with ex-members, *"Joeka"* was founded in 1980. This organization decided, after having been in touch with the S.O.S. to set up a center to receive ex-members. *Joeka's* goal was determined to be helping people, who had come under the influence of a religious group in which systems and structures were used that presumably hindered the development of an individual's personality, leaving him or her without a "view on the future."

Publicity and Information

The S.O.S. for the most part occupied itself with publicity and information. In the first period it issued many folders about the NRMs and gave many interviews. The S.O.S. also had contacts with broadcasting companies and could in this way influence the public.

Furthermore, in this period many books with a critical attitude towards the NRMs were translated into Dutch (for example, Enroth, 1977; Conway and Siegelman, 1978).

However, more important was the request put to the Dutch Government by the S.O.S. to investigate the NRMs. On June 26, 1980 a commission was established by the Department of Health for this purpose. The S.O.S. asked the government to (a) control the activities of the movements, (b) to restrain the propaganda made by the movements, (c) to forbid the NRMs to allow foreign members to enter the Netherlands, (d) to create the possibility to place members under legal restraint, (e) to impose a trial period before one becomes a member of a group, (f) to provide information at the schools, (g) to subsidize the private information groups, and (h) to finance the S.O.S.

The Commission investigated the Divine Light Mission, Bhagwan Shree Rajneesh's movement, the Hare Krishna movement, Transcendental Meditation, the Church of Scientology, the Unification Church, and the Jesus-children (a small Dutch group). Some Christian movements, intended to be investigated, were not studied. On July 12, 1984 the Commission's report was ready. The conclusion was clear: there was no reason whatsoever to take measures against the NRMs because in general they did not present a major danger to public mental health. Moreover, no proof was found that NRMs used violence in recruiting members or that members had significant psychological problems. The Commission suggested that the S.O.S. had to be better informed about the NRMs and that the S.O.S.'s attitude interfered with a dialogue with the groups.

At that time, the S.O.S. heartily supported a similar investigatory motion in the European Parliament, which was accepted by Parliament on May 22, 1984 in a weakened form. It served only as an advisory statement. However, soon after that, the European Parliament lost interest in the NRMs.

With the case of the Tai Chi-group the anti-cult mentality reached a climax. For many years a Tai Chi-group which lived as a communal group led by a teacher existed in Amsterdam. (Tai Chi is a traditional Chinese form of patterned calasthentics with both aerobic and martial arts benefits.) In this group there were many women and little children. The parents of one of the members had many questions about this little understood group, and they were afraid the little children were not educated properly. In 1982 the parents contacted the S.O.S. and together they drew up a list of complaints. Eventually they came forward with the following accusations: the leader had too much psychological influence on the members, the women were humiliated, the leader frequently had sexual intercourse with the women, little children were separated as soon as possible from their mothers in order to make them more independent, and the children were physically and mentally neglected. On October 7, 1983 twenty children were taken away by the police and the Child Welfare Council for observation. Around the same time, two of the women-members seemed to have disappeared. The publicity was enormous. However, after a while it became clear that none of the children had any problems. The other accusations also were found to be groundless. The two members who had allegedly vanished had actually been kidnapped by their parents and deprogrammed. In February 1984 it was more or less admitted that mistakes had been made by the officials. Ironically, at the end of the whole affair, one of the fathers of a Tai Chi group member became the president of S.O.S.

The Reaction and the End of the S.O.S. (1984-1991)

The year 1984 was a turning point for the S.O.S. On many fields, it appeared that the situation with the NRMs was different than generally was thought. Moreover, it was clear that the ACM ideology had not won popular or official appeal. We can signal the decline of S.O.S. by the following developments:

(1) In 1979 when the S.O.S. was founded there also were people, mostly scholars, who thought the problems with the NRMs minimal. In 1981 a psychological analysis of NRM members was published, which took the edge off the theory of brainwashing. A year later the president of a health care commission defended a thesis in which it was shown that NRMs were small and not very strange and more was written about the phenomenon of NRMs in both a historic perspective and the perspective of the science of religion. By 1984 the already-mentioned report of the Commission was available. All this publicity also counterbalanced the books critical of various NRMs and showed that what had happened in NRMs was not as disturbing as it seemed. It became clear that irregular things happened in other groups besides NRMs and that Dutch law could provide for those difficult cases.

(2) The report of the Commission put an abrupt end to much of the negative publicity. Since that time almost nothing has been written about the dangers of NRMs. Apart from those cases which were of local interest, this lack of interest in NRMs can also be illustrated by the fact

that it took many months before the Commission's report was discussed in the Dutch parliament. The SOS was heavily disappointed, because it did not receive financial support and was attacked in its view about the NRMs. The S.O.S. had to face the fact that it would stand alone and could only continue as a small organization for mutual assistance.

(3) The failing of the reception center in 1983 also came as a shock to the anti-cult ideology. If there really had been so many problems with the ex-members as was said, at least some people should have been treated; but no ex-member was ever seen. The case of the Tai Chi-group also demonstrated that there were no major problems. Of course, individual situations arose which were not pleasant in terms of family dynamics and disagreement, but these were merely incidents in need of special measures or special treatments, not wholesale shifts in policy.

(4) Since 1977 a movement of ex-members of Jehovah Witnesses, parallel to the S.O.S., had been set up. In many cases the S.O.S. helped them and they in turn assisted the S.O.S. However, in 1987 this movement ("The Dutch Association of Disappointed People") ended its existence by joining a new religious movement called "Eben Haëzer," an evangelical group, based on the "Concordant Greek Text" of Adolph Ernst Knoch. The fact that another anti-cult movement became a "cult" itself shocked the S.O.S.

However, there were other developments:

(5) The report of the Commission made people aware that freedom of religion is a very important thing and that it would be not desirable to "remedy" anything in this situation.

(6) People also realized again that pluriformity is a fundamental aspect of Dutch society, and that this pluriformity implies the existence and tolerance of NRMs.

(7) Besides that, Dutch society realized in the eighties that many foreigners from different religions were in Holland to stay permanently. Hindus and Moslems belong to the Dutch culture now, and they have their own beliefs, their own customs, and their own special ways of life. The existence of these religions also gave room to the acceptance of the NRMs.

(8) Furthermore, it became recognized that NRMs could change themselves. Scientology became more subdued, the Unification Church was more open than before and looked for cooperation with the churches, and the Hare Krishna's and the Divine Light Mission were

now either very small or disappeared altogether. Moreover, it became clear that within the groups, ideas and practices existed which were of some merit and which could be used outside the setting of the NRM itself.

(9) Finally, it is interesting to note that in the second half of the eighties much attention was paid to the problems of members and ex-members of the stronger, reformed churches. It appeared that many of them suffered from fear and feelings of guilt and needed psychiatric help. So, when people from generally respected churches could get entrapped in significant problems, why should one bother to single out small NRMs?

Thus, anti-cult ideology largely disappeared from Dutch society. The S.O.S. did not see itself as an ACM anymore. In 1985 the S.O.S. publicly declared to fight NRMS no longer and denied having the wish both to influence the government in matters dealing with NRMs and to propagate kidnapping or deprogramming. The S.O.S. only wanted children within groups to be conscious of what they were doing and to learn why they had become members. Furthermore, the S.O.S. wanted to give information about the way some NRMs recruit their members and to help people, mostly parents, who have problems with children or other relatives who are involved in NRMs. After 1985 even the desire to help and the need to be helped appeared to wither away. The S.O.S. fell from 200 members in 1980 to 40 half a decade later. Thus, the S.O.S. decided to end its activities. On January 12, 1991 the S.O.S. was disbanded; people with problems dealing with NRMs were advised to go to another Dutch organization which in a broader sense helped people with acute problems.

What have been the results of the S.O.S. in the Netherlands? First of all, the organization has helped many people who really had problems. As a self-help organization it functioned well, even if its vision of the NRMs has been one-sided. Second, the report of the Commission requested by the S.O.S. made the government and parliament aware that the churches in general still had some privileges. This was not considered to be in keeping with the separation of church and state. Therefore, the decision was made to end these privileges. Although the S.O.S. did not intend this, ironically it changed the position of the churches in Dutch society. Finally, the S.O.S. contributed in establishing a negative image of the NRMs in the media. Although nowadays not much is written about the dangers of the NRMs, many people still have the idea that NRMs are strange and dangerous organizations. (I personally found this image still vivid when a reporter of a journal from a provincial town phoned me about the end of the S.O.S.) The view of the NRMs was still exactly the negative image that the S.O.S. had built up. This image will likely last for a long time. Otherwise, however, in general the S.O.S. had little influence in Dutch society. When the end of the S.O.S. had come, none of the important journals made mention of it.

NOTES

1. As an illustration, between 1975 and 1979 the police officials responsible for juveniles obtained 30 complaints nationwide (almost all regarding the Children of God and the Unified Family). The national government's Welfare Council received during this period only 12 complaints (about the same groups).

2. Taken from an unauthored S.O.S. brochure, circa 1979.

3. In this folder the following groups, familiar to North American anti-cultists, were mentioned as dangerous "sects:" Bhagwan Shree Rajneesh's movement, the Hare Krishnas, the Divine Light Movement (at that time already very small in the Netherlands), the Unification Church, Transcendental Meditation, and the Children of God (later the Family of Love), by then non-existent in the Netherlands.

4. Deprogramming was primarily conducted by American deprogrammers (mostly the work of one person, E. Barbo). One of the reasons deprogramming was never done very much had to do with finances. (It appeared to be prohibitively expensive.) After some time there appeared a Dutch deprogrammer, Ms. Barbara Bisschot, a member of the S.O.S. and responsible for rehabilitation. She did not use the word deprogramming but preferred to say, "Stepping out with evaluation-counseling" or "Rescue operations." She left the Netherlands in 1985, after which the S.O.S. abandoned the practice of deprogramming completely. As the S.O.S. secretary told me in an interview, deprogramming is illegal, it is threatening to the private life of the member, it is not certain that deprogrammers are capable enough in human relations, it does not always work, and it is very expensive. Nowadays, "deprogramming" refers to a method which is used on a voluntary basis, or what in the United States is now termed "exit counseling."

REFERENCES

Beckford, James A., 1983. "The 'Cult Problem' in Five Countries: The Social Construction of Religious Controversy," in Eileen Barker, ed., *Of Gods and Men: New Religious in the West.* Macon, GA: Mercer University Press, pp. 195-214.

Conway, Flo and Jim Siegelman, 1978. *Snapping: America's Epidemic of Sudden Personality Change.* Philadelphia: J. B. Lippincott.

Enroth, Ronald, 1977. *Youth, Brainwashing, and the Extremist Cults.* Grand Rapids, MI: Zondervan.

Shupe, Jr., Anson D. and David G. Bromley, 1983. "Moonies and the Anti-Cultists: Movement and Countermovement in Conflict," in Jeffrey K. Hadden and Theodore E. Long, eds., *Religion and Religiosity in America.* New York: Crossroad, pp. 70-83.

Shupe, Jr., Anson D., and David G. Bromley, 1980. *The New Vigilantes: Deprogrammers, Anti-Cultists, and the New Religions.* Beverly Hills, CA: Sage.

Shupe, Jr., Anson D., Bert L. Hardin, and David G. Bromley, 1983. "A Comparison of Anti-Cult Movements in the United States and West Germany," in Eileen Barker, ed., *Of Gods and Men: New Religious Movements in the West.* Macon, GA: Mercer University Press, pp. 177-93.

MODERN ANTI-CULTISM IN THE MIDDLE AND FAR EAST

CHAPTER XI

ALIEN GODS, ALIEN IDENTITIES: THE "ANTI-CULT" LOBBY IN ISRAEL

Benjamin Beit-Hallahmi

The development and impact of new religions can be assessed by looking at the reactions they bring about in various segments of society (Beit-Hallahmi, 1992b). In response to the growth of new religions in Israel since the early 1970s, a countermovement appeared in the form of an "anti-cult" lobby, similar to their counterparts in the United States, and modeled after them in some ways (see Shupe and Bromley, 1980; Robbins, 1988). In this chapter, I will survey the history of the movement through looking at its various components, including the Israeli government and non-governmental organizations. New religions in Israel had to contend with the hostility of the religious establishment, the hostility of the public, the hostility of families of members, and the hostility of the media, which were guided by all of the above. The opposition started, naturally enough, with Jewish religious groups, then came from parents' organizations, and then involved the media, Israeli government, and the public.

RELIGIOUS COMMUNITIES IN ISRAEL

In Israel, where there is no constitution, no separation of religion and state, and a Ministry for Religious Affairs, there is a clear legal definition of new religions. This applies to all religious communities not formally recognized by the state. According to Israeli law, all residents of the State must belong to some religious community, whose rules they then must follow in regard to marriage, divorce, and burial. A majority of Israeli residents, 82% as of 1992, are classified as Jewish, but most of them are non-observant beyond following tradition in the major lifestyle rites of passage.

The Israeli system of religious divisions uses the "millet" system, taking the religious community as a basic unit. This notion is borrowed from Turkish law (Cahnman, 1944). Under the "millet" system, the Israeli government recognizes certain established religious groups whose leaders are accorded special status, even when they represent tiny minorities. These religious communities are also entitled to government financial support for keeping their churches or mosques (including tax exemptions), for maintaining their separate legal systems, and for paying the salaries of clergy. They have an official standing and their leaders are treated as dignitaries. All other groups, ranging from Reform Jews to ISKCON (International Society for Krishna Consciousness), are not recognized.

The boundaries of religious legitimacy in Israel (Sobel & Beit-Hallahmi, 1991) are delineated in Israel Pocket Library's *Religious Life and Communities* (1974) which contains material taken from the *Encyclopaedia Judaica.* The religious communities described are Jews, Muslims, Christians, Samaritans, Karaites, Druze, and Bahais. Conversions from one "millet" to another are possible under the system but have to be registered with the State to be legally valid. This occurs according to the legal authority of the British Mandate of 1922. All these orders have been kept in force by the Israeli government since 1948. The British Mandate government recognized ten religious groups, namely Jews and nine Christian denominations. Since 1948, the Israeli government has recognized the Druze (in 1957), the Evangelical Episcopal Church in Israel (in 1970), and the Bahai Faith (in 1971). Moslems have not been officially recognized, but their religious courts have been, and they have been empowered by two Israeli laws in 1953 and 1961 respectively. Cases of conversion from one recognized group to another number under 300 a year, and most of them are conversions from one Christian church to another. About 5 cases of Jews converting to Christianity, about 15 cases of Christians who adopt Judaism, and about 10 cases of Jews converting to Islam, are officially registered every year.

As Pfeffer (1974) correctly points out, in Israel legitimation of a marginal religion is accorded by the government, and he chooses the good example of non-Orthodox Jews who in Israel are members of a marginal religion, not accorded legitimacy by the state. The common division of Jews in the United States into three denominations, Orthodox, Conservative, and Reform, has little bearing on religious life in Israel. Reform Judaism and Conservative Judaism, imported from the U.S., thus would be counted among the other new religions. They are subject to either opposition (from the Orthodox establishment) or indifference (from most Israelis) and have shown little success in attracting members. Liebman and Don-Yehiya (1984:19) state: "The institutional monopoly of the Orthodox (Conservative and Reform rabbis are not recognized as rabbis in Israel . . .) is not a major political issue. There are no more than two or three thousand members of non-Orthodox synagogues . . . ." As of 1992, there were 17 Reform and 30 Conservative synagogues in Israel. Their histories in Israel are similar to those of other new religious movements. They were imported by foreigners, who have been trying to convert the natives to their viewpoint, with limited success. Most members of these Jewish movements have been immigrants from English-speaking countries. As of 1992, there are probably fewer than 3,000 Israeli adults in both. In a sense, Reform Judaism has a harder task "selling" itself to Israelis than even ISKCON. The former tries to present itself as an authentic form of Judaism, while the latter is clearly an alternative and in opposition to Judaism. Most Israelis have not responded to the Reform and Conservative messages, apparently because they do not feel the need for another Judaism in addition to the readily available Orthodox version. The Reform and Conservative movements also express quite strongly values characteristic of U.S. culture, such as anti-authoritarianism and feminism, which are foreign to Israeli experience and culture. The opposition to Reform Judaism in Israel thus comes from the Orthodox since it threatens their dominance and monopoly. Opposition to new religions is almost universal, because they threaten the unity provided by the Jewish identity common to secular and religious Israelis.

In summary, Israeli society clearly exhibits a low tolerance for non-Jewish old religions and even for non-Orthodox branches of Judaism. New religions present a direct challenge to the religious establishment. And in Israel this challenge is more serious because it is directed towards Jewish identity and Zionism and thus touches the ideological base of the state itself.[1] Alternately, most new religions in Israel have been imported from the outside. Not all of them have been treated in the same way by the Israeli establishment. Some have been singled out for harsher treatment, and they are those that present a threat through their basic message and their mere existence.

ANTI-CULT V. ORGANIZATIONS

Concerned Parents Against Cults

This organization, modeled after similar grassroots family-based groups in the U.S.A., was founded in 1980 in Haifa and became formally incorporated as a non-profit organization in 1982. In July 1981 it had fifteen members, but by late 1981 membership had grown to sixty families. The organization has been active in lobbying the media and the government. Its chairman, whom I shall call N.B., has made numerous media appearances, including appearances on television, in which his face and full identity were always hidden from the cameras.

Concerned Parents Against Cults has published its own leaflets, containing information about various new religions. The leaflets refer also to *est* as a cult, and their general level of accuracy and sophistication is rather low. N.B. has also been active in addressing letters to newspapers whenever any favorable or even neutral mention was made of any of the new religions. The organization has been instrumental in bringing Israel the film "Ticket to Heaven," which drew much media attention, including television coverage. There can be little doubt that effective lobbying by Concerned Parents was instrumental in the creation of the government commission of inquiry in February 1982, and members of the organization appeared several times before the commission and kept informal contact with its staff. Meanwhile, Concerned Parents was effective in creating contacts with other government agencies, such as the Health Ministry.

On May 12, 1983 a day-long symposium was held in Tel-Aviv, titled "The Problems and Treatment of Cult Adepts." It was organized jointly by Concerned Parents Against Cults and by the mental health division of the Health Ministry. It was addressed, among others, by the latter's director and by the legal counsel for the Health Ministry. Other participants included psychologists, psychiatrists, and former "cult" members. The intervention practices of "cult exit counseling" and "deprogramming" were introduced and explained by individuals who wanted those to be imported to Israel. The individuals presenting and advocating "deprogramming" were North Americans who were ready to discuss their own experiences in practicing it and offered their services. Among those present, however, strong doubts were expressed about the legality of such procedures in Israel.

Materials distributed to the audience at the symposium consisted of articles published in the U.S.A., such as a much-cited article in *Psychology Today* by Singer (1979) and an annotated bibliography of books on cults, again published in the U.S.A. and well known to persons studying the new religions. The overall solution offered at the symposium, which I personally attended, was the medicalization and psychologization of the new religions phenomenon. There is no evidence that this perspective was indeed adopted by either government authorities or the public.

Yad La'Ahim and the New Religions

Yad La'Ahim is a non-profit organization, with eight branches in Israel. Its members fight against abortions, drafting women into military service, autopsies, and other issues of concern to the Orthodox community. Yad La'Ahim constitutes an "anti-missionary" lobby in Israel, active since the 1950s. The ideology of the organization is clear: it represents Orthodox Judaism, and anything incompatible with it should be eliminated from the State of Israel. Any group which presents a challenge to the loyalty of Jews to Orthodox Judaism (including other Jewish traditions) should be confronted. (Thus Yad La'Ahim is similar to the conservative religious wing of the North American anti-cult movement as described by Shupe and Bromley [1980:65-70].) There is no differentiation, within the ideology of Yad La'Ahim, between old and new religions. Their struggle against the new religions since the 1970s has been a continuation of their struggle since the 1950s against Christian missionary groups, which culminated in the passing of an anti-missionary law by the Knesset in 1977. The only way in which the new religions may be different, and more dangerous, for Yad La'Ahim, is in that they do not carry the old cultural stigma attached to Christianity and its millenia-old conflict with Judaism. Thus, they are not as easily recognized for what they are, and may be able to attract Israelis. In fact, this is exactly what has happened.

Yad La'Ahim activities include media relations, publications, and actual harassment of new religions. The most obvious and noticeable activity is that of initiating newspaper articles about new religions. Some of the articles sound like press releases, and include wild claims about the success of new religions. Yad La'Ahim publishes a monthly bulletin of activities against "missions and cults," which includes information about alleged Christian missionaries, Messianic Jews, and new religions. It also publishes special reports and reprints articles appearing in the press. In 1982, a special booklet containing testimonies of former members of new religions, who were now Orthodox Jews, was published. It contained seven personal stories. A special report listing 17 "cults" operating in Israel was also published in 1982. Yad La'Ahim submitted a memorandum to the commission of inquiry investigating cults. The memorandum included 12 recommendations for actions against new religions, from close police surveillance to declaring Scientology's E-Meter illegal. In addition to this document, the organization also arranged for witnesses to appear before the commission.

The Kibbutzim and New Religions

The kibbutzim, communal settlements which invest much energy and concern in the education of their young people (Rabin & Beit-Hallahmi, 1982), make up less than 3% of the Israeli population. Nevertheless, they are much more visible in Israeli society and much more visible in the world of the new religions. It is hard to determine the exact representation of kibbutz-born and raised individuals in the new religions, but they clearly make up more than 3%, perhaps 10% in some groups, and thus are clearly overrepresented. Joining a new religion means usually leaving the kibbutz, and the kibbutzim, which are justifiably concerned about desertions, have reacted to this threat.

One large kibbutz reached an important policy decision in 1983. Since kibbutz members usually do not have private funds, the kibbutz used to cover membership dues in any external organization. In the case of new religions, members who had joined them while still in the kibbutz applied to the kibbutz Education Committee, claiming that membership in Transcendental Meditation, or the Emin Society, was an educational activity. Concern was shown by Education Committees when the training courses never ended and when more became known about various new religions. The kibbutz in question decided to stop any such payments and thus force the member to choose between the kibbutz and the outside group.

The kibbutzim have their own centralized educational organizations as well as their own psychotherapy clinics. Policies in regard to new religions have been formulated by educators, psychiatrists, and social workers. An anti-cult task force was created in 1982. This task force has been active in organizing symposia and lectures to kibbutz educators and to kibbutz members. In addition, there are treatment groups for families whose children have joined new religions and lectures for high school students in the kibbutzim. Training courses for professionals have also been organized by the Kibbutz Child and Family Clinic in Tel-Aviv, under the heading of "Mystical cults—how to prevent and treat." Most of the 260 kibbutzim in Israel belong to two large federations. As of 1984, there was an anti-cult task force in each federation, staffed by educators and mental health professionals.

MEDIA COVERAGE OF NEW RELIGIONS

An inspection of the Israeli press reveals that references to specific new religions, or "cults" in general were sparse before 1973. The only new religions whose existence in Israel can be gathered from the Israeli media before the 1973 war were ISKCON and Transcendental Meditation. The first wave of media attention to new religious groups followed the 1973 war. Press attention to Transcendental Meditation was positive or neutral, and the first press campaign against new religions in the spring of 1974 actually singled out the Divine Light Mission. No similar campaign is to be found in the Israeli press until 1982-83, when no group is singled out, and the topic is "cults" in general.

This second wave of media coverage, totally negative in tone, coincides with the creation of the government commission of inquiry, and the increased activity by Yad La'Ahim. It also coincides with the formation of the Concerned Parents Against Cults organization, active since 1980. The articles ranged from news reports covering the new religions and their relations with the community and government authorities, to interviews with professionals and academics, to reports on lectures by professionals with different orientations. In many of the articles, the inspiring hand of Yad La'Ahim can be immediately recognized. In a few cases, it was the parents' organization that initiated such articles.

The electronic media, which in Israel are owned and controlled by the government, have also entered the fray. Radio and television programs have discussed "cults" with illustrations taken from the activities of specific new religions. ISKCON, Transcendental Meditation, and Emin (Beit-Hallahmi, 1992B) have been singled out on these programs. Most major Israeli newspapers have carried not just major articles on "cults," but also a series or two on "cults in Israel."

1983 was a banner year for newspaper articles about cults. In addition to hundreds of articles about specific groups, there was an eight-part series in *Haaretz,* Israel's leading daily. The confidential *National Police Intelligence Report* on cults (Soffrin & Yodfat, 1982) was leaked to the press as soon as it was ready, and excerpts were duly published.

The tenor of all newspaper articles was negative, some of them purely sensational. The only exceptions to the moral crusade in the newspapers were those articles in which the new religions were defended on the basis of general democratic principles and on the basis of their similarity to the Judaization movement (Beit-Hallahmi, 1992b). While Zaretsky and Leone (1974) suggest that the North American media have given new religious movements an appearance of legitimacy, in Israel, for cultural and historical reasons, the situation is totally different. The media present new religions as definitely illegitimate and deviant. There has been one notable exception, however. Thanks to its dynamic leader, Yeshaiahu Ben-Aharon, the field of Anthroposophy in Israel has gained, by the 1990s, the status of a respectable philosophical-scientific approach. Ben-Aharon was often invited to a variety of events and even academic symposia and through him the late Rudolph Steiner's occult "discoveries" thus won a measure of legitimacy. For example, a popular symposium held at Tel-Aviv University in the summer of 1990 on the question of academic success included a presentation by Ben Aharon, who presented Steiner's "educational philosophy." Ben-Aharon shared the podium with authors, psychologists, mathematicians, and philosophers. The audience was treated to a lecture on Rudolph Steiner's occultist philosophy of education and greeted it with serious attention. Ben-Aharon skillfully managed to avoid any mention of the group's beliefs in reincarnation, or its ties to Christianity, which would have aroused a negative reaction in Israel.

THE INTERMINISTERIAL COMMISSION OF INQUIRY ON CULTS

This commission was appointed by Education and Culture Minister Zebulun Hammer on February 5, 1982. Miriam Glazer-Ta'asa, Deputy Minister for Education and Culture, was appointed to head the commission. The commission was assigned to investigate "Eastern cults" and its mandate was formulated as follows:

> Determining the extent of cult
> growth in Israel, their locations
> and dimensions.
>
> Locating the causes for this growth.
>
> Obtaining information on the nature of the cults:
> modus operandi, significance of effects,
> actions, and aims.
>
> Consequences of cult activities for the individual and
> for society.
>
> Determining ways for coping, by the educational
> system, with the cults.
>
> Recommending treatment modes (legal, public,
> educational, etc.)
>
> (Hammer, 1982)

The appointment of the commission of inquiry was the result of lobbying by Concerned Parents Against Cults, by individual parents whose children had joined the new religions, and by Yad La'Ahim. It is possible that in view of media attacks on the new religions and public sentiment in some communities, the creation of the commission was seen by some members of the government and by its chairperson, former school teacher and principal, Mrs. Glazer-Ta'asa as an opportunity for gaining some popularity. It should be pointed out here that Mrs. Glazer Ta'asa had, since her appointment as Deputy Minister for Education and Culture in July 1981, earned a certain notoriety. Affiliated with the Herut right-wing party, she had become the spokesperson for reactionary and nationalist views and had gained the enmity of intellectuals and liberals in Israel. For example, she expressed views critical of nudity in the theater, explicit sexual references in poetry, and the lack of nationalist spirit in Israeli culture.

The first indication of an interest by the Ministry of Education and Culture in new religions came on October 29, 1981, when newspapers reported on a meeting at Mrs. Glazer-Ta'asa's office to discuss the "Guru Maharishi cult." The meeting was held following requests from Yad La'Ahim and Concerned Parents Against Cults. On January 14, 1982, the director-general of the Ministry issued a special memorandum to all high schools in Israel, titled "Educational Measures in View of the Trend of Some Youth to Turn to Various Cults" (Shmueli, 1982). The memorandum, which was clearly inspired by the October 1981 meeting, alerted teachers to the existence of cults and recommended general measures of "reinforcing value education" and helping the institution of the family to prevent cult involvements. It should be pointed out that most new religions in Israel do not recruit high school students in any case.

The first session of the commission took place on February 22, 1982 in Jerusalem, and about 30 sessions of the full commission were held. The commission heard representatives of Concerned Parents, Yad La'Ahim, the kibbutz task forces on new religions, ex-members of new religions, and parents of members and ex-members. In addition, the leadership of two new religions, Transcendental Meditation and Emin (Beit-Hallahmi, 1992b), volunteered to appear before the commission in order to persuade its members of the non-religious nature of their activities. The commission was not persuaded. The commission received written reports and memoranda from the National Police, Yad La'Ahim, Concerned Parents Against Cults, and several of its own members.

After the commission had been at work for five years without publishing a report, public curiosity had been aroused and several newspaper stories dealt with the delay. Normally, such a commission is expected to release a report within a few months following its appointment. When the Commission Report was finally released in February 1987, it was a long and cumbersome document holding 503 pages, including a 74-page bibliography. It contained detailed background surveys on Scientology, Emin, *est,* Transcendental Meditation, Rajneesh, Ananda Marga, the Unification Church, ISKCON, Divine Light Mission, and Divine Intervention.

The Commission regarded *est* as a religious cult, despite the fact that there is nothing religious in its teachings or practices. The Commission recommended more energetic enforcement of consumer protection laws, the laws governing not-for-profit organizations, tax laws, and immigration laws in Israel as ways of limiting the activities and influence of new religions. In addition, the Commission recommended government activities in collecting and circulating information about new religions, educational activities, and help to former members, families of members, and "vulnerable populations." Following the publications of the Commission Report, the two groups that cooperated with the Commission, Emin and Transcendental Meditation, published lengthy rebuttals. The Emin document held 63 pages, and the Transcendental Meditation Report (titled "The Truth about TM versus the Commission Report") held about 100 pages of documents, including a list of 355 "scientific studies" of TM.

LOOKING BACK: NEW RELIGIONS AND THE BOUNDARIES OF RELIGIOUS LEGITIMACY IN ISRAEL

Looking back at the development of new religions in Israel, we can reach the following conclusions:

First, there is (not too surprisingly) a reverse relationship between the degree to which a group deviates from majority norms and its success in recruiting members in Israel. There is also a positive relationship (again not too surprising) between the degree of deviance and the degree of opposition to the group, regardless of its size. Thus, ISKCON, the Divine Light Mission, and Ananda Marga have achieved only limited success but have aroused considerable opposition.

In Israel, the new religions have been regarded as threatening cultural uniformity and, more seriously, because of the nature of Israeli identity, as threatening basic loyalties to the state. There is one cultural factor which determines the nature of reactions to new religions in Israel, and this factor is the cultural uniformity of Israeli society around the core of Jewish identity (which does not mean Orthodox observance).

Second, the successful new religions are those that combine a medium degree of deviation from the majority in regard to beliefs and lifestyle with a medium degree of separation from the member's previous social attachments. Such groups are Transcendental Meditation, Scientology, and Emin. That is to say, they do not make "totalistic" demands of members, such as dropping out of the conventional workforce or living separately and communally.

Third, the appearance of new religions in Israel can be described in a most basic way as a cultural innovation. It is an innovation because it represents behaviors previously unknown in the culture which within a relatively short time have become established as the norm for a significant minority. This innovation has appeared together with several others (e.g., return to Orthodox Judaism) and thus should be analyzed within a broader context (Beit-Hallahmi, 1992b). The appearance of new religions in Israel in a major way is much more radical in its implications than the growth of new religions in the U.S.A.

Fourth, the styles of these groups, in both internal management and recruitment, give rise to opposition and antipathy. In some of these groups, members remind outsiders of aggressive salesmen, especially when the membership is growing rapidly. Other "new religions," such as Anthroposophy and Jehovah's Witnesses, do not arouse these reactions because of their "gentle" manners and low-pressure civility. Christian missionary groups, which have been active in Israel for a long time, are often referred to in the Israeli media as "cults," but the way they are treated in practice is totally different. New religions have been clearly more successful than old style Christian missions in recruiting young Israelis. One reason is that the new religions do not suffer from the cultural stigma attached to Christianity. Their lack of a long history, and lack of historical contact (and conflict) with Judaism, works in their favor.

In most Western societies today, new religions are perceived as a threat, first by relatives (usually parents) of members and to an often lesser extent by various government authorities (e.g., Beckford, 1983). Parents' organizations, commissions of inquiry, and legal actions are indications of that. In Israel, in addition to the threat to the family, the new religions pose a threat to the basic Jewish identity of the State of Israel and to basic loyalty to the state. While in the U.S.A., opposition to the new religions since 1970 focused on their activity as posing a threat to the family, namely parent-child relations, Israel opposition to the new religions focuses not only on the apparent threat they pose to family loyalty but also on the threat to loyalty to the State of Israel and to the Israeli identity.

Concern about losing Jews to other religions is as old as Judaism itself. Diaspora Jews, living in the midst of the majority culture, always lose in the battle against it. In the modern State of Israel, there has always existed concern about Christian missionaries, and the term "mission" (pronounced mee-ssee-yon) has become part of the spoken language in Israel since the 1950s. Any Christian coming to live in Israel and any Christian organization active in Israel have been suspect. The lessons of Jewish history have not been forgotten, and for orthodox and non-observant alike, this proselytization issue has become a prime concern. When Billy Graham visited Israel in the late 1950s, for example, he was denied the use of a city auditorium in Tel Aviv and was allowed only an appearance in Nazareth, before an audience of Christian Arabs.

The concept of "Jewish unity" is used by both religious and secular Jews in Israel. It is the basis for overall cultural and political unity. Jewish identity, and specifically religious symbols and actions, unify Jews from all ethnic origins and cultures and also differentiate Jews from Arabs (Deshen, 1978; Liebman, 1975). The very existence of the new religions are seen as undermining the solidarity and uniformity of Israel society. They present the prospect of an alternative loyalty or at least a divided loyalty.

Action has been taken against groups that challenged military service obligations (universal in Israel), loyalty to the state, or loyalty to Jewish identity. In Israel, one can be a secular Jew but still preserve a nominal Jewish identity. Joining a new religion means, for an Israeli Jew, a rejection of Jewish identity. The positive step of joining ISCKON or Ananda Marga, for example, is a religious conversion, leaving behind the conventional Jewish identity and the attachment to the Jewish collective. Any ideology offering an alternative identity will be subject to vigorous attack and persecution. And as we have seen, where there is no real claim of an alternative identity, reactions to a new religion have been milder, regardless of course. Thus, ISKCON, with a score of members but which rejects the Israeli identity, is perceived as more of a threat than Emin, with hundreds of members who still keep the Israeli identity. Ironically, the largest new religions (i.e., most successful)—Emin, Scientology, and Transcendental Meditation—have been treated more leniently by surrounding Israeli society (and have thus become the largest) because they are more ambiguous in the challenge they pose to the traditional Israeli identity. These groups do not offer the members an exclusive new identity, and allow them to still claim loyalty to the State of Israel (either wholeheartedly or not, this claim is explicit).

Eister (1974:612) has suggested that new religious movements are likely to flourish in societies which are undergoing culture crises in the form of "Dislocations in the communicational and orientational institutions." The historical period of the crisis of Zionism gives rise to both the success of new religions in Israel and the crusade against them (Beit-Hallahmi, 1972a). The new religions can be regarded as breaking up the old monolithic ideology and pushing Israeli culture towards pluralism. The other part of the process has been the resistance to such a push. In this way, the new religions are a symptom of social stress as well as personal distress.

NOTES

1. In a 1984 survey of Israeli youth, only 11% of respondents regarded joining new religions positively, while 85.6% regarded it negatively. On the other hand, a return to Orthodox Judaism was viewed positively by 61.5%, while 32% viewed it negatively. In another public opinion survey in 1984, Israelis were asked whether they considered certain actions to be damaging to Israeli society. Among the acts listed was "converting away from Judaism." Among those aged between 20 and 24, 52% considered it as damaging to society, while among those over the age of 24, the percentage was 66% (Beit-Hallahmi, 1992b).

2. The history of the "anti-cult" movement in Israel can be summarized chronologically:
   1974 (Spring) First hostile media campaign. The main target: Divine Light Mission
   1974 Confidential police report on the Divine Light Mission
   1980 Concerned Parents Against Cults—first informal organization
   1981 Concerned Parents Against Cults—formal incorporation
   1982 (February) Commission of Inquiry appointed by Education Minister
   1982 Report by Yad La'Ahim on "cults in Israel"
   1982 Confidential national police report on "cults in Israel"
   1982 "Anti-cult" task forces created by kibbutz federations
   1982/83 Second media campaign against new religions
   1987 Commission of Inquiry Report is published.

REFERENCES

Beckford, James A., 1983. "The 'Cult Problem' in Five Countries: The Social Construction of Religious Controversy," in Eileen Barker, ed., *Of Gods and Men: New Religious Movement in the West.* Macon, GA: Mercer University Press, pp. 195-214.

Beit-Hallahmi, B., 1992a. *Original Sins: Reflections on the History of Zionism and Israel.* London: Pluto Press.

-----, 1992b. *Despair and Deliverance: Private Salvation in Contemporary Israel.* Albany, NY: SUNY Press.

Cahnman, W. J., 1944. "Religion and Nationalism," *American Journal of Sociology* 49:524-529.

Deshen, S., 1978. "Israeli Judaism: Introduction to the Major Patterns," *International Journal of Middle East Studies* 37:141-169.

Eister, A. W., 1974. "Culture Crises and New Religious Movements: A Paradigmatic Statement of a Theory of Cults," in L. I. Zaretsky and M. P. Leone, eds., *Religious Movements in Contemporary America.* Princeton, NJ: Princeton University Press.

Hammer, Z. 1982. Personal correspondence to Miriam Glazer Ta'asa, February 5 (in Hebrew).

Israel Pocket Library, 1974. *Religious Life and Communities.* Jerusalem: Keter Books.

Liebman, C., 1975. "Religious and Political Integration in Israel," *Jewish Journal of Sociology* 17:19-26.

----- and E. Don-Yehiya, 1984. "Separation of Religion and State in Israel: A Program or a Slogan?," in C. S. Liebman and E. Don-Yehiya, eds., *Religion and Politics in Israel.* Bloomington: University of Indiana Press.

Pfeffer, L., 1974. "The Legitimation of Marginal Religions in the United States," in L. I. Zaretsky and M. P. Leone, eds., *Religious Movements in Contemporary America.* Princeton, NJ: Princeton University.

Rabin, A. I. and B. Beit-Hallahmi. *Twenty Years Later: Kibbutz Children Grown Up.* New York: Springer.

Robbins, Thomas, 1988. *Cults, Converts and Charisma.* Newbury Park, CA: Sage.

Shupe, Anson D., Jr. and David G. Bromley, 1980. *The New Vigilantes: Deprogrammers, Anti-Cultists and the New Religions.* Beverly Hills, CA: Sage.

Singer, M. T., 1979. "Coming Out of the Cults," *Psychology Today,* January:72-82.

Sobel, J. and B. Beit-Hallahmi, 1991. *Tradition, Innovation, and Conflict: Jewishness and Judaism in Contemporary Israel.* Albany, NY: SUNY Press.

Soffrin, G. and H. Yodfat, 1982. *Cults in Israel.* Confidential Intelligence Report, Intelligence Department, Israel National Police Headquarters, August 22 (in Hebrew).

Zaretsky, L. I. and M. P. Leone, eds., *Religious Movements in Contemporary America.* Princeton, NJ: Princeton University Press.

CHAPTER XII

THE ANTI-CULT
MOVEMENT IN JAPAN[1]

Michael L. Mickler

INTRODUCTION

The 1980s witnessed a relative "cooling" of cult controversies in the United States. As a result of stagnating membership growth, lingering negative stereotypes, the natural progression of family and career formation, costly legal disputes, and the deaths or incarceration of prophet-founders, many of the most highly visible cults of the 1970s began to mute their radical teachings and moderate their practices. During this same period, the loosely-based, largely family coalitions comprising the anti-cult movement (ACM) began to deemphasize coercive deprogramming, became more discriminate in their application of "cult" and "brainwashing labels," looked to move away from its "parochial, isolated position," and "professionalized" to the extent of seeking grant fundings, establishing a research base, and opening a dialogue with opponents (Bromley and Shupe, 1987; Robbins, 1988).

The situation in Japan is much different. In 1971, the practice of kidnapping and deprogramming began there, the same year as in the U.S. As in the U.S., it was started by parents taking action on their own to prevent their offspring from joining what they considered to be an undesirable religious group. There have been numerous parallels in the methods of kidnapping in both countries. The differences, however, are more striking. Chief among these is the fact that in Japan kidnapping and deprogramming is still increasing, whereas in America these have declined. Thus, a major thrust of this chapter has been to discover why in the United States there are now only a handful of cases, whereas Japan claims 300 per year.[2]

A second difference between the situation in the U.S. and Japan is the latter's virtually exclusive focus on the Unification Church (UC). In the U.S., certain anti-cult organizations designated the UC their "primary target and arch nemesis" not only because it embodied "more objectionable 'cult' characteristics than any other single group," but also because successful repression . . . could serve as a precedent for attacking other marginal religions" (Shupe and Bromley, 1980:31). In reality, however, the American ACM took on all manner of groups including more established sects (thereby allowing the ACM's critics to label it an "anti-religion" or "faith-breaking" movement). Attempted deprogrammings of reputed converts to radical politics and lesbianism also discredited the American ACM. Since Japan has proliferated numerous new religious movements (the so-called *shinko shukyo* or "newly arisen religions"), another question to be answered is why the UC has been singled out.

A third major difference between the situation in the U.S. and Japan relates to the involvement of Christian ministers. In the United States, Christian clergy have not hesitated to flay the UC on doctrinal and sociopolitical grounds. Some have counseled counter-evangelism, and most have flatly rejected the UC's ecumenical overtures. Nonetheless, there has been great reluctance on the part of clergy to involve themselves with deprogramming. In fact, numerous clergy and religious organizations have come to the UC's defense on civil liberty grounds. Again, the situation in Japan is quite different. There, especially since 1985, Christian ministers from a wide range of denominations have participated in coercive deprogrammings. Moreover, they have established interdenominational networks and committees "for rescue and consultation," some of which have budgetary support from parent religious bodies. In more extreme cases, church-owned buildings have been utilized for incarceration, and deprogramees "bound with rope" have been "taken to Sunday Service" (Uchida, 1985). Given these extremities, a final thrust of this research has been to account for the involvement of Christian ministers.

Basically, the ACM in Japan has passed through three distinct stages (Hirose, 1988). The first stage, extending from 1967-1977, began with an article in the prestigious *Asahi Shimbun* which stated that the UC or "Genri Undo" (Principle Movement) was the cause of family breakdown. The chief anti-cult vehicle set up during this period was "Parents of Victims of the Unification Association" ("Zenkoku Genri

Undo Higaisha Fubo no Kai") established in 1973. Although engaging in violent deprogramming and given support by the Japanese Communist Party (JCP) which opposed the UC politically, "Parents of Victims" and a subsequent group, "Parents Opposed" ("Hantai Fubo no Kai"), established in 1975, were relatively isolated and ineffective.

Following disclosure in America of the UC's alleged links with "Koreagate," the Japanese ACM entered a second stage. Now able to attract more influential persons, "People Concerned about the Principle Movement" ("Yurgo suru Kai") emerged in 1978 as the leading anti-cult association. Intending to cancel the UC's religion corporation status, the group adopted a strategy of holding UC adherents in mental hospitals for deprogramming. Deprogramming cases involving Christian clergy also began to proliferate during this period. Nonetheless, the UC continued to register far more impressive rates of growth than any of the established denominations.

A third stage of the ACM in Japan, beginning in 1987, followed a scathing 41-page report issued by the Japanese Bar Association against the so-called "Spiritual Sales Method" *(reikan shoho),* a practice which induced buyers to pay inflated prices for marble pagodas, name stamps, or ginseng tea as a means of avoiding misfortune and placating restless ancestors. The implication of the UC and UC-connected businesses in this practice further legitimated the ACM and led to an all-out attack on the UC by opposing groups, in particular Christian ministers who began to account for a major portion of the "rescues." This appears to have had more of an effect, although there also is evidence of public reaction against deprogramming.

THE BEGINNINGS OF THE
ACM IN JAPAN: 1967-77

The ACM in Japan, as noted, derived initially from two separate groupings: the families of converts and the JCP. Families of converts were aroused because the UC, contrary to other Japanese New Religions, recruited individual young adults and removed them from jobs, colleges, and families. Most of the "newly arisen religions," as James Beckford has noted, "are composed mainly of family units, and members are encouraged to retain their secular employment[.]" As a result, "the vast majority of New Religions are considered not to represent a serious threat to any of the country's most important social institutions" (Beckford, 1983:207-8). The UC, however, quickly set up communal enclaves, developed independent means of financial support, and promoted "pioneer" witnessing in distant cities. Moreover, by the early 1970s, much to the consternation of parents, adherents were departing Japan as missionaries to other parts of the world. Even more disturbing was the participation of converts in UC-sponsored "mass weddings." As a result of these and other practices, the *Asahi Shimbun* depicted the UC as "Oya Nakase Genri Undo" ("the religion that makes parents weep").

In a recent study, "Deprogramming as a Mode of Exit from New Religious Movements," David Bromley notes:

> The opposition of parents to their offsprings' conversions . . . did not translate directly into a means for countering those conversions. The development of a means for extricating individuals from these groups . . . awaited the appearance of a moral entrepreneur who would develop viable tactics for achieving this end (1988:189).

Within the U.S., he adds, "The individual who serendipitously appeared at the propitious moment to fill this role was Ted Patrick, who created the term *deprogramming.*"

A similar dynamic was at work in Japan. However, there were two "moral entrepreneurs" rather than one. The first of these was Teruko Honma (b. 1922), a housewife and erstwhile political activist from Noshiro City, Akita Prefecture. In April 1971, she kidnapped her daughter, Hatsuko, who had recently joined the UC. She subsequently admitted her daughter to Shimada Mental Hospital and had her held there for 65 days. While there, her daughter discovered a Bible with an inscription written by a cousin, who was also a UC member and former inmate. This led her to conclude, after escaping, that she was being subjected to a practice already in place (Honma, 1988). In April 1972, Teruko Honma started a group called "Parents Against the Principle" ("Yokokai") and in 1973 helped set up "Parents of Victims of the Unification Association." In 1975, she founded "Parents Opposed" (also translated "Parents for Doing Something about the Principle Movement"). Taking a more publicly activist posture, Honma, with others, broke into Japanese UC headquarters, carrying stickers, trampling furniture, breaking windows, and tearing down pictures. Apart from organizing parental opposition, she was a key connecting link to the JCP (Fukuda and Meno, 1984; Honma, 1988).

The other significant early ACM figure was Tomigoro Goto (1909-84). Whereas Honma was primarily an instigator and organizer, Goto was a professional deprogrammer. He first became involved when his son joined the UC. After his son left, he remained active, publishing such tracts as *Bury the Bloodsucker Sun Myung Moon.* With Honma, he founded the "Parents of Victims" association, becoming its first president. Goto broke from Honma in 1975 and with an ex-UC associate, Takashi Maryuyama (b. 1925), established the "Shinsei-kai (New Life) Home" in 1976. There, they practiced a particularly violent form of deprogramming. Modified with iron bars on every window, the single house at 4-1-11 Mukoyama, Nerima-ku, Tokyo functioned as a deprogramming and "rehabilitation" center until 1978 when it closed down as a result of UC-initiated *habeas corpus* suits and unfavorable publicity stemming from Maruyama's alleged rape of a 23-year-old female church member. Other escapees reported being handcuffed and tied with ropes and chains. After his institute closed, Goto continued to incarcerate UC adherents in established mental institutions (Uyeno and Fukuda, 1984).

The JCP began to attack the UC in 1978 after establishment of the International Federation for Victory Over Communism (IFUOC) which it termed, "just another name of the Unification Association" (Sasaki, 1977). Before then, the JCP had taken little notice of the UC or any "newly arisen religion" besides Sokka Gokkai, whose proselytizing ("shakuhuku") campaigns and "Komeito (Clean Government) Party" had threatened its working class foundation. Nonetheless, as the UC gained a base on university campuses through its "Collegiate Association for the Research of Principle" (CARP), confrontations ensued. The UC later reported physical attacks, obstruction of worship services and witnessing (sometimes by propaganda vehicles with loudspeakers), spying, and suspected infiltration. More significant were the links being forged between the JCP and anti-church groups (mainly through Teruko Honma) and the JCP's resolution of conflict with Sokka Gokkai in 1974. Honma, active in the JCP-connected "New Women's Movement," began to be featured in the JCP's party newspaper *Akahata* ("Red Flat"). By the mid-1970s, JCP elected officials began denouncing the UC in the Japanese Diet.

Family-based opposition to the UC, then, in the course of a decade had coalesced into the beginnings of the ACM in Japan. Given an initial impetus by the *Asahi Shimbun's* stigmatization of the UC as "the religion that makes parents weep," a network of organizations had been set up, a class of quasi-professional deprogrammers emerged, and important alliances were established. In particular, the ACM gained access to the resources of the powerful JCP. However, despite these gains, the ACM was relatively isolated and ineffective. Significantly, though having successfully conducted clandestine deprogrammings, noisy demonstrations, and even having brought their concerns before the Diet, ACM adherents were not able to mobilize the Japanese establishment into any kind of direct action. In fact, the UC retained a degree of support within the ruling Liberal Democratic Party (LDP) and within certain universities (Beckford, 1983; Mitsuo, 1985). More importantly, the general perception was that anti-UC agitation was a family issue best left for families to resolve. Confrontations between the UC and JCP were likewise seen as simple conflicts of interest and political ideologies.

THE MOUNTING IDEOLOGICAL OFFENSIVE: 1978-85

A major weakness of the ACM in Japan during its initial stages was the lack of a viable ideology. As a result, its heavy-handed tactics lacked sufficient legitimation and broad-based appeal. This situation changed radically after 1978. Following the disclosure in America of the UC's alleged links with "Koreagate," the Japanese ACM entered a new stage. Now able to attract more influential persons, it mounted an ideological offensive which labeled the UC an organ of the KCIA and its membership as "brainwashed." To some extent, this process resembled developments in the United States where the cult controversy "rapidly transcended the clash of interests and evolved into a social scare." The key element in effecting this transformation in the U.S. was "the construction of a subversion mythology . . . premised on the existence of a conspiracy" (Bromley, 1988:186-87).

This same dynamic was at work in Japan. There, immediately after the Fraser Subcommittee of the U.S. House released a March 15, 1978 investigative report, the JCP launched a large-scale, anti-UC campaign. Previously, its attacks had been sporadic, consisting mainly of support for Teruko Honma's activities, student-directed campus confrontations, and occasional rhetorical flourishes in the Diet. Now, the JCP (ironically) branded the UC a "heretical organization" and called upon the entire party to "isolate and annihilate" it. In June, JCP Chairman Kenji Miyamoto stated that "Stamping [out] VOC is a Historical War for Justice" (Hirose, 1988). The best indicator of the JCP's dramatically escalated ideological attack is the following computation of articles on the UC in *Akahata* (*Red Flag,* the JCP's newspaper): 16 for 1970, 6 for 1971, 18 for 1972, 3 for 1973, 4 for 1974, 13 for 1975, 21 for 1976, 71 for 1977, and 1,716 for 1978. According to UC sources, "the JCP attacked the Unification Church on 5 pages of the 16-page *Akahata* everyday throughout 1978!" (Fukuda and Ueno, 1984).

In addition to escalating its attack, the JCP also altered its approach. Before it had attempted to expose IFUOC as a UC front. Now, by popularizing an "unevaluated" United States CIA report released by the Fraser Committee that the UC had been "founded" by the KCIA, the JCP fanned the flames of traditional Japanese-Korean antagonizing and raised the specter of foreign interference, effectively parlaying what had been a communist party struggle into a cause for all "democratic" and "progressive" forces in Japan. The impact was substantial. CARP, in particular, was cut off from programs on numerous university campuses, including activities at Tokyo University, the nation's most prestigious university. The UC likewise reported "suppressive actions" taken against it by women's groups, labor unions, national student groups (i.e., the Zengakuren), self-governing university associations, teacher's unions, peace and cultural groups, JCP-influenced sectors of the film industry, reformist municipalities, the Liberal Bar Association, "left-leaning" journalists, and "pro-JCP organizations in the media" (Fukuda and Ueno, 1984).

By the end of 1978, this ferment had coalesced into another ACM organization, "People Concerned About the Principle Movement" ("Genri Undo wo Yuryo suru Kai"). Unlike "Parents of Victims" or "Parents Opposed," this group included influential figures such as Sukenaga Murai, former President of Waseda University; Chitose Kishi, chairman of the Japanese Bible Association; and Ayako Miura, a novelist. It also included among its organizers two professors from Rikkyo University and Nagoya Engineering College, an administrator from Hiroshima University, two independent Christian ministers, two others associated with the United Church of Christ in Japan (UCCJ), and the indefatigable Teruko Honma. It also utilized medical doctors and lawyers. Publicly, this group was committed to "ostracize" the UC by canceling its religious corporation status. Short of that, it resolved: "UC members are mental patients, therefore, cooperation with medical doctors will be the way of opposing from now on" (Kobayashi, 1991).

Based on this officially adopted "resolution," numerous UC adherents were kidnapped and committed to mental hospitals for "deprogramming" between 1979-85. Once there, they were isolated, disoriented by drug injections, and when deemed sufficiently "recovered," forced to endure "rehabilitation" under professional deprogrammers such as Tomogiro Goto. Hospitals involved were Kurumegaoka and Kingoka; Kichijoj Hospital in Tokyo; Koyama-Fujimada Hospital in Tochiga Prefecture; Wakasuka Hospital in Miyagi; Seibu Hospital in Inuyama City; and Midorigaoka Hospital in Tomakomai City (Fukuda and Ueno, 1984; Davies, 1990).

Eventually, through writs of *habeas corpus* being issued or escape, 25 such cases were recorded, a figure regarded by UC spokespersons as "only the tip of the iceberg" (Kobayashi, 1991). *The Gulag in Japan* (1984), a UC-published volume, contains the testimonies of "survivors." In addition to hospitalization, another method utilized was forced confinement of adherents in make-shift cells at parent's or relative's homes. These were cheaper and less conspicuous, especially given the UC's surveillance of suspected hospitals and success in obtaining *habeas corpus* writs.

Deprogramming cases involving Christian clergy also proliferated during this period. Although representing only a tiny percentage of the Japanese population, it is not difficult to understand how expertise possessed by trained clerics might be of use to the ACM both in delegitimating UC religious claims and in "hand-to hand" combat with recalcitrant deprogramees over doctrine. There were additional reasons why ministers offered their "services." Some, especially those associated with the National Christian Council (NCC), were far left politically and regarded the UC as a fascist organization with militarist leanings. More conservative clergy took advantage of deprogramming as a proselytizing option. Whatever the motivations, there is clear evidence associating Christian clergy, churches, and organizations with the ACM from the mid-1970s. In 1975, for example, Tokyo Yamanote Church hosted the first national conference of "Parents of Victims." Reference already has been made to clergy participation in "People Concerned" which, in fact, was organized in a NCC meeting room. Five clergy were directly implicated in mental hospital cases (Fukuda and Ueno, 1984). Over time, particular clergy took a leadership role in the deprogramming movement. Sadao Asami, a Harvard Divinity School graduate, was the earliest, having been active since 1975. Shin'ya Waga, a Seventh Day Adventist minister, adopted the practice of having parents sign a memorandum stating that should their son or daughter leave the UC they would "not raise objections to him/her joining the Seventh Day Adventists." He later set up the "Ekulesia Kai" to coordinate his efforts. Activity in Hokkaido was especially intense. There, the Church of the Twelve Apostles in Sapporo readily acknowledged that 24 people in all (including their 12-person choir) had "escaped" the UC because of their activities. Still, members of the congregation expressed astonishment to see one not yet "converted" UC member "bound with rope when . . . taken to the Sunday Service" (Uchida, 1985). In June 1984, Rev. Sanai Hashimoto set up a Hokkaido branch of "People Concerned," installed Mitsuo Toda, a professional deprogrammer, as president, and reported 7 successful cases out of 10 within the month of September (Hashimoto, 1984).

None of these clergy were disciplined by any church governing body. If anything, they reflected the general tenor of their churches' official positions. Christian "establishment" relations with the UC in Japan had been strained since 1974 when a Rev. Moriyama began "severe attacks" in *The Christian Weekly* against the UC as being "heretical" (Fukuda and Uyeno, 1984). They deteriorated further following the NCC's 1979 "Reconfirmation of the View on the Unification Church" which denied the UC status as a Christian body. In 1985, Japan's Bishops Conference issued an eight-page statement which termed the UC not a Christian Church, stated that it was not subject to ecumenical outreach, and warned Catholics not to participate in its activities or meetings. Finally, in November 1986, the United Church of Christ in Japan (UCCJ), the largest grouping of Protestant bodies, released an "Official Statement" which apart from the standard disassociation "in faith" and "in organization" from the UC, criticized its converts' "rapid personality changes" and "deceptive" sales practices, activities which "are causing damage to many citizens." The UCCJ committed itself "to work on this situation" (Nakajima, 1986).

Thus, during its second decade the Japanese ACM made impressive strides. Based on disclosures of alleged UC links to "Koreagate," the

JCP effectively isolated CARP on college campuses and within sectors of Japanese society. "People Concerned," a more broadly based and influential organization than the earlier parents' groups, successfully enlisted the cooperation of certain medical and legal constituencies. In addition, Christian ministers emerged as an significant resource. Yet despite these gains, there were still problems. First, the UC's KCIA connection was by no means a given, and some mass-circulation publications printed retractions or qualifications once more facts were known. Second, although "People Concerned" utilized "brainwashing" terminology, it lacked expertise with more sophisticated models of "coercive persuasion." As a result, the UC had only minor difficulties in securing writs of *habeas corpus* which eventually put an end to forced hospital confinements. Third, despite clergy attacks, the UC registered far more impressive rates of growth than any of the established denominations. If anything, the UC was thriving. By the mid-1980s, CARP had reasserted itself on university campuses, innovative "video centers" had boosted recruitment, and UC-connected "salespeople" were annually bringing in what was estimated to be in the billions of yen (Mitsuo, 1985; Masataka, 1987). Given this situation, ACM activity was at most only a minor irritant.

ALL-OUT ATTACK: 1987-PRESENT

These conditions changed dramatically in 1987, following a blistering 41-page report issued by the Japanese Bar Association (JBA) against the so-called "spiritual sales method" *(reikan shoho),* a practice which influenced buyers through high-pressure sales tactics and "fortune-telling" to purchase items at highly inflated rates. Implication of UC-related businesses in this practice reinvigorated the Japanese ACM and led to an all-out attack by opposing groups, particularly Christian ministers who organized themselves into relatively higher-profile, interdenominational "rescue" networks. Although this situation has yet to play itself out, the combination of undercutting the UC's financial and personnel bases appears to have had an effect. On the other hand, there is some evidence of public reaction against "deprogramming."

Concern about salespeople preying on "religious anxieties" was first voiced by the Japan Consumer Information Center which reported that more than 2,600 complaints about the sale of marble vases, ivory seals, and miniature pagodas had been lodged with them between 1976-82 (Burgess and Isikoff, 1984). The center published pamphlets to warn consumers about the sales of these items but did not directly link such incidents with UC operations. However, in 1984, a former executive of the UC-affiliated newspaper *Sekai Nippo* (World Daily News) reported that the UC in Japan had transferred "at least $800 million over the past nine years into the United States." He further stated that the money was generated "primarily through a Tokyo-based business operation that uses church members to sell . . . religious icons . . . represented as having supernatural powers" (Burgess and Isikoff, 1984). In 1986, eight housewives from Kanagawa Prefecture brought suit against "Happy World," a UC-related import trading company, and its selling agencies, demanding a refund of 18,051,000 yen ($130,000), the total amount they paid for products from Korea (*Mainichi Shimbun,* 1986).

The JBA report further substantiated these claims, and was followed by "horror stories" of mostly middle-aged women mortgaging homes, cashing in insurance policies and otherwise ruining family fortunes. This, in turn, led to a renewed demand for refunds. In 1988, two women filed suit against the UC in Tokyo District Court alleging that they were "systematically deceived into buying a lucky stamp, a treasure pagoda, Ginseng concentration, pictures, and leather." Both charged that they were forced to sell their real estate by "so-called psychic mediums." Although the UC maintained that church was limited to "legal religious propagation" and that the suit was "unreasonable," it settled out-of-court, receiving 83 million yen ($590,000) from salespersons of "Inspiration Business," who had membership in the UC and who had sold goods to the women. The UC paid that money to the plaintiffs, stressing again that the church had no involvement in "money business" (*Yomiuri Shimbun,* 1988). In 1989, the "Fukuda Lawyers' Party for the Salvation of Victims of the Spiritualist Sales Method" reported a settlement between 61 buyers and several dealers of marble vases according to which the dealers would refund the full amount of paid money (*Asahi Shimbun,* 1989a).

Implication of UC-related businesses, as noted, reinvigorated the ACM and led to renewed attacks, especially by Christian ministers who began to account for most "rescues." The UCCJ, which already committed itself to "work on the situation," played a leading role. In late 1987, it formed a "Liaison Committee on the Problem of the Unification Movement" and started counseling meetings for parents concerned about offspring in the UC. Approximately 30 clergy, involved in "rescuing activities," met the following March at Tokyo's Japan Christianity Hall to compare methods, offer reports, and make recommendations. The Hokkaido region reported that in conjunction with "People Concerned," they had persuaded 150 UC adherents to turn from their beliefs. Kyushu reported 120 applications for "consultation," and 15 cases then under "persuasion" by them. A total of 31 cases in Tokyo and 11 in Osaka "were accepted for consultation," and in Tokyo, "the rescue ratio hit 70%." Significantly, it was confirmed by participants, "that the UCCJ would deal with the problem of the Unification Movement in the context of our Missions." They also decided to promote "countermeasures" within the UCCJ as a whole, using *Shinto no Tomo* (Friends of the Faithful) magazine to list locations and contacts of "Rescuing Activities Offices" for each region; and to submit a request to the UCCJ standing committee asking for an "annual donation campaign" (UCCJ Liaison Committee on the Problem of the Unification Movement, 1988).

Rather than simply being available, the UCCJ began aggressively "soliciting." A letter addressed "To All Congregations of the Osaka Parish," for example, noted that if prospective UC converts had not yet attended a 7-day workshop,

> there is some room for parents to get them back . . . Otherwise, it would be too late for you to change their minds. The Unification Movement is not mere measles, but cancer. Please consult a Christian minister as quickly as possible (UCCJ Osaka Countermeasure Committee Against Unificationism, 1988).

The "National Liaison Committee for Christians Opposing the Principle Movement" ("Gen-Tai-Kyo') was founded in October 1989, basically for those Protestants outside the UCCJ fold. Its stated purpose was "to save and consult the lost souls taken by the Unification Church and their families." With this organization in place, ministers who were deprogramming individually gained a nationwide support system. The UC alleged 96 identified cases of deprogramming by Christian ministers in 1989 (and "about 300" since 1985) in a 1991 petition to the World Council of Churches. Some of the main churches involved were the UCCJ; the Japanese Evangelical Lutheran Church; the Japanese

Lutheran Doho Church; the Japanese Church of Jesus Christ; the Assembly of God, Japan; the Catholic Church; the Japanese Union Conference of Seventh Day Adventists; and the Evangelical Alliance Mission (Kobayashi, 1991; Davies, 1990).

Although, as mentioned, this situation has yet to play itself out, the combination of undercutting the UC's financial and personnel bases has had an effect. The drying up of the marble vase-miniature pagoda-ginseng tea-name stamp market, expensive lawsuits, and the simultaneous necessity of supporting overseas projects have reportedly led to huge debts and slashed UC operating budgets worldwide. At the same time, escalating clergy opposition has forced the UC to acknowledge that it has a deprogramming problem and to request outside help. In a petition to the World Council of Churches (WCC) protesting "the situation of violent deprogramming by Japanese Christian ministers," the UC asked that it "take proper measures against this matter" (Kobayashi, 1991). The UC also has approached Western scholars for assistance.

Although the activities of the ACM after 1987 clearly put the UC on the defensive, the former's situation is not uniformly bright. In particular, there is some evidence of public reaction against "deprogramming." *Zembo,* a conservative magazine, attacked groups "whose profession is 'deprogramming'," referred to them as "witch-hunting," and "exposed" a Gen-Tai-Kyo "converting manual" (Zembo, 1989). In Hokkaido, Mitsuo Toda, former president of "People Concerned" was forced out and his organization's "deprogramming apartment" closed as a result of a suit brought by two female UC adherents in December 1987 (*Asahi Shimbun,* 1989b). In 1989, Rev. Takeo Funada, clergyman of Kyoto Seito Church, appeared to testify about a deprogramming incident, "the first time a so-called anti-UC clergy was questioned in court." Under questioning, he admitted having spoken to 11 UC members under conditions of incarceration. He also admitted having used "a part of Kyoto Seito Church for incarceration, himself" (*Chuwa Shimbun,* 1989).

CONCLUSION

Having considered the ACM in Japan, we are in a better position to address the questions posed at the beginning of this paper.

(1) Why, in Japan, are kidnapping and deprogramming still increasing, whereas in the United States these have gone into decline? This question can be examined from the UC side, from the ACM side, and from the perspective of Japanese society. From the UC side, at least two considerations are relevant. First, the UC in Japan has not been subject to (or resisted) pressures which have led some of the most highly visible cults in the West to "accommodate." In particular, it has maintained its conversion rate and avoided "routinization" by enforcing a rigid communalism, postponing family-formation, and regularly sending members overseas. Hence the UC has not only afforded a pool of available "deprogramees," but also has perpetuated the practices most objectionable to anti-cultists. Second, the UC, until recently, has basically chosen to ignore the problem. Perhaps part of this may relate to a desire to "save face." More likely, UC leaders accepted deprogramming as an unfortunate, but necessary, price to be paid for their substantial monetary and membership gains.

From the ACM side, the increase in deprogrammings should not be viewed as a token of success but of failure. The fact that after 20 years, the countercult movement was still reduced to vigilante-style kidnappings signified the utter lack of response it had been able to garner from governmental authorities. This reliance also pointed to the continuing paucity of the movement's ideological resources.[3]

On the other hand, the ACM's very crudeness and lack of sophistication functioned to inhibit critical rejoiners from the academy. Hence, the Japanese ACM avoided the kind of delegitimization endured by its Western intellectual counterparts. At the same time, though conceptually thin, the ACM exhibited a certain pragmatic effectiveness in "piggy-backing" first on the JCP and later on various clergy organizations. It also varied its tactics, moving initially from forced hospital confinements to "rehabilitation" centers to private homes. More recently, Christian ministers have "sanitized" the practice, referring to it as "rescue" or "consultation" and contextualizing it as "mission."

From the perspective of Japanese society, conventional wisdom might hold that there exists a mentality relatively insensitive to civil liberties or individual "rights" which would favor, or at least tolerate deprogramming so long as it reinforced traditional loyalties. This view, of course, may be a product of Western ethnocentrism. Nonetheless, it is a fact that the Japanese court system, though undermining certain practices through *habeas corpus* rulings, has by no means taken an activist posture against deprogramming or issued any precedent-setting decisions. Moreover, unlike in the U.S., there appears not to be a single case of a deprogrammer being prosecuted, much less convicted. Part of this has to do with the fact that Japan is a far less litigious society than the U.S., and informal "apologies" often suffice in lieu of lawsuits. Still, the lack of significant reprisals against deprogrammers has helped to proliferate the practice.

(2) Why has the UC been singled out? James Beckford, in an early 1980s study. "The 'Cult Problem' in Five Countries," argued "first and foremost" that opposition to the UC in Japan derives from "a deep rooted suspicion of anything closely connected with Korea." Publicly, the UC was "accused of being an attempt to further Korean interests by underhanded methods." At the personal level, these feelings were "translated into the view that association with the UC is 'shameful' and brings dishonor on the family." As a result, many "hostile parents" could "not bring themselves to admit publicly that their child has joined a Korean religious movement," a factor which, in Beckford's estimation, prevented the anti-cult campaign from "accelerating" (Beckford, 1983:206). Although unaware of deprogrammings and the scope of the ACM in Japan, Beckford rightly fingered prejudicial feelings as a contributing factor.

A second "source of resistance" to the UC, according to Beckford, "is the way in which it is felt to usurp the functions and status of the family." This, he noted, "is particularly acute with regard to the practice of allowing the movement to select marriage partners independently of the family's preferences." Connected to this is the objection that the UC frequently sends abroad many hundreds of Japanese adherents, widely regarded as "an intolerable affront to the value of family unity and family-centeredness" as well as a very real "disruption of traditional relations with sources of potential patronage and lifelong employment." This, Beckford points out, is contrary to most Japanese New Religions which "are composed mainly of family units" and encourage members "to retain their secular employment" (Beckford, 1983:206-207).

The UC's isolation and lack of support networks, particularly within the religious sphere, also have contributed to its being singled out. Though a new movement, the UC is not readily identified among Japan's "newly arisen religions," most of which are "syntheses of ancient Buddhism, Shinto and folk religion" (Beckford, 1983:202). Nor, in spite of its efforts, is it counted among the Christian denominations.

Viewed from another angle, the UC is conspicuous because it stands in a midway position between well-established, indigenous New Religions and sects such as the Mormons and Jehovah's Witnesses which have made few inroads into Japanese society. Neither minor enough to be dismissed nor formidable enough to intimidate opposition, the UC has had to weather wide-ranging attacks. It is undoubtedly the case that hostility towards and isolation of the UC has led to the escalation of deviance and mutual distrust.

(3) How to account for the involvement of Christian ministers? There is clear evidence associating Christian clergy, churches, and associations with deprogramming since the mid-1970s, first on a limited and later on a wholesale basis. I have already noted that the expertise possessed by trained clerics was of significant utility to the ACM both in delegitimating UC religious claims and in verbal "combat" with recalcitrant deprogramees over doctrine. This was especially the case in Japan where the religious *qua* Christian base was so slight. Buddhist priests, occasionally called in by distraught parents, could offer little more than appeals to familial loyalties. Secular Japanese had no clue what was at stake *theologically* for struggling deprogramees. Ministers, however, could ease the trauma of prospective apostasy by supplying alternative salvific scenarios. For this reason, they were eagerly sought.

There were also compelling reasons why ministers offered their "services." Some clergy, as noted, were practically left-leaning and convinced that the UC, if unchecked, would lead the nation into a fascist militarism reminiscent of the 1930s. Other more conservative clergy took advantage of the deprogramming option as means of "soul-saving" or "church growth." Two other factors are important. First, the UC has persistently proselytized Christian churches, in particular, targeting its newer converts. The UC also has maintained a covert posture in doing so. This, understandably, has led to intense strain. In deprogramming new UC converts, Christian clergy simply escalated an already-existing competition. Finally, the Christian churches, like the UC, occupy a mid-range position in Japanese society. Neither large enough to intimidate opposition nor obscure enough to go unnoticed, they have endured attack, particularly from nationalist groups. From this standpoint, ministers' attacks on the UC might be understood as a means of gaining legitimation *vis-a-vis* the larger society and as a way of taking the focus off themselves. Whether these clerics have found a niche in an otherwise uncomprehending and unresponsive social environment or whether their activities might provoke a reaction is as yet an unanswered question.

While Japanese society has a reputation for being "tolerant and pragmatic" in religious matters, and although the constitution of 1947 guarantees freedom of religion, religious conflict is not exactly unprecedented within the Japanese setting. Beckford (1983:205) reminds us that in 1951 Rissho Kosei-kai banded together an alliance against Soka Gakkai, "blamed for bringing all other New Religions into disrepute." Competition, actual violence, and speculation about "a religious war (Shukyo Senso) of "attrition" subsequently led to mutual accommodations, though less robust growth figures. It may be that the deprogramming conflict will before long move into the accommodation mode. One can already detect certain chinks in the armor. The UC has admitted that it has a problem. The ACM is facing a degree of public reaction against deprogramming. One might expect to see a scramble for respectability on both sides.

NOTES

1. This chapter was originally prepared for presentation at a seminar on New Religious Movements in Global Perspective, Buelton, California, May 16-17, 1991.

2. Numbers of deprogramming cases are notoriously difficult to determine, in part due to high rates of voluntary defection in most new religions. One less-than-scientific method which the UC in Japan utilized to distinguish between voluntary and deprogrammed defectors was to count those who returned for their belongings. It was assumed that those who left on their own would have taken their things with them originally. If the UC-claimed figure of 300 coercive deprogrammings per year is accurate, it dwarfs U.S. figures by a considerable margin. David Bromley (1988) reports 396 coercive deprogrammings of UC adherents in the U.S. between the years 1973-86. The peak year was 1976 with 108 deprogrammings.

3. "Brainwashing" has served as a baseline staple of ACM ideology in the West. How effectively this line of argument can function in a society extolling the virtues of absolute obedience and loyalty is questionable. James Beckford (1983) noted, "When comparisons are made with anti-cultism in other countries, one is struck by the relatively insignificant weight given in Japan to the argument that recruits are gained by brainwashing or psychological manipulation" (207).

REFERENCES

Asahi Shimbun, 1967. "The Religion that Makes Parents Weep" (*Oya Nakase Genri Undo),* July 7.

------, 1988. "Concerning Spiritualist Sales Method, Unification Church is Sued by Two Women for Its Systematic Illegal Business," May 8.

------, 1989a. "Reconciliation in Spiritualist Sales Method Problem at 14 Million Yen," March 2.

------, 1989b. "The Investigation is Over on 'Restraining Unification Church Members,'" March 17.

Beckford, James, 1983. "The 'Cult Problem' in Five Countries: The Social Construction of Religious Controversy," in Eileen Barker, *Of Gods and Men: New Religious Movements in the West.* Macon, GA: Mercer, pp. 195-214.

Bromley, David, 1988. "Deprogramming as a Mode of Exit from New Religious Movements: The Case of the Unificationist Movement," in David Bromley, ed., *Falling From the Faith: Causes and Consequences of Religious Apostasy,* Newbury Park: Sage, pp. 185-204.

Bromley, David and Anson Shupe, 1987. "The Future of the Anticult Movement," in David Bromley and Phillip Hammond, eds., *The Future of New Religious Movements,* Macon, GA: Mercer, pp. 221-234.

Burgess, John and Michael Isikoff, 1984. "Moon's Japanese Profits Bolster Efforts in U.S.," *Washington Post,* Nov. 16.

Chuwa Shimbun, 1989. "Rev. Funada Admitting His Practices of Curbing and Relationship with Deprogramming by Violence," Dec. 15.

Davies, Andrew, 1990. "Kidnappings in Japan and America," Unification Theological Seminary, Barrytown, NY, photocopy.

Fukuda, I. and Ueno, T., 1984. *The Gulag in Japan: Religious Persecution by the Communist Party,* Tokyo: Research Institute on Communism and Religious Issues.

Hashimoto, Sanai, 1984. "The Rampant Unification Association Principle Movement Which is the Same as IFUOC and the 'People Concerned." Report on the 9th Mission Conference on Social Issues, Hokkaido Christian Center, The Committee for Social Issues of the Hokkai Region, The United Church of Christ in Japan.

Hirose, Akira, 1988. *The Revealed Facts of Opposing Ministers,* Tokyo: Committee of Comparative Study of Religions.

Honma, Hatsuko, 1988. "My Testimony," *Shintenchi-Zokando,* Nov. 15.

Kobayashi, Akio, 1991. A Petition, Addressed to Dr. Kyung Seo Park, Executive Secretary for Asia, World Council of Churches, April 10.

Mainichi Shimbun, 1986, "Housewives Demand Refund from Selling Agencies," Nov. 11.

Masataka, Ito, 1987. "On the Track of 'Divine Sales' People," *Japan Quarterly* 34:300-304.

Mitsuo, Kasahara, 1985. "The Moonies Make a Comeback," *Japan Quarterly* 32:46-50.

Nakajima, Masaki, 1986. Official Statement concerning the Unification Association and the Unification Movement, United Church of Christ in Japan, Nov. 18.

Robbins, Thomas, 1988. *Cults, Converts, and Charisma: The Sociology of New Religious Movements.* Newbury Park: Sage.

Sasaki, T., 1978. *Strategic Organizations of South Korea: IFVOC and the Unification Church.* Communist Party of Japan.

Sekai Nippo, 1988. "Reconciliation in Inspiration Business Problem: The Plaintiffs and UC Reached a Reconciliation," May 22.

Shupe, Anson and David Bromley, 1980. *The New Vigilantes: Deprogrammers, Anti-Cultists, and the New Religions.* Beverly Hills: Sage.

UCCJ Liaison Committee on the Problem of the Unification Movement, 1988. "Let the Issue be Dealt with in the Context of Our Missionary Work," *Krisuto Shimbun,* April 9.

UCCJ Osaka Countermeasure Committee Against Unificationism to all Congregations of the Osaka Parish, 1988, April.

Uchida, Kazuhito, 1986. "A Church with a Coffee Shop," *Fukuin Senkuo* (The Gospel Missions), May, pp. 53-58.

Yomiuri Shimbun, 1988. "Reikan Shoho (Spiritualist Sales Method) Problem: Two Women File a Suit Against Unification Church, Requesting 75 Million Yen as Compensation," May 7.

Zembo, 1989. "The Identity of the Groups Whose Profession is 'Deprogramming'—Kidnapping and Confining Unification Church Members-Today's Witch-Hunting," Jan., pp. 34-41.

CONTRIBUTORS

BENJAMIN BEIT-HALLAHMI, currently affiliated with the University of Haifa (Israel), received his Ph.D. in clinical psychology in 1970 from Michigan State University. Since then he has held appointments in the United States, Israel, and France. His recent books include *Despair and Deliverance: Private Salvation in Contemporary Israel* (1992) and *The Psychoanalytic Study of Religion* (1994). In addition to his academic publications, he has written about political affairs, including his book *Original Sins* (1992).

RICHARD BERGERON is a graduate of St. Paul University (Canada) and of l'Universite of Strasbourg (France). He is currently Professor at the Faculte de Teologic de l'Universite de Montreal (Canada) and both founder and president of the Centre d'Information sur les Nouvelles Religions in that same city. He has published numerous books and articles on Christianity and new religious movements.

DAVID G. BROMLEY is Professor of Sociology at Virginia Commonwealth University (U.S.A.) and the University of Virginia. In addition to maintaining a prolific writing agenda on religious controversies of the cult-sect type, he is editor of the *Journal for the Scientific Study of Religion.* Most recently he coedited (with Jeffrey K. Hadden) *Religion and the Social Order: The Handbook on Cults and Sects in America* (1993) from JAI Press.

PRISCILLA D. COATES is the former Executive Director of the Citizens Freedom Foundation and is currently Chairperson of the Cult Awareness Network, Los Angeles Affiliate (U.S.A.). This chapter was originally presented as a luncheon talk entitled "The History of the Cult

Awareness Network" at the conference on New Religions in a Global Perspective, Buellton, California, May 16, 1991. The views presented in this paper are those of the author and are not intended to represent the Cult Awareness Network.

SOSHANAH FEHER is a sociology graduate student at the University of California, Santa Barbara (U.S.A.). She is working on a doctoral dissertation entitled "Drawing the Line on Community Boundaries: A Case Study of Messianic Judaism and the Jewish Community," as well as beginning work on a project examining ethnicity within the Shepardic Jewish community in the United States.

STEVEN HASSAN is a licensed Mental Health counselor based in Boston, Massachusetts (U.S.A.). He holds a master's degree in counseling psychology from Cambridge College. His book, *Combatting Cult Mind Control: The #1 Best-Selling Guide to Protection, Rescue, and Recovery from Destructive Cults*, was published in 1988 and has been translated into Spanish, German, and Japanese. A former member of the controversial Unification Church, he is active as a lecturer, author, and consultant.

MASSIMO INTROVIGNE is director of the Center for Studies on New Religions, or CESNUR (Italy), an international network of scholars based in the city of Torino. He also teaches a seminar on sociology and religion at the Instituto Superiore de Scienze Religiose, Foggia, Italy. He is the author or editor of eleven books in Italian (three of them translated into French) on new religious movements and the occult.

REENDER KRANENBORG is a research professor of the Faculty of Theology of the Free University in Amsterdam (the Netherlands). He is editor of the journal *Religieuze Bewegingen in Nederland* (Religious Movements in the Netherlands).

MICHAEL L. MICKLER is Assistant Professor of Church History and Communications at Unification Theological Seminary, Barrytown, New York (U.S.A.). He is the author of *The Unification Church of America: A Bibliography and Research Guide* (1987) and *A History of the Unification Church in America, 1959-1974* (1993), as well as articles and reviews on the Unification Church and other movements.

JAMES T. RICHARDSON is Professor of Sociology and Judicial Studies at the University of Nevada, Reno, where he also directs the Masters of Judicial Studies Degree Program, as well as the Center for Justice Studies. He received his Ph.D. from Washington State University in 1968, and his J.D. degree from Nevada School of Law, Old College, in 1986. His research interests span many sociological and legal topics related to religion, including how legal systems deal with and impact minority religions. He has authored or edited six books, and about 100 articles and chapters in journals, many of them jointly with other scholars in the field.

JOHN A. SALIBA (S.J.) is Professor of Religious Studies at the University of Detroit (U.S.A.). He has written extensively on new religious movements from both social scientific and Roman Catholic perspectives. Among his recent publications is the comprehensive reference text *Social Science and the Cults: An Annotated Bibliography* (1990) published by Garland Publishing, Inc.

ANSON SHUPE is Professor of Sociology at the joint campus of Indiana University-Purdue University Fort Wayne, Fort Wayne, Indiana (U.S.A.) He is the author, coauthor, or coeditor of two dozen books on religious movements as well as on family violence. In addition, he has written extensively for professional journals, magazines, and newspapers. His most recent book is *The Violent Couple* (with William A. Stacey and Lonnie R. Hazlewood), published by Praeger Publishers, (1994).

BAREND VAN DRIEL is a doctoral student at the University of California, Santa Cruz. He is from The Netherlands, where he has earned degrees from the University Nijmegen in psychology. His research interests include the way media treat religious groups and the way religious groups develop within specific societal structures. Van Driel has published papers in the *Journal for the Scientific Study of Religion, Journal of Communication,* and *Sociological Analysis,* among others. He visited for a year at the University of Nevada, Reno, where he and Richardson did some joint research, including that reported herein.